Working on Earth

CLASS AND ENVIRONMENTAL JUSTICE

EDITED BY
Christina Robertson
AND
Jennifer Westerman

UNIVERSITY OF NEVADA PRESS RENO & LAS VEGAS

University of Nevada Press, Reno, Nevada 89557 USA
Copyright © 2015 by University of Nevada Press
All rights reserved
Manufactured in the United States of America
Design by Kathleen Szawiola

Library of Congress Cataloging-in-Publication Data

Working on earth : class and environmental justice /
edited by Christina Robertson and Jennifer Westerman.
     pages   cm
Includes index.
ISBN 978-0-87417-963-7 (paperback) — ISBN 978-0-87417-964-4 (e-book)
1. Environmental justice. 2. Human ecology. 3. Working class.
4. Working class—Social conditions. 5. Working class—Canada—
Case studies. 6. Working class—United States—Case studies.
I. Robertson, Christina, 1960–   II. Westerman, Jennifer.
GE220.W67 2015
363.700973—dc23   2014032929

The paper used in this book meets the requirements of American National Standard
for Information Sciences—Permanence of Paper for Printed Library Materials,
ANSI/NISO Z39.48-1992 (R2002). Binding materials were selected for strength
and durability.

FIRST PRINTING

24   23   22   21   20   19   18   17   16   15
5   4   3   2   1

FOR JOHN, CR   FOR JIM, JW

CONTENTS

Working on Earth owes its origins to personal convictions, friendship, and fate. Long before we became coeditors of this volume, a belief in activist scholarship drew each of us to enroll in the Literature and Environment Graduate Program at the University of Nevada, Reno. Interdisciplinary, bridging boundaries between the humanities and the environmental sciences, and unapologetically inclusive, the program attracted students from around the world. In addition to influencing a generation of scholars, teachers, activists, and authors, the extracurricular aspects of the program inspired partnerships, marriages, children, and many strong friendships. Our friendship is one of them. When we met fifteen years ago, our convictions took root in a shared passion for literature, environmental justice, and long walks in Reno's foothills, with Jen's husky, Mila, leading the way. All those footsteps precede this book.

Quite by chance, each of us chose to explore the intersection of labor, nature, social class, and environmental justice. While we approached these issues from distinct angles—as a literary and cultural critic and as a creative nonfiction writer—the workplace stories we encountered led us to consider the impacts of work on people and landscapes. We observed that environmental literary and cultural criticism focused on race, gender, and ethnicity, but was less engaged with class. At the same time, we were coming to understand that social class often determines levels of disproportionate exposure to environmental hazards for poor workers and working-class people of all races, genders, and ethnicities.

We saw, too, that conversations about job security, wages, and benefits tended to ignore the long-term impacts of extractive and polluting industries on worker health and safety, on the natural landscape, and on surrounding communities. When we found scholars already at work defining an emerging field called *working-class studies,* we recognized common ground with our growing interest in environmental justice studies. We wondered what restorative cultural work might emerge if we explored the confluence of working-class studies and environmental justice.

Many environmental literary and cultural critics insist that scholars, writers, and teachers have a responsibility to engage the worldwide ecological crises of our age in cultural texts and in everyday life. This project takes that stance. Like the graduate program that brought us together, this essay collection is interdisciplinary and inclusive, and aims to link the environmental sciences with the humanities. Scholars working in literary studies, history, anthropology, cultural studies, creative nonfiction, political science, journalism, environmental justice, and sustainability studies have contributed essays to *Working on Earth.* We sought to practice narrative scholarship, to include essays from both academic and creative writers, and to support exploration of the personal and the political. Drawing on myth, history, research, and personal experience, the writers gathered here attest to the power of storytelling to transform the ways we work and live on Earth. These essays urge us to reinhabit an environment where working-class people are visible and where the land sustains the connections we build, the systems we create, and the planet we inhabit.

How have we labored in the past, and how must we, in the future, work on Earth? How do our land management practices promote or hinder social equity and ecological diversity? How are environmental justice and social justice intertwined? *Working on Earth* has its origins in these questions, these conversations. We believe this book takes a new step toward exploring these ideas.

Whereas we assembled these essays primarily for students and scholars in the environmental humanities, we hope that this book will be read beyond those classrooms. Even as these essays are authored by people who, it must be said, work as academics, many of the voices featured in this volume belong to working-class people whose experiences often go unrecorded, and so unaccounted for. We also hope that this book will inspire further work at the intersection of working-class studies and environmental justice. One such volume of stories might illustrate the interdependence of union workers and the environment. Our aim here is to make the case that class—a marker of identity, culture, privilege, access, and agency—is inextricably linked to environmental justice. Environmentally and socially just economic practices will remain the exception until including the voices and stories and experiences of working-class people becomes the rule.

We would like to thank all of our contributors for their intellectual curiosity, creative insights, and dedication to seeing this project through to publication. Their words and their work continue to inspire us.

We would also like to extend our gratitude to our faculty mentors in the Literature and Environment Program at the University of Nevada, Reno, including Michael P. Branch, Michael P. Cohen, Cheryll Glotfelty, and Scott Slovic.

We also thank our colleagues at the Association for the Study of Literature and Environment, in the English Department at the University of Nevada, Reno, and in the Sustainable Development Department at Appalachian State University.

Our writing and planning for the book have been enriched thanks to the work of anonymous reviewers for the University of Nevada Press, and we are grateful for their time and thoughtful suggestions. We thank our editor Joanne O'Hare for her guidance. We also thank the staff at the press, including Kathleen Szawiola and Alison Hope, for their stewardship of this book.

We are also indebted to a group of environmental literary scholars, environmental sociologists, environmental historians, and scholars of environmental justice and the working class whose work has greatly influenced our own, including Joni Adamson, Julian Agyeman, Elizabeth Ammons, Robert J. Bruell, Robert Bullard, Renny Christopher, William Cronon, Daniel Faber, Sherry Lee Linkon, Carolyn Merchant, Chad Montrie, Kathleen Dean Moore, David Pellow, John Russo, Julie Sze, Tom Wayman, Richard White, and Janet Zandy, and the many scholars and activists working across the globe to make visible the relationship between work and nature.

We are especially thankful for the support and encouragement we have received from our families, and we offer our most profound thanks to them for providing both grounding and levity.

Finally, this volume has been a true editorial collaboration between us, and we are deeply appreciative of the ways that this project has challenged and expanded our understanding of class, justice, and environment.

WORKING ON EARTH

Introduction

Toward a Working-Class Ecology

**CHRISTINA ROBERTSON AND
JENNIFER WESTERMAN**

When Norma Fiorentino's private water well exploded, Dimock, Pennsylvania, became the flashpoint for hydraulic fracturing, widely known as fracking, the controversial process used to extract natural gas from shale formations. Residents in this Susquehanna County township argued that methane from Cabot Oil & Gas Corporation's hydraulic fracturing operations contaminated their drinking water, while Cabot contended that naturally occurring methane tainted the wells. Royalties from lease payments, industry jobs, and impact fees created economic incentives for natural gas development in Dimock, but residents like Fiorentino felt betrayed by the industry's promises. The community splintered, as so often happens when development issues are framed in terms of jobs versus the environment. As natural gas developers tap shale gas deposits in the United States and Canada, the jobs versus environment controversy sparked by hydraulic fracturing divides community after community. From Washington and Radford Counties in Pennsylvania, and Killdeer and Dunn Counties in North Dakota, to Beaver and Clearwater Counties in Alberta and along the Peace River in British Columbia, working-class people face both economic insecurity and the unequal risk of exposure to environmental hazards that are largely unregulated and poorly understood.

Working on Earth explores the ideological, cultural, and actual space where class identity, the material conditions of work, and environmental justice issues intersect. As a group, working-class people are marginalized by their lack of access to political power, by their economic status, and by the common perception that they lack ecological knowledge. Even well-paid union jobs don't often entitle blue-collar workers to participate in decisions about the consequences—bodily or environmental—of their work. As Janet Zandy observes in *Hands: Physical Labor, Class, and Cultural Work,* "The white-collar middle class may endure long hours and job insecurity, but they do not lose fingers, destroy their mouth cavities, and poison their bodies because of their paid labor. And the rich, of course, never have to make such trade-offs."[1] Working-class people on the front lines face such hazardous conditions on a daily basis.

Social class is intertwined with and defined by what kind of work we perform, and manual wage labor is a key identity marker in our society. Getting one's hands dirty, doing the heavy lifting, and working on and living off the land is the realm of the working class. This physical work carries inherent risks. Workers in closest contact with the land, including miners, loggers, farmers, ranchers, agricultural workers, fishermen, construction workers, ironworkers, roofers, sanitation workers, power linesmen, and shift workers face the greatest environmental dangers.[2] Indoor laborers, such as chemical or manufacturing plant workers, housekeepers, and night-shift workers, also face environmental hazards. Whether outdoors or on the factory floor, exposure to toxic chemicals, airborne pollutants, and artificial light are just a few of the many threats to workers' health. And such exposure is rarely contained within factory gates. Toxins can follow workers home, polluting their communities, along with the air, water, and land.

Sustainable economic and community development, long-term job security, and living wages often elude working-class people. Consider that communities dominated by coal mining, such as those in Mingo County, West Virginia, are some of the poorest in the state and in the United States.[3] Environmental and public health consequences, including water and air contamination and respiratory illnesses and cancers, are also higher in nearly every county in West Virginia where mining is the dominant industry.[4] Workers come to accept the environmental and public health consequences as the terms of doing business, of making a living. As Robert D. Bullard argues, environmental justice "is not about poor people being forced to trade their health and the health of their communities for jobs. Poor people and poor communities are given a false choice between having, on the one hand, no jobs and no development and, on the other hand, risky low-paying jobs and pollution. In reality, unemployment and poverty are also hazardous to one's health. This jobs-versus-unemployment scenario is a form of economic blackmail."[5] Indeed, the business-as-usual policies that drive industrial capitalism, in West Virginia and elsewhere, fail to account for indicators of human well-being and ecological health, such as aspirational needs and biological diversity. Working-class people face a dual injustice: the economic insecurity that accompanies boom and bust and disproportionate exposure to environmental hazards.

As the contributors to *Working on Earth* suggest, these injustices are rooted in the ways we have used and valued nature over time. They are reinforced by a social hierarchy where the most affluent groups amass wealth and dominate decision making while assuming less risk of exposure to environmental hazards. Working-class people sustain advanced economies, yet they receive less compensation for their labor and possess little control over policy making. The aim of this collection is to explore the costs of pitting jobs against the environment and to expose how this "false choice" exploits working-class people and the more-than-human world. Why, for example, do we so often accept worker exploitation and environmental pollution as necessary consequences for economic growth?

The essays in *Working on Earth* advance the need for what we term a *working-class ecology*. Working-class ecology calls attention to the ways in which class structures, access to power in the workplace, the material conditions of work, and the more-than-human environment interact.[6] A working-class ecology challenges industrial policies and practices that divide economic security from environmental health, forcing workers, communities, all sentient beings, and the land to pay dearly for the cost of making a living. As Devon Peña suggests, "The environmentalism of everyday life does not divide the environment into disembodied parts like 'nature,' 'work,' and 'home.'"[7] The writers in this volume illustrate how dividing nature, work, and home produces environmental and social crises.

The Intersection of Working-Class Studies and Environmental Justice

The writers in *Working on Earth* illustrate a fluid understanding of what it means to talk about class. For John Russo and Sherry Lee Linkon, working-class studies "is not only about the labor movement, or about workers of any particular kind, or workers in any particular place—even in the workplace. Instead, we ask questions about how class works for people at work, at home, and in the community." Working class describes not just a socioeconomic category, but also a rhetorical category. Class serves as an identity marker that reflects and reinforces social and political hierarchies in relation to other identity markers, such as gender and race. Zandy observes, "Our understanding of class identity is incomplete without the interplay of these other identities, but these other subjectivities cannot be properly studied without a class dimension." The writers in this volume collectively assert that we must consider environment—places that shape and are shaped by the lives of working-class people—as an equally significant identity marker alongside gender, race, and class. Richard White has written that "our work—all our work—inevitably embeds us in nature."[8] When we separate economy from environment, making a living from realizing social justice, we fail to see how our class identities are mutually constituted not only by our labor, but also by the natural world. When we make working-class ecology visible, we come to see how the work that we do determines uneven exposures to social and environmental risks.

The environmental justice movement confronts the unequal distribution of environmental hazards in marginalized communities and challenges the structural inequalities that perpetuate such harms. "Access to a healthy and clean environment," contend David Pellow and Robert J. Bruelle "is increasingly distributed by power, class, and race."[9] Scholars and activists in the environmental justice movement examine connections between social, political, and environmental inequalities, contesting practices and policies that exploit people of color, indigenous communities, women, the poor, and the working class. The environmental justice movement exposes one of the primary contradictions of economic globalization: as poor workers and working-class people become more dependent on modern industrial capitalism, they are increasingly susceptible to exploitation by that system. A second contradiction follows: "Under capitalism 'the greater the social wealth, the functioning capital, the extent and energy of its growth,' the greater are capital's ecological demands, and the level of environmental degradation."[10] In other words, global industrial capitalism engenders worker exploitation and environmental degradation. As the environmental justice movement makes clear, many environmental issues intersect with working-class struggles—where we work, what kind of work we perform, and what materials we work with—yet the environmental justice movement has historically focused on discussions of environmental racism and engaged less vigorously with analyses of social class. The contributors to *Working on Earth* aim to demonstrate the necessity of analyzing class in relation to environmental justice.

The Cultural Work of Stories

Working on Earth is grounded in the belief that stories have the potential to illuminate—and to change—our values and practices. Stories perform cultural work. This cultural work is distinct from other forms of discourse that undervalue personal experiences and individual and community truths. A successful story can make us feel, on a visceral level, what's at stake. As Zandy writes, "No book can reattach the human hand severed on the job, but it can trace the process of dis/memberment and remembering, and see the hand's potential for graceful movement, its delicate rough beauty, and its hidden wisdom." Stories framed by working-class ecologies link body and memory, landscape and labor. In other words, stories challenge us to recognize and examine the ways that work and environment intersect. Lawrence Buell argues that environmental change "requires a climate of transformed environmental values, perception, and will. To that end," he continues, "the power of story, image, and artistic performance and the resources of aesthetics, ethics, and cultural theory are crucial."[11] This transformation will only come about if people doing all kinds of cultural work argue, collectively, for a wholly reimagined relationship with the environment.

How, then, can stories challenge us to reimagine a world in which we view work and environment in relational terms? Working-class and environmental justice scholars hold in common the belief that stories of marginalized, poor, and working-class people are vital sources of knowledge, insight, and evidence. For example, Russo and Linkon emphasize the centrality of the "lived experience of working-class people" to current efforts in working-class studies, noting the importance of "collecting and studying representations that capture the voices of working-class people, such as oral histories, songs, poems, and personal narratives." Robert D. Bullard and Damu Smith cite the fundamental leadership of women of color in the environmental justice movement, emphasizing, "It is important that these women's stories be told in their own words, in keeping with the environmental justice principle that demands that people be allowed to speak for themselves."[12] Scholars and activists in both fields also ask questions about whose voices go unaccounted for in social and environmental decision making. Such questions confront dominant narratives of human progress, narratives in which economic growth takes precedence over the well-being of both workers and the environment. As Charles Waugh, whose essay "Raining in Vietnam: The Personal Politics of Climate Justice" opens this book, remarks, "In short, stories about climate change and climate justice sparked in us a global consciousness that highlighted the positions of power and privilege that otherwise remain hidden in most of our everyday decisions."

Our Working Lives, Our Living Earth: Essays in This Collection

Based in cultural theory, criticism, narrative, and research, the essays in this volume illustrate the impacts of the ways we work on Earth. Drawing on historical, societal, cultural, ethical, literary, and personal perspectives, these essays chronicle environmental histories that reveal social inequities in land management. These essays bear witness to lost landscapes and to family members who died making a living. They recover working-class stories and assert their importance in reimagining sustainable jobs and communities. They present solutions to the global climate crisis that do not divide worker from wilderness, labor from landscape. They offer examples of once-degraded landscapes, now reinhabited with sustainability and human welfare in mind. These essays call for new narratives, reframed around the collective survival of human beings and the more-than-human world.

Working on Earth begins with a historical reckoning of the jobs versus environment dichotomy, moves on to an accounting of unintended consequences for workers and the land, and concludes with a range of perspectives that reimagine relationships between work and nature. The contributors to Part I, "Working for a Living: Class, Justice, and Environment," suggest that any analysis of class must be contextualized by how we value and manage land. Historically, those jobs linked with the land—farming, fishing, mining, ranching, and forest work, for instance—have been filled by people who identify as and are perceived as either working class or the working poor. Yet, in most cases, a close association with the land has not afforded these groups political or social power. Instead, as corporate-owned or public land increases in value—whether for economic or aesthetic reasons—those whose livelihood depends on continued access to this land or its resources are often excluded from decisions about its management. The writers in Part II, "The Ways We Work: Toxic Consequences," call attention to everyday industrial practices that comprise occupational and environmental hazards that disproportionately impact laborers designated—culturally and on the job—as the working class. Indeed, the narrative arc of *Working on Earth* suggests that understanding and valuing working-class struggles must be an integral part of achieving environmental justice and sustainable development. The writers in Part III, "The Workers and the Land: Toward a Just and Sustainable Future," examine shifts in the ways we value labor and nature. They document how human and environmental forces are challenging perceptions about how to achieve climate justice, cultivate class consciousness, and reinhabit exploited landscapes.

■ Across ages and around the globe, human beings have organized themselves around myth, parable, legend, and story. The stories we hear and tell about culture, history, work, and ways of living on the land frame our belief systems, our relationships, and our actions. One worldwide story now finally being told distills what ecologists have recently named the Anthropocene era, the geological blink of an eye that accounts for the sum effects of human activity on Earth. We know that the destiny of humans and the fate of the natural world are inextricably bound. We can continue to perpetuate the existing model of global economic capitalism, which will relegate the laboring classes to the basest of working conditions and consign the planet to ecological catastrophe. Or, we can change. Our collective survival depends on our capacity to make ethical decisions that consider all sentient beings and the land. To this end, the larger cultural narratives we live by will sustain us or destroy us. The future of our planet has its roots in the stories we tell: we need new narratives that reinforce the necessity of cooperation, of reciprocity, of respect for all beings, and of living within ecological limits.

NOTES

1. Janet Zandy, *Hands: Physical Labor, Class, and Cultural Work* (New Brunswick, NJ: Rutgers University Press, 2004), "The white collar," 29.

2. U.S. Department of Labor, Bureau of Labor Statistics, Economic News Release, "Census of Fatal Occupational Injuries Summary, 2012," http://www.bls.gov/news.release/cfoi.nro.htm.

3. Sean O'Leary and Ted Boettner, West Virginia Center on Budget & Policy, "Booms and Busts: The Impact of West Virginia's Energy Economy" (July 2011), http://www.wvpolicy.org/downloads/BoomsBusts072111.pdf.

4. For more information, see Michael Hendryx, "Poverty and Mortality Disparities in Central Appalachia: Mountaintop Mining and Environmental Justice," *Journal of Health Disparities Research and Practice* 4 no. 3 (2011): 44–53; Keith J. Zullig and Michael Hendryx, "Health-Related Quality of Life Among Central Appalachian Residents in Mountaintop Mining Counties," *American Journal of Public Health* 101 no. 5 (2011): 848–53; and Keith J. Zullig and Michael Hendryx, "A Comparative Analysis of Health-Related Quality of Life for Residents of U.S. Counties with and without Coal Mining" *Public Health Reports* 125 no. 4 (2010): 548–555; Michael Hendryx, E. Fedorko, and A. Anesetti-Rotherme, "A Geographical Information System-Based Analysis of Cancer Mortality and Population Exposure to Coal Mining Activities in West Virginia," *Geospatial Health* 4 no. 2 (2010): 243–256.

5. Robert D. Bullard, "Environmental Justice in the Twenty-first Century," in *The Quest for Environmental Justice: Human Rights and the Politics of Pollution*, ed. Robert D. Bullard (San Francisco: Sierra Club Books, 2005), "is not about," 42.

6. Michael Zweig, *The Working Class Majority: America's Best Kept Secret*, 2nd ed. (Ithaca, NY: Cornell University Press, 2012), 1–4.

7. Devon G. Peña, "Tierra y Vida: Chicano Environmental Justice," in Bullard, *The Quest for Environmental Justice*, "the environmentalism," 190.

8. John Russo and Sherry Lee Linkon, "What's New about New Working-Class Studies?" in *New Working-Class Studies*, ed. John Russo and Sherry Lee Linkon (Ithaca, NY: IRL Press, 2005), "is not only about," 10; 11–12; Janet Zandy, ed., *What We Hold in Common: An Introduction to Working-Class Studies* (New York: Feminist Press at CUNY, 2001), "Our understanding of," xiii; Richard White, "'Are You an Environmentalist, or Do You Work for a Living?': Work and Nature," in *Uncommon Ground: Rethinking the Human Place in Nature*, ed. William Cronon (New York: W. W. Norton, 1996), "our work," 185.

9. David Naguib Pellow and Robert J. Bruelle, eds., *Power, Justice, and the Environment: A Critical Appraisal of the Environmental Justice Movement* (Cambridge, MA: MIT Press, 2005), "Access to," 2.

10. John Bellamy Foster, "The Absolute General Law of Environmental Degradation Under Capitalism," *Capitalism Nature Socialism* 3 no. 3 (1992): "Under capitalism," 79.

See also John Bellamy Foster, Brett Clark, and Richard York *The Ecological Rift: Capitalism's War on the Earth* (New York: Monthly Review Press, 2011); Kenneth A. Gould, David N. Pellow, and Allan Schnaiberg, *The Treadmill of Production: Injustice and Unsustainability in the Global Economy* (Boulder, CO: Paradigm Publishers, 2008); and Zweig, *The Working Class Majority*.

11. Zandy, *Hands*, "No book can," 5; Lawrence Buell, *The Future of Environmental Criticism: Environmental Crisis and Literary Imagination* (Hoboken, NJ: Wiley-Blackwell Publishing, 2005), "requires a climate," vi.

12. Russo and Linkon, "What's New about New Working-Class Studies?," "lived experience," "collecting and studying," 11; Robert D. Bullard and Damu Smith, "Women Warriors of Color on the Front Line," in Bullard, *The Quest for Environmental Justice*, "It is important," 65.

PART I

Working for a Living

Class, Justice, and Environment

Raining in Vietnam

The Personal Politics of Climate Justice

CHARLES WAUGH

n the mythical past of Vietnam, the spirits of things roamed as freely on the Earth as did humans. So it was when on one particularly fine day the spirit of the mountain, Son Tinh, decided to stroll along the beach to enjoy the fresh sea air in his lungs and the warm sand beneath his feet. Eventually he came upon several fishermen eagerly discussing the great price a large, unusual fish caught in their net would fetch at the market. Longer than a man, with powerful thrashing muscles, the fish seemed determined to rise up from the beach and return to the sparkling water. Its glistening scales flickered from brilliant green one moment to vibrant blue the next, and when Son Tinh looked into its eyes, he saw something there he could not ignore. He said to the fishermen, "Don't try to sell this fish at the market; it won't end well for you." The fishermen scoffed at this advice and told Son Tinh where and how he might find his own end. Seeing they could not be swayed, Son Tinh changed course. He doubled their price and bought the fish himself, with the condition that they put the fish back into their boat and take Son Tinh with them out to deep water. On the rolling waves, half a mile from shore, Son Tinh slit open the net and rolled the glittering fish back into the sea. With a mighty splash, the fish leapt from the water, and hovering in air transformed into the shape of a man shimmering with liquid light. "I am Thủy Tinh," said the spirit of the sea with a slight bow. "Thank you for saving my life." As a token of gratitude, he presented Son

Tinh with a large and ancient tome, telling him it held the power to grant him anything he desired. Then Thủy Tinh disappeared beneath the waves.

Not long after that, Emperor Hùng Vương and his court toured the country, traveling from the capital to the coast and into the mountains to announce a contest to find a husband for Princess Mỵ Nương, whose beauty outmatched all other Earthly beauties. To prove his worthiness, the suitor would have to present the court with ten white elephants, ten giant tunas, ten tigers, ten sailfish, ten trees that were one hundred meters tall, and ten green pearls. Surely it would take someone rich and powerful to amass so many treasures from both the land and the sea. Smitten by the beauty of the princess riding in her palanquin along one of his jungle paths, Son Tinh decided at once to use the magic book to complete the challenge. But Thủy Tinh had also been captivated by the beautiful Mỵ Nương as she had sailed along the coast. Using the many fingers of his rivers, he painstakingly gathered each of the contest items. When he arrived at Hùng Vương's court, he was surprised to discover he'd already been bested, and by his former savior no less. Unaccustomed to losing, he refused to admit defeat, especially considering Son Tinh had only been able to win by using the tome that had once been his. In his fury, he sent all the winds and waves he could muster crashing into Son Tinh, who raised his stony shoulders and shrugged the water back to the sea. When the storms subsided, Son Tinh remained unbroken, and it took another year before Thủy Tinh regained the strength to attack again. But attack again he did, and the next year, and the next year, and the year after that, and every year thereafter. And even though the mountains have always survived, the yearly monsoons have always returned, and the people caught in between have always suffered the most.[1]

■ On the corner of Le Loi Street and Cua Dai Road in Hoi An, Vietnam, torrential rain pours from the sky like wet cement, splattering on the pavement all around. My family and I are on the southeast side of the intersection where it's usually easier to hail a taxi but whose businesses have all closed up for the night—a *bia hơi* (beer garden) shut down by the rain, and a bank and an agro exchange with regular hours—so the only light comes trickling down from storefront fluorescents half a block away. My six-year-old son bounces between a filthy concrete telephone pole and one of the brick columns of the *bia hơi*'s fence. Black grime drips from his hands and red from the clay of the poorly fired bricks streaks down the back of his T-shirt. When I urge him to stop, he steps off the curb into the gutter stream of god knows what swept along by the downpour, submerging his sandaled feet to the ankles. My sixty-seven-year-old father, diagnosed with multiple sclerosis five years before, hobbles in circles on the broken pavement nearby, unable by natural disposition to stand still, and yet unable to make his right leg move properly. When he does stop for a moment, he takes all his weight on his good leg, his torso skewed like a house with a washed-out foundation. He's thoroughly soaked. My wife, my mother, my son, and I have umbrellas, and we've tried to shield him as much as possible, but with rain like this there's not much we can do. My father didn't want to have to carry anything besides his walking stick and felt too hot to wear a raincoat.

It's the night of the full moon festival, so thousands of tourists and townspeople alike have packed into this tiny old town on the central Vietnamese coast, and now, with the rain, they have taken every taxi, too. At some point the taxi companies simply give up answering their phones. We are stranded, stuck in a rainstorm like the moronic tourists we've become, and my blood boils as my dripping-wet yet ever-optimistic father says for the twelfth time, "Getting there is half the adventure!"

I want to strangle him. I am no tourist. I am not on an adventure. I've lived in Vietnam this time for three and a half months, and all together more than two years spread out over four stays, the longest a year in 2004 and 2005. I speak the language. I know this town. I have friends here. At this moment in my life, I *live* here. Normally, we'd have hopped on our motorbike an hour ago, before the storm even started, my son Owen up front, my wife Jen behind, and zipped home to our bungalow just outside town so we could be snug and dry listening to the rain pounding the tiles of our roof. Normally, we wouldn't even bother with taxis, unless we were making the trip up to Danang, and sometimes not even then. Normally, it doesn't rain like this in April, the driest month of the whole dry season.

■ Only a people resigned to suffering extreme weather could originate and maintain a legend like the one about Son Tinh and Thủy Tinh. Only a people devoted to their ancestors, fulfilling their duty to create a new generation despite the insurmountable challenges nature poses could carry on in the face of such perpetual danger. But seasonal monsoons are one thing. Some estimates suggest that, with a one-meter sea level rise and all the extra energy in the system that goes with it, hundred-year storms may hit Vietnam as frequently as once every four years.

In fact, according to the Intergovernmental Panel on Climate Change (IPCC) and the World Bank, the climate change prognosis for Vietnam is in many ways as bad as it gets. Their researchers have predicted a one- to three-meter rise in sea levels over this century, which means a significant portion of Vietnam's arable land will be inundated. With just a one-meter rise, 5 percent of Vietnam will be under water, and with the IPCC's worst-case scenario, a five-meter rise, 16 percent of Vietnam disappears beneath the waves. In all cases, the areas hit first and worst are the fertile river deltas where much of the nation's crops are grown, and where most of the people live. In the five-meter scenario, nearly 40 percent of the population—over 34 million people—will be displaced. Taking these predictions into account, the World Bank believes Vietnam will be one of the five countries most impacted by climate change, with the world's worst impacts in lost GDP, displaced people, and destroyed urban areas.[2]

As dire as this forecast sounds, at least the effects are spread over decades, allowing the Vietnamese time to plan for them in some way. Other aspects of global warming have even more immediate catastrophic impacts on Vietnam. Yearly weather patterns over the past forty years have demonstrated an intensification of extremes, and in Vietnam this has meant longer, more-intense periods of drought and heat wave as well as more-frequent and more-intense rains, typhoons, and flooding. So while the overall number of rainy days has decreased, when it does rain, it pours.

Thủy Tinh just might have his revenge after all.

◼ In February I had flown from my snowed-under home in Utah to Hanoi, where I reunited with friends and colleagues, finished translating a collection of narratives about Agent Orange exposure, and began several new projects, including one that compared traditional Vietnamese attitudes toward the environment found in folk literature and culture with the attitudes in contemporary Vietnam that seem more rooted in global development, tourism, manufacturing, and consumerism. Three weeks later, Jen and Owen joined me to visit with friends for ten days before we moved on to the next phase of our research and writing trip three hundred miles to the south in Hoi An.

Hanoi is cool and wet in February, the temperature sometimes dropping to the fifties or below, but feeling colder because of the damp. Vast blankets of moisture-rich clouds roll in from the Eastern Sea, then settle into the Red River valley, reducing visibility to the hand in front of your face for days on end. These are the days when nothing seems better than piping hot bowls of pho for breakfast and as many cups of thick, chocolaty Vietnamese coffee as your racing heart can stand. But Hoi An is protected from much of this winter chill by Hai Van Pass, where the Truong Son Mountain Range bulges east all the way out to the sea. The mountains keep the cold air to the north, and the warm air to the south. Between Hue, north of the pass, and Danang, south of the pass, just fifty miles apart, the temperature can vary by up to thirty degrees Fahrenheit. We flew into Danang International Airport late on a warm Sunday afternoon, and had made the twenty-mile trip by car down to the old town of Hoi An by nightfall.

We'd been there twice before. We spent Christmas in Hoi An in 2004, and returned the following May with friends visiting from the United States. Owen had been two at the time, just a pudgy little monkey with downy blonde hair, getting his first taste of the ocean. At the beach, a Vietnamese family who owned a restaurant adopted us. Cô Mãn, or Aunty Mãn, cooked whatever Bac, her fisherman husband, had caught that morning, and in the frequent lulls of the day played with Owen in the sand. We dined on clams steamed with lemongrass and chilies, grilled crab and shrimp in lemon and pepper, and tuna and snapper so fresh they melted on the tongue. At the end of our second visit, I promised Cô Mãn when our family returned to Vietnam we would come see her again. But it wasn't Cô Mãn's friendship alone that drew us back. Hoi An has an intriguing, intercultural history that makes globalization visible in the distant past as well as in the present, plus a unique geophysical location that makes the interdependence of our global fates abundantly clear.

Two large, intertwining rivers—the Thu Bon and the Vu Gia—drain the Truong Son Mountains in Quang Nam Province, flowing into the now well-developed harbor at Danang and the smaller, older harbor at Hoi An. Along the way they course through the Go Noi area, renowned for over a thousand years for its mulberry trees and *Bombyx mori,* the silkworms that eat the leaves. The silk made from these caterpillars attracted traders from China, Japan, India, the Netherlands, Portugal, England, and France, and in the sixteenth century, Hoi An became a bustling seaport, with sizable

Chinese and Japanese neighborhoods. Farther into its past, in the fourth century AD, the same Indian-Hindu influences that led the Khmer to build the temple complexes in Cambodia called Angkor Wat inspired the neighboring Cham people to construct a similar, though smaller temple complex here called My Son (pronounced Me Sun). The seventy or so buildings that composed My Son served as a religious and cultural center that helped disseminate Champan iterations of Hindu philosophy, religion, art, and customs throughout Southeast Asia.

Vestiges of this 1,600-year-old cultural mixing are everywhere in Hoi An. In 1999 the United Nations Educational, Scientific, and Cultural Organization (UNESCO) declared the city a World Heritage Site, citing its blend of local and foreign architectural styles, upkeep of traditional handicrafts, and preservation of cultural customs such as the full moon festival, when people float paper lanterns carrying their wishes upriver with the tide and then watch as the tide shifts and the lanterns rush out to sea. In My Son, also a UNESCO World Heritage Site, many of the temples remain intact, having survived centuries of decay and, for the most part, even the onslaught of American bombs.[3]

Even so, there have been some changes since we last visited in 2005. Of course, the old town remains intact—it's protected by law—but the city around the old town has grown. A new four-lane highway now travels along the coast from Danang, providing access to the dozen or so luxury resorts that have sprung up. Each of them appears to be trying to find its international niche, catering to the aesthetics of the tens of thousands of Chinese, Japanese, Korean, French, and American tourists who visit every year. But much has remained the same, too, especially when you consider the land surrounding this development and the millennia of agricultural work that has been performed on it.

■ The night we were stranded in the rain, we had decided to take a taxi into town since our last excursion hadn't worked out very well. A few days previous, we had split up, with my father and me on the motorbike, and Jen, Owen, and my mother on bicycles. Mom and Dad had just arrived the day before, and we wanted them to experience all the things we love about living in Vietnam. Traveling by bike or motorbike happens to be a surprising joy, even in a busy city like Hanoi, but especially in the countryside. The wind feels wonderful on your face, and that intense rice paddy green vibrates with sunshine all around you. Nearly everyone in Vietnam gets around this way too—it's just a part of the texture of Vietnamese life.

As we'd hoped, the ride in *was* lovely. The sun had just begun to sink into the mountains, lighting up the sky in hazy pinks and blues that shimmered in the reflection off the river. Our route ran along a quay where fishermen and tour guides tie up their brightly painted boats (each with eyes on the prow to "see" where the rocks and fish are), and because the road runs out before reaching town, requiring the use of a couple narrow alleyways to get back to the main streets, there's no traffic. Just a lovely, peaceful trip into town. Perfect.

Or, at least, perfect until it was time after dinner to return home. We had eaten at a leisurely pace, savoring the green papaya salad, pineapple shrimp, and grilled bananafish, only to further indulge ourselves with treats from our favorite patisserie for dessert. Just on our way out of the old town, the storm hit like the sky had been torn open, gushing with rain. The streets flooded instantly, two to three inches deep. We ducked under a balcony near the Ceramics Museum on a street that doesn't stay open late, the shops having already boarded up their fronts in the old Chinese way—with thick horizontal slats that can be slid into grooves along the jamb. Some light came from behind the shuttered windows and from down the block, near the market, where four or five women had kept booths open to sell rambutan and mangosteen to tourists.

With the rain my mother and Jen could not get enough momentum to generate enough power for their bicycle headlamps to light their way. They decided to wait for a break under the balcony, but they encouraged my father and me to return home without them. An hour later, when the rain hadn't stopped and they still hadn't returned, I was just about to go out looking for them when they dragged themselves in, soaked and visibly shaken.

They had finally realized the rain wasn't going to let up. Neither had any money or a cellphone, so they couldn't have called a cab even if they were willing to leave the bikes. Owen's patience had run thin, manifesting in a series of tired complaints, but the real kick in the pants came from a rat scrabbling up from the rushing gutter and on to their same higher, drier concrete porch. By this point, their ability to feel compassion for the similarity of their fates had already washed out. They scrambled onto their bikes and shoved off into the Nguyen Thai Hoc Street current.

Every pothole hidden beneath the surface of the water threatened to send my mother flying off the bike; she had no headlight to speak of, and her glasses had become so splattered with rain it wouldn't have mattered if she'd had a battery-powered Krieg light strapped to the handlebars. She tried to stay right behind Jen the whole way home, but even so, the ride had rattled her so badly, she took a shower and went straight to bed.

So far, sharing our Vietnam with my parents was not working out.

■ Much of traditional Vietnamese culture arises from the thousands of years of sustainable work people have put into the land, making it produce food and the materials for clothing and shelter without artificial inputs, without pushing it to exhaustion. Both work and land feature heavily in the traditional form of poetry called *ca dao* (pronounced ca zow), still sung by laborers all over the country. And in traditional Vietnamese literature—the folktales, legends and myths that form the backbone of Vietnamese identity—work and the land intermingle. How people work and live on the land is so important to Vietnamese culture that today even most city folk continue to regard some place in the countryside as their *quê nhà*—their home land, the place of their ancestors—intuitively registering that the land and the work on it are integral parts of who they are.

A substantial portion of this work means rice production. The *ca dao*, "Lullaby," recorded and translated by John Balaban, captures this rice-work-culture nexus:

> Little one, go to sleep. Sleep soundly.
> Mother's gone to market. Father plows the fields.
> For rice and clothing. So the land yields a good home.
> Study hard, little one, grow up
> to tend our native place, these mountains and rivers.
> Become worthy of our Lac-Hong race
> so our parents' faces can widen in smiles.[4]

Hoi An has not become so globalized as to forget these roots. In fact, several rice and vegetable fields remain even within the city limits. Outside of town they stretch to the mountains on the western horizon in a patchwork of diked paddies, linked by the irrigation canals that run between them. Rice seedlings grow first in soil, then get transplanted to the muddy bottom of flooded paddies. At harvest, workers drain the paddies, crop the rice plants and husk them for the grain, then burn the husks and stubble to return nutrients to the soil before flooding them again. Some farmers introduce other organic material such as straw into the soil, or grow fallow crops like mung beans to turn into the soil before replanting rice. The only other fertilizers traditionally come from the dung of grazing buffalo and ducks. Like a several thousand–year-old running commentary on the work being performed, each step along the way has been immortalized in some *ca dao,* or in some folktale or legend. In the course of telling how Vietnam came to be, even Hanoi's famous water puppet theater reenacts the life cycle of rice.[5]

As Vietnam has joined the global economy—by embracing market capitalism, using cash flows from world development agencies such as the World Bank and the International Monetary Fund, and by joining the World Trade Organization—not all Vietnamese farmers have chosen to retain these traditional forms of agriculture, and many have felt pressure to give them up.[6] Costs for staples and medical care have risen steeply in recent years as the state has given up on trying to subsidize them. Doctors who can charge for their services at private hospitals have refused to work at state hospitals, and the state stores that used to be the only retailers in town have completely disappeared. The desire by some, and the need by others, to take a larger part in the economy of cash, with all its material trinkets and outward signs of success, have led many to invest in high-tech, high-yield, industry-dependent rice strains that can be sold for export; so many, in fact, that most rice now grown in Vietnam is of this inferior, export quality, and the rice most Vietnamese like to eat has to be imported from Thailand.[7]

Some farmers have turned to other food-related industries such as catfish or shrimp farming, betting that the world market for these products will at least earn them some much-needed cash, if not make them rich. One farmer who made this transition is Mr. Bích, from the Vinh Chau District in the Mekong Delta.[8] After hearing a story about a distant neighbor who had made a fortune by converting to shrimp farming, he decided to do the same. When an international shrimp food producer came through Vinh Chau offering start-up loans in exchange for long-term contracts to buy their shrimp pellets, Mr. Bích signed up. He used the loans to clear his land of all its vegetation and to bulldoze the paddies into shrimp ponds. Now the blazing hot dry season sun bakes his land, keeping the growing shrimp warm, but it also bakes his house. Since he no longer has any place on his land for rice or fruits or vegetables, the money he earns from the shrimp has to cover the loan payments and the pellet contract, plus all the food he and his family eat, which now comes from as far away as Thailand, China, or maybe even the United States. The shrimp pellets come from ground up "trash fish" that are caught in the company's commercial fishing operation off the Pacific coast of South America. If the price of shrimp goes back up, says Mr. Bích, he can make enough to pay off the loans and get on top of the pellet contract. If it doesn't, he'll just continue to work off the debt, however long it takes. Even after joining the global economy, Mr. Bích's margin for survival is still quite small. Most Vietnamese farmers earn only about $300 per year, leaving little room for failure.[9]

The landscape is just as unforgiving. Approximately one-fifth of Vietnam is flat enough for agriculture, the rest being hilly and mountainous and frequently covered by triple canopy jungle. Often the transition between these two extremes is miniscule, with the paddy land stretching right up to immense limestone karsts that jut up from the Earth, prompting high praise from Paul Theroux, who wrote in *The Great Railway Bazaar,* "Of all the places the railway had taken me from London, this was the loveliest," but making for some hard limits to what can and can't be farmed.[10] Typically, flat paddy land in Vietnam can be found on average less than twenty-five feet above sea level. In the Mekong and Red River Deltas, where the majority of Vietnam's rice—and now shrimp—is grown, much of the land is at or just above sea level, putting farmers like Mr. Bích who live there at great risk from storms and floods. If sea levels rise as the IPCC has predicted, many of these farms will be under water. Even if the dangers of rising waters can be averted, studies by the International Rice Research Institute have shown that paddy yields decrease by 10 percent for every one degree Celsius increase in growing-season minimum temperature. For those living closest to the margins, farmers working the land much as their ancestors did for the past three thousand years, global warming not only constitutes a life-or-death situation, but also threatens to wipe out the very basis of Vietnam's traditional culture.[11]

■ Eventually, after a long, wet hour of standing in the rain, a taxi slowed to a stop right in front of us. The driver knew already where we wanted to go, so despite the wait apparently my initial call to the taxi company had got us into the queue. We just needed to be patient. Or, I did. Maybe it was just *my* calls that the taxi company stopped answering. At any rate, we arrived back at the bungalow safe and sound, and for the most part dry, except for my father.

But the frustration and anxiety I felt over how to get my family back home in the pouring rain—about doing something stupid, about being in the wrong place at the wrong time, about having my parents visit us in Vietnam during the dry season when all it did was rain—made possible a more personal examination of the consequences of a warming world.

On that corner I had been worried about Owen staying clean, both physically and medically. I admit to occasional bouts of germaphobia, and the gutters of any country that still has frequent outbreaks of cholera, dysentery, and typhoid tend to bring out those feelings fairly strongly. In a reverse parenting sense, I also felt responsible for keeping my mother and father safe and healthy, and for their being in Vietnam in the first place. And for myself, I felt the humiliation of being the type of person who allows himself to get stuck on a corner in the rain. Vietnamese know better: they either sit in a café somewhere and wait it out, or they throw on their tent-shaped rain gear and take off. (It even fits over the motorbike handlebars, and some come with two hoods for two Vietnamese-sized adult riders and enough room for a child or two in between.) As much as I want to fit in there, to live there, to be at home there, my family, my size, and ultimately my privilege all exclude me from ever really fitting in, no matter how much I want it to be otherwise. I fool myself when on the surface I live like a Vietnamese, but certain moments, like this one, make the differences stand out in vast relief. In the end, I discover I am just another oversized American who wants the luxury of having a car immediately at my disposal. And the larger discovery is also true: I won't be the one whose house is submerged by the changing weather patterns of global warming, my work and my culture won't be ruined by higher sea levels, and when the big, one-hundred-year storms come for real, I will likely be eight thousand miles away, tucked safe, warm, and dry in my mountain valley home.

But Hoi An, like much of Vietnam, will have to face the threats of global warming full on. Not only is it still largely agricultural just outside of town, but also most of its surroundings are only a meter or two above current sea level, meaning that the medium-case sea level rise scenario will have much of the historic old town underwater. Its beaches will become sandbars, the agricultural land behind them, lagoons. Cô Mãn's restaurant, like Hoi An itself, will be gone. Even if the highest parts of the area survive, if the old town, the beach, and the mulberry trees are all under water, its traditional ways of working will have been destroyed.

In Vinh Chau, not only will Mr. Bích's shrimp farm most likely be submerged, but also perhaps Vinh Chau itself, along with many other Mekong Delta districts. Already living on the margin, Mr. Bích has taken out loans from a multinational corporation to try to make a better life for his family. But the production practices the corporation engages in, along with all the subsidiary impacts that diminish local food production, mean that Mr. Bích and his neighbors are caught in a carbon-intensive process that actually increases the likelihood of their own destruction. Will the multinational take any responsibility for turning Mr. Bích into an ecological refugee? More than likely, the corporation will instead hold him responsible for whatever remains of his loan and his contract for shrimp food.

It goes without saying that rural Vietnamese in places like Vinh Chau and Hoi An have not contributed significantly to the accumulation of greenhouse gases that are heating up the planet. Compared to the carbon output of China and the United States, even Vietnam's turn toward unsustainable food practices doesn't make much of an impact. A large portion of Vietnam's electricity comes from hydropower.[12] Many people still use bicycles, though most ride motorbikes, often whole families at once, and unlike in the big cities, very few people in these small towns own private cars. Many farmers still use buffalo to plow their fields. And while Vietnam's manufacturing sector continues to grow, requiring more electricity and producing more greenhouse gases, most of that activity occurs around the big cities, and a significant portion of the demand for those products comes from the United States and other Western countries. For certain, the past few centuries' worth of industrial coal and oil burning occurred almost exclusively in the West, not in the paddies of Vietnam. In short, as they might put it, the rural, working-class people of Vietnam did not sow the breeze that has reaped this whirlwind of climate change.

■ As significant as these problems are, my parents and I don't discuss them much while we're in Hoi An. After all, we don't have a lot of time together, there's much to see and do and soon enough the weather does actually clear, and it's Mother's Day.

When I reconstruct it in my mind, we spend the day on the beach under a clear blue sky, eating crab and drinking rice wine, soaking up the sunshine and enjoying ourselves immensely. We play cards and build sand castles and enjoy sharing Cô Mãn's hospitality with my parents. When Mom and Dad return to the United States, I do email them some of the forecasts for climate change impacts on Vietnam, and, having been so captivated by the beauty of this place that is so meaningful to me, my father, who owns and runs a quality assurance business that certifies the proper and timely manufacture of big equipment orders for clients mainly drawn from the oil industry, calls each of his clients one by one, admonishing them to stop building oil pumps and to start investing in solar panels and wind farms. He sells the Lincoln Navigator he's been driving all over Ohio, Indiana, and Kentucky for his clients, buys a Prius, covers the roof of the house with solar panels, plants a garden, and goes into retirement off the grid.

Okay, since I'm in fantasy land, I may as well have him peaceably and single-handedly end the wars in Afghanistan and Iraq, convince fundamentalists everywhere to mellow out, find meaningful work for every adult on the planet, and at the same time stabilize global temperatures somewhere around their eighteenth-century, preindustrial levels.

But . . .

. . . what really happens goes more like this: A few days after the big storm, the weather in Hoi An does in fact clear. We spend Mother's Day at a Western friend's place on the beach under a clear blue sky, eating steaks from Australia and drinking white wine from France, because truth be told Cô Mãn's place is hard on my parents—the bathrooms are tiny stalls with pit toilets down a treacherous set of stairs and the food is strictly Vietnamese, which doesn't quite agree with my father's stomach. But we do soak up the sunshine and enjoy ourselves immensely, playing cards and swimming in the Eastern Sea. When my parents leave a few days later, they drive to Hue in a hired car, just the two of them. They drive all over Hue, visiting the imperial palace and the funeral grounds of the last emperors of Vietnam before flying south to Saigon to take a car to My Tho to embark for a three-day tour on the Mekong. Tourism's down this year so the whole boat belongs to them alone, the whole crew, the whole thirty-occupancy vessel with all the diesel it takes to chug its way upstream. Then they float back, return to Ho Chi Minh City by car, and fly out for home. At each point along the way, they pick up souvenirs, stay comfortable with air conditioning, and make ample demonstration of the carbon-intensiveness of travel. It is not my Vietnam, but it *is* magic for them, and at least now they have some personal appreciation for the place that is such a huge part of my life. They can see the Vietnamese as people, not as former enemies, and see the place for all the remarkable things it is, not as a war, and not as the kind of hell on Earth most Americans of their generation imagine it to be, even if what made life difficult for them there on their vacation only reinforce how privileged—or, to use their word, how *blessed*—they feel for living in America.

When they return home, Dad goes back to work; in fact, he takes on a few more jobs with a few more days of driving to pay off the vacation and to make some headway on paying for the next one, my parents still wanting to get as much travel in as they can before my father retires and they lose that income, or worse, before his mobility is further diminished. The last thing on his mind is replacing the Navigator. The fuel economy may be bad, but the higher seats make it easy for him to get in and out, the four-wheel drive lets him travel for clients all through whatever the nasty Ohio winter can dish out, and, let's face it: the luxury package reminds him that he's finally come a long way from where he started.

As far as I can tell, by the nature of his day-to-day work interactions, no one he converses with regularly really believes that there's much we can do about a warming planet. In fact, I'm sure that many of his clients are outright climate change deniers. But the feeling of helplessness that arose from standing in the pouring rain in the middle of the dry season continues to surface in my memory, and knowing that he must now feel some stake in the place we all shared together, I have to know more about what he thinks about climate change. When I phone him, unsurprisingly I catch him at work, in Indianapolis, inspecting a control valve assembly for a client in Taiwan. The next day, he returns my call while driving the two hundred plus miles home. As we speak, I can hear the staticky hiss of his tires on Interstate 70, and can imagine the vast white fields stretching out to the north and south, the endless rows of crumpled cornstalks poking sporadically through the snow.

A kind of awe creeps into his voice as he reacts to my news about the forecasted sea level rise and the impact it will have on the places he thinks most fondly of when he recalls his trip to Vietnam. To my surprise, he doesn't disparage or even dispute the IPCC predictions; rather, he tells me that he recognizes the warming of the world, that he has seen proof of it for himself in the fact that the Ohio River hasn't frozen over since the winters of his youth, and that he views it as part of the larger cycles of temperature fluctuation the Earth has always had. He concedes the greenhouse effect, and even that humans have helped speed up the rate of warming through the release of the carbon from all the coal and oil burned since Western industrialization. But he doesn't want to trade the lifestyle he has now for one from his lower-impact, poorer past, let alone the preindustrial past, and he feels at a loss to imagine a way to solve the problem.

"What about an economy of scale," I ask, "where individual actions don't matter so much by themselves, but when multiplied by billions of people across the planet *can* have a big impact?"

"Sure," he says, "but that works only when you can actually get enough people to act, and most people have a hard time seeing the need to do anything. Convince people here, now," he says, referring to the dozens of storms and subzero days Ohio's had this winter, "that the world is getting warmer."

"But if you do know," I say hesitantly, imagining the bulk of the vehicle around him, the V-8 under the hood, the large tires I can hear over the phone, "shouldn't you do something, even if only to save yourself the gas money?"

"Yeah," he says with a laugh. "I let my heart make the decision to buy my truck, not my head. If they make a hybrid with the clearance and weight and four-wheel drive to get me through the winters, I probably should've bought it."

I'm so impressed, shocked even by how much we agree on in this conversation, that I decide not to scold him by saying he should've bought the hybrid Escape or Highlander, not to push ourselves outside the agreement we've found. (I can do that later, in an email . . . maybe.) Yet those same concerns I felt on the street in Hoi An are the ones he cites for buying his suv: safety, convenience, and maybe most of all how it makes him feel inside about who he is.

The story he would tell about himself that culminates in driving the Navigator is a story of success, of rising from a home made from blue-collar jobs among the steel mills of the Ohio River valley to white-collar jobs in customer relations, and eventually to running his own business. Of having parents who hadn't finished high school, to raising children who graduated college and beyond. The protagonists and minor characters are all drawn from his own family and a small group of friends, and it's unlikely that any of the subplots involve anyone else from outside this very close-knit, local group, or that any particular outward sign of success has anything to do with anyone but himself, his family, or his faith.

And what I realize from having this conversation with him about global warming and the possible imminent demise of a livelihood, culture, and connection to land in Vietnam is that so many of all our stories are like my father's, where the people involved are limited to those we know personally, and the crises, failures, and triumphs tend to revolve around ourselves. But the moment he and I began to talk about climate change, the range of characters in our stories widened dramatically, the triumphs and failures had broad, rhizomatic sweeps, and we could begin to see how the stories themselves gave us an expanded view of the world and our role in it. In short, stories about climate change and climate justice sparked in us a global consciousness that highlighted the positions of power and privilege that otherwise remain hidden in most of our everyday decisions.

A climate scientist named Mike Hulme has made this connection to narrative too: "We need to reveal the creative psychological, ethical and spiritual work that climate change is doing for us. Understanding the ways in which climate change connects with foundational human instincts opens up possibilities for re-situating culture and the human spirit at the heart of our understanding of our changing climate."[13] He suggests using stories to open up these exact kinds of conversations, to help us better see who's involved, who's impacted, and most of all, how we can all inspire one another to achieve something better. These stories might be from our own recent past, the present, or our hopes for the future. Or they might be the stories from our collective, mythic past, stories that we can repurpose toward understanding what climate change and climate justice will mean for all human beings everywhere in the world.

Once my father and I began to tell our stories about our time in Vietnam and the climate challenges we will all face in the near future, we also began to see just how central our work is to understanding the scope of the problems and imagining solutions. Discussions about work get us to think about what we do *every* day, whether that means how we commute and how far, or where the things we make end up and how they get there, or who we work with or for, and how those coworkers make these same decisions. In my own case, my work to improve relations between the United States and Vietnam requires me to travel there occasionally. But I can find ways to maximize the productivity of my time in Vietnam by working simultaneously on as many projects as I can, and to minimize the number of trips by working with colleagues from home by email or Skype. While there, if I think about how my work intersects with others' and what climate impact results, I can choose to operate in a way that has the best outcome for everyone involved. The same goes for my daily work at home in Utah. Cô Mãn, Mr. Bích, and traditional Vietnamese farmers face a variety of local and global threats related to climate change, and it's obvious that for them and others living on the margins that personal, household economics as well as international corporate and governmental power will have to be significant drivers of all climate change solutions, but also that they need the help of people like my father who have to this point not given much thought to their own carbon footprints. Only when we can imagine all these examples at once and see the larger implications of our work's relationship to climate change and a more complete picture of everyone whose lives our work touches can we begin to imagine better ways to do what we must to make a living, while at the same time ensuring that we will all still have a place on this planet in which we can live.

■ A long time ago, a boy named Chú Cuội lived in a small village near the edge of the forest, providing for himself by tending the buffalos of his neighbors and roaming the forest hunting small game and cutting firewood to sell in the village market. A caring and gentle soul, Chú Cuội made a special bond with all the buffalo in his charge, speaking to them in low whispers while feeding and bathing them so that they always came to him and did his bidding without fail.

One day in the forest, Chú Cuội had chopped enough firewood to fill the two large baskets of his shoulder pole and started down the path along the river toward home when he heard a strange, bawling sound coming from the bushes ahead. Gently lowering his axe and baskets, he peeked through the leaves and discovered three tiger cubs growling and pouncing and tumbling over one another. When the first bit the tail of the second, then turned and bounded out of the clearing with the second in pursuit, Chú Cuội decided in an instant to dash in and snatch the third, imagining the price he could demand for it at the market and how this one amazing act would finally establish him as one of the great hunters in their valley. It was only after taking the cub firmly by the scruff of its neck and holding it out so it could not turn its razor sharp claws and teeth on him that the cub's impressively large and ferocious tigress mother let out a bone-melting snarl from the riverbank nearby. In panic, Chú Cuội tossed the cub aside and scrambled up the nearest tree. When he looked down, he saw that the carelessly tossed cub had collided with a rock and been knocked unconscious.

The mother entered the clearing and nosed the cub, but it did not stir. She licked it and prodded it, but still it would not move. Chú Cuội flushed with the dread of what he'd done, his heart aching with remorse, and watched as the tigress, unperturbed, left the cub and approached a banyan tree growing near the river. She bit off several leaves and chewed them while returning to the cub, then deposited them on the unconscious cub's head. After just a few seconds, the cub raised itself up, shook all over, then pounced after its mother's swishing tail as she disappeared in the direction of its siblings.

Chú Cuội climbed down and went straight to the banyan, wondering whether its leaves were magic or if it had just been a coincidence that the cub had leapt up when it did. Nevertheless, he picked a handful of leaves and put them in his pocket before gathering up his firewood and returning to the village.

Along the way, he found the favorite dog of one of the families whose buffalo he tended lying dead beside the path, a swipe of blood across its throat. Knowing the children would be inconsolable, he decided to try the banyan leaves before telling them what he'd found. He chewed the leaves, patted them onto the dog's wound, then stood amazed as the wound closed and the dog stirred back to life. In just seconds the dog was on its feet, wagging its tail and licking his hand. Chú Cuội immediately dumped his firewood, ran back to the tree, and carefully dug it up, wrapping the roots in wet leaves and slinging the whole bundle between the baskets to carry it home, where he planted it in the best spot in his garden.

Over the years, Chú Cuội became rich as the news of his miraculous healing power spread throughout the land. Every day people came from all over with all sorts of incurable diseases, weak hearts, and broken bones that took just a bit of the chewed-up banyan leaves to cure. Chú Cuội never charged a cent, but in gratitude the people always paid him something, or brought him some delicious dish to eat. And despite the attention and the many demands made of him during each day, he set aside time every morning to care for the tree, pruning branches, picking off insects, and giving it just the right amount of water to keep it healthy, knowing that if he stopped caring for it, one day the tree would simply fly away and disappear.

And then one day he forgot to water the tree. It was a festival day and there was a contest he wanted to win and he'd been thinking for weeks about it and about the girl he hoped to impress, and so when he finally remembered that he hadn't watered, he was already on the other side of the valley. The contest would start any minute. In an instant, he decided the tree could wait; he would just race back home as soon as it was over. Which he did, just in time to see the withered branches of the tree quiver, the trunk start to shake, and then, unbelievably, the roots just let go of the Earth as the tree began to float up into the sky. Chú Cuội shouted in alarm and made a fantastic, desperate leap to clutch the last roots dangling down. He hauled himself up to the root bundle, hoping to weigh the tree back down to the ground, but instead the tree just kept rising, all the way up into the heavens. A moment later, Chú Cuội found himself sitting at the base of the tree in the barren golden land of the moon, with the Earth shining in the distance far below. To this day, you can still see him sitting there, playing sad songs on his flute, pining for his terrestrial home.[14]

■ Sometimes we need a shift in perspective to see how remarkably we are sustained by the world around us, how even the smallest of our actions can have enormous impacts, and how ultimately it is our obligations that preserve us. Like Chú Cuội, if we don't want to find ourselves lost in space, sadly looking back at the Earth we once knew, we have to realize that Mr. Bích's and Cô Mãn's fates are tied to our own, that we must think of them too when we think about the things we want, and that our successes and failures are not simply our own.

NOTES

1. My retelling of the Son Tinh–Thủy Tinh folktale is based on several retellings. See, for example, Alice Terada, *Under the Starfruit Tree* (Honolulu: University of Hawaii Press, 1989), 50–53; Sherry Garland, *Children of the Dragon* (New York: Harcourt, 2001), 20–28; and Nguyen Nguyet Cam and Dana Sachs, *Two Cakes Fit for a King* (Honolulu: University of Hawaii Press, 2003), 27–32.

2. R. V. Cruz, et al., "Chapter 10: Asia," *Climate Change 2007: Impacts, Adaptation*

and Vulnerability. Contribution of Working Group II to the Fourth Assessment Report of the Intergovernmental Panel on Climate Change, ed. M. L. Parry et al. (Cambridge, UK: Cambridge University Press, 2007), 469–506, http://www.ipcc.ch/pdf/assessment -report/ar4/wg2/ar4-wg2-chapter10.pdf; S. Dasgupta et al., "The Impact of Sea Level Rise on Developing Countries: A Comparative Analysis," in *World Bank Policy Research Working Paper 4136* (February 2007), World Bank, Washington, DC, http://www-wds .worldbank.org/external/default/WDSContentServer/IW3P/IB/2007/02/09/000016406 _20070209161430/Rendered/PDF/wps4136.pdf.

3. World Heritage Convention, "Hoi An Ancient Town," UNESCO, http://whc.unesco .org/en/list/948; and World Heritage Convention, "My Son Sanctuary," UNESCO, http:// whc.unesco.org/en/list/949.

4. Anonymous, "Lullaby," in *Ca Dao Vietnam: Vietnamese Folk Poetry,* ed. John Balaban (Port Townsend, WA: Copper Canyon Press, 2003) 31. Recordings available at http://www.johnbalaban.com/ca-dao.html.

5. In water puppet theater, the puppeteers stand behind a curtain in a pool of water and use submerged control rods to make their puppets appear to be moving on the water. More information on this thousand-year-old art form can be found at http:// www.thanglongwaterpuppet.org/?/en/Home/.

6. Ngo Thi Phuong Lan, "From Rice to Shrimp: Ecological Change and Human Adaptation in the Mekong Delta," paper given at the *International Conference on Environmental Change, Agricultural Sustainability, and Economic Development in the Mekong Delta of Vietnam,* Can Tho University, Can Tho, Vietnam (March 25–27, 2010).

7. Vietnam News Service, "Imported Rice Brands Dominate Markets in the Mekong Delta," *Viet Nam News,* http://vietnamnews.vnanet.vn/Economy/195638/Imported-rice-brands-dominate-markets-in-the-Mekong-Delta-.htm.

8. Mr. Bích, interview with the author and other participants of the *International Conference on Environmental Change* (March 25, 2010).

9. Ngo, "From Rice to Shrimp."

10. Paul Theroux, *The Great Railway Bazaar* (New York: Penguin, 1975), 289.

11. International Rice Research Institute, "Coping with Climate Change," *Rice Today* 6(3): 10–15.

12. World Bank, "Vietnam and Energy," Energy & Mining in East Asia and Pacific (World Bank, Washington, DC, 2013), http://go.worldbank.org/S6Z88J3HC0.

13. Mike Hulme, *Why We Disagree about Climate Change: Understanding Controversy, Inaction and Opportunity* (Cambridge, UK: Cambridge University Press, 2009), 326.

14. My retelling of the Chú Cuội folktale is based on several retellings. See, for example, Garland, *Children of the Dragon,* 11–19; Do Van Ly, *The Stork and the Shrimp* (New Delhi: Siddharta Publications, 1959), 82–84; and The Gioi Publishers, *Vietnamese Legends and Folktales* (Hanoi: The Gioi Publishers, 1997), 39–42.

2

Working in Nature, Playing in Wilderness
Race, Class, and Environmental History in the Apostle Islands

JAMES W. FELDMAN

To me, the Apostle Islands have always been a wilderness. I first visited the islands in the early 1980s on a summer-camp hiking trip to Stockton Island. A population of black bears had recently taken up residence on the island, and the chance of seeing a bear—or having it rob our food supplies—added a thrill to the trip that I remember to this day. I have returned to the islands many times since, eager for the chance to walk the lonely beaches, to explore the overgrown forests, and to experience Lake Superior's notoriously furious storms. I spent two summers working at Apostle Islands National Lakeshore, giving tours of the Raspberry Island Lighthouse by day and exploring the island after hours. With no camping permitted on the island, I had the place to myself at night, and the island forest—a patch of old-growth hardwood/hemlock rare in the western Great Lakes—makes for quite a playground. Solitude, old-growth forests, and the powerful moods of Lake Superior make a potent set of wilderness characteristics.

Many others cherish the same attributes. In 2005 a panel of experts gathered by *National Geographic* named Apostle Islands National Lakeshore as the most appealing park in the United States. "In good shape ecologically. Not over-visited," commented one expert. "No man-made lights visible," stated another. "Visitation to the Apostle Islands is limited . . . keeping them in natural, pristine condition," added a third. "The aesthetic appeal of the land and water interaction is both dramatic and comforting." Apostle

Islands National Lakeshore ranked far ahead of more-well-known parks like Shenandoah, Yellowstone, and the Grand Canyon. These more famous parks confront dire threats from over-use, invasive species, and misman-agement. Fewer than 200,000 people visit the Apostle Islands each year, so the park does not face the crowds found elsewhere. This has helped main-tain the park's appeal.[1]

The twenty-two islands off Wisconsin's Bayfield Peninsula are sur-rounded by the cold, blue waters of Lake Superior. Red sandstone cliffs jut from the lake at several points around the archipelago. Pounding waves have carved caverns and arches where the sandstone faces the open lake. Quiet beaches line the shore in more-protected areas. A rich forest mosaic covers the islands, including several patches of old growth. Bob Krume-naker, the park's superintendent, explains that "some of the islands in this park are literally snapshots—very rare ones—of the original forests that once covered vast parts of this state and the larger Great Lakes region." The island environments are whole and healthy, an ecological integrity that amplifies the islands' allure. The Apostles have relatively few invasive spe-cies and provide a home for several endangered and threatened ones.[2]

And yet the islands were not always seen as a wilderness—that is, as a place to cherish wild nature, enjoy solitude, or camp and kayak in a primitive setting. Native Americans used the islands for centuries, and the Ojibwe Indians regard Long Island as a sacred site for its role in their migration to Wisconsin. French traders and missionaries arrived in the 1600s and Madeline Island served as a center of the fur trade through the 1830s. Euro American residents of the Chequamegon Bay fished, farmed, and logged in the Apostles after the 1850s. All of these people made homes and workplaces in the islands, each with their own ways of using and valu-ing nature. While the Apostles might have been a place to recreate or to contemplate the power of nature, they were also a place to live and work. The valuation of the islands exclusively as a wilderness developed only in the second half of the twentieth century, as resource extraction dwindled. The wilderness where I find solitude and wild nature was created out of a landscape shaped by the lives, and livelihoods, of men and women who once called this place home.[3]

The transitions among these ways of using nature have not always been easy. The success of extractive industries such as logging and commercial fishing required the suppression of local, subsistence-based ways of using nature, while the emergence of wilderness in the Apostles demanded the cessation of extractive activities. These economic shifts have had both social and ecological consequences. When methods of using and valuing nature come into conflict, some people have their access to resources prescribed in favor of others. Lines drawn by class, region, and race often lie at the root of these disputes. For more than a century, questions about how to best use the Apostle Islands and their resources have pitted locals against outsiders, whites against Indians, and working-class residents of the region against tourists visiting from elsewhere. Those with greater economic and political power—usually the outsiders, whites, and tourists—have consistently outmaneuvered locals, Indians, and working-class residents in these debates.

Analyzing histories like this one need not call into question the value of nature protection or other environmental causes; the Apostle Islands remain vitally important because of the healthy and wild nature that flourishes there. Rather, these stories illuminate the social and environmental consequences of conservation and environmentalism. As the historian Karl Jacoby explains, "By analyzing the class relationships embedded in conservation, we can take some preliminary steps toward illuminating the manner in which ecological relations and social relations interlock with one another, constructing together the material reality we call nature." The conservation and environmental movements have brought important changes to the way that people of different classes and groups interact with the natural world, changes to which we need to pay attention so that we may better understand the human place in nature.[4]

In the past twenty years, environmental historians have undertaken the important task of untangling these complicated social and ecological relations by illuminating the ways that class, race, gender, and region shape our interactions with nature and how these interactions have changed over time. Among its many insights, this scholarship has produced two related sets of observations about the relationships between the lives of working people and the environments in which they work. First, the way that we use and value nature reflects divisions within human society. Nature protection and other forms of environmental action have had social consequences, benefiting some and harming others. The creation of parks and preserves both in the United States and elsewhere, for example, has often led to the dislocation of people who used resources that the parks aimed to protect.

Large parks like Shenandoah and Yellowstone have followed this pattern, as have lesser-known places such as the Apostles. Environmental historians have also explored the parallels between the alienation of nature and the alienation of labor. The same economic processes—most importantly the expansion of market relations—have caused both the natural world and human labor to be treated as costs of production in the drive to accumulate capital. These two sets of observations are linked. Changing economic processes such as the expansion and corporatization of resource extraction or the emergence of mass consumption prompted a reorganization of the relationships between humans and the natural world, a reorganization that reflects power structures within human societies. These historical insights help explain how environmental injustice—in this case, the suppression of some methods of using and valuing nature in favor of others—became embedded in the economic and political structures of conservation and nature protection.[5]

At moments of significant economic transition, with the economic future of northern Wisconsin at stake, people with power used conservationist and environmentalist logic to impose their vision of the "proper" economic relationships with nature on people with different ideas and ways of using nature. The Apostle Islands region faced two such transitions. In the late nineteenth century, the shift from a mixed subsistence economy to one more focused on resource extraction and market sales secured access to resources for powerful sport and commercial interests by restricting access for local residents of the region. In the 1950s the decline of resource production and the rise of the consumer economy brought a new debate on whether to manage the islands as a wilderness. In both of these transitions, those with economic and political power ensured their own access to diminishing resources at the expense of those without such advantages. And yet the environmental history of the islands also shows that lines drawn by class, race, and region are not absolute. The designation of Apostle Islands National Lakeshore in 1970 generated a diverse opposition coalition defined more by attachment to place than by social factors. All of these forces—social difference, unequally distributed power, attachment to place—came into dynamic conflict at times of economic transition. The environmental history of the Apostle Islands provides a case study of the relationship between environmental injustice and nature protection, and also serves as a reminder that these relationships are not confined to the distant past or to other parts of the world.

Market Production, Recreation, and the Costs of Conservation

Contests over the use of island resources arose with the first steps toward governmental management of natural resources—the regulation of sport and commercial fishing. In the late nineteenth century, resource managers across the nation championed the ideology of conservation, calling for the maximization of public utility from public resources. The logic of conservation provided an important tool for resource managers seeking to use the growing regulatory authority of the state to guide the economic transformation of rural areas like the Apostle Islands toward a greater connection with the national market.[6] The state of Wisconsin became active in conservation in 1874, when the legislature created the Wisconsin Fish Commission (WFC). Commissioner James Nevin explained the application of conservation to Wisconsin's fisheries: "Conservation does not mean hoarding fish or game as a miser does his gold; it means to permit the taking, catching, and killing of fish and game in such a manner, at such times, and in such quantities, as will conserve the supply for future years." It also meant the prioritization of market production and recreation over subsistence.[7]

Nevin and the WFC had two tools at their disposal: supplementing fish stocks with artificial propagation, and changing how fishermen caught fish. Both fisheries experts and fishermen preferred propagation, and this became the initial focus of the WFC. But even the most devoted pisciculturalist recognized that artificial propagation alone would not restore badly damaged fisheries. The habits of fishermen needed to be changed, too. "What we need is protection for the small fish," Nevin recommended, "and artificial propagation will keep the lakes and streams well supplied." It was a difficult task. Fishermen supported artificial propagation far more enthusiastically than regulation, and laws outlawing specific equipment and the sale of small fish were notoriously hard to enforce. Nevertheless, the state legislature passed the first laws regulating the fisheries in 1879, setting minimum weights for marketed fish and banning small mesh nets. Over the next several decades, the WFC and the state legislature tightened these restrictions.[8]

State regulation privileged some fishermen—especially full-time fishermen focused on market production—over others. Fishermen used different types of equipment, depending on their available capital and the amount of time they spent fishing. Pound nets, for example, required a significant investment and a crew of two to three men, and were used only by the most well-capitalized fishermen. Seine nets, on the other hand, could be used from the shore, required little investment, and were more common among itinerant fishermen who drifted in and out of the industry. A limit on the mesh size that applied to seine and pound nets affected fishermen of different means disproportionately. Independent, part-time fishermen could not refit their rigs to comply with tightening regulations. Closed seasons allowed large fish-dealing and fish-packing companies to sell frozen fish while no fresh fish reached the market. One Lake Superior fisherman explained the consequences of a closed season as "detrimental to a great many poor families, who live, from year to year, on the fish caught." For the small-scale and part-time fisherman, he explained, the closed season "might not be the best regulation."[9]

A similar pattern of state regulatory authority developed in the sport fisheries. In 1879 the WFC started a propagation program for game fish, such as brook trout and wall-eye pike, and introduced sport fish popular elsewhere. The motivation was explicitly economic. "Hundreds of sportsmen from beyond our borders annually visit [northern Wisconsin], and leave thousands of dollars within our confines," the commissioners explained. The commissioners viewed their work as vital to the expansion of the tourist trade: "These summer dwellers and throngs of transient sporting tourists who bring so large a revenue to our state, seek not only fine scenery, boating and fresh air. Our lakes and rivers are also attractive to them because of their fish supply. This supply needs continual protection as well as reinforcement."[10]

The commissioners made an apt observation. In the late nineteenth century, as railroads reached every corner of the state, the railroad companies promoted northern Wisconsin as a sportsman's paradise. Fishermen would find the rivers of the Chequamegon Bay "literally swarming with the finest brook trout. . . . Five hundred of the epicurean dainties in one day is by no means an extraordinary catch." The channels between the islands offered a form of fishing found nowhere else between the ocean coasts: trolling, or fishing for lake trout with a hook and line. "Parties who have tried it say there is no finer sport to be had than that of trolling for lake trout among the islands," commented the *Bayfield County Press*. In the early years of railroad tourism, only the wealthy could afford the time and expense of journeys to remote destinations. After the turn the century, however, as the economy matured and became more modern, leisure time and disposable income became markers of the emerging middle class. To attract this new group of travelers, the railroad companies erected luxurious hotels in Ashland and Bayfield. They promoted these hotels widely, as well as the recreational opportunities of the islands.[11]

Like the changes in the commercial fishing industry, the growing tourist trade in the Apostles coincided with the economic shift toward the market. For residents of Bayfield and other nearby towns, the tourist trade opened new opportunities for wage work. Locals earned money by guiding tourists on camping and hunting expeditions, working in hotels, caretaking for summer residents, and selling supplies and foodstuffs. The editors of the *Bayfield Press* explained that tourists "aid in consuming our produce, in giving employment to laboring men and in helping business generally." The tourist trade provided important opportunities to earn money in an economy that was moving away from subsistence.[12]

To help preserve sporting opportunities, the WFC complemented its stocking programs with a continual call for the regulation of sport fishing. Beginning in the 1870s, the legislature set closed seasons on sport fish, prohibited the use of nets on inland waters, and outlawed the sale of game species. As in the commercial fisheries, these regulations privileged some activities—and some people—over others. The commissioners were quite explicit in this goal: "While these inland waters have a local importance as yielding food, their value as a means of sport and recreation is much greater, both to the state and to the community in which the lake is situated. For this reason, the aim of legislation for many years has been to preserve the fishing rather than to cause the lakes to yield a maximum amount of food." Sporting provided a better use of game fish than did subsistence. Rural residents—who often depended on fish and game to supplement their meager incomes—saw their access to commonly held resources restricted.[13]

One group in particular suffered from the regulations put into place by the WFC: the state's Ojibwe Indians.[14] Ojibwe had used the fisheries of Lake

Superior for generations, for both subsistence and for wage work. They had labored in the commercial fishery in the Apostles since its inception in the 1830s. As they integrated into the American economy, Ojibwe blended subsistence with the opportunities presented by the market. Fishing stands as an example of this balancing act. The ice that formed over the channels between some of the islands provided ideal conditions for spear fishing. The Ojibwe were so successful in this enterprise that they made the Chequamegon Bay the only site of commercial spear-fishing on Lake Superior. One fisherman described the winter fishery in the 1890s: "Considerable many half-breeds—Indian blood. There would be probably upwards of 150 people engaged in this fishing in the winter. There will be 1/3 of that number who do not sell any fish—just fish for their own use." The mixture of subsistence and market activity constituted an essential component of Ojibwe economic life.[15]

Both federal Indian agents and state conservation officials disapproved of Ojibwe methods and their tendency to drift in and out of the commercial fishery, and they leveraged conservation laws to impose their ideas of proper behavior on Native Americans in Wisconsin and elsewhere. Federal Indian policy in the late nineteenth century had the stated goal of assimilating Ojibwe into mainstream society. The ability of the Ojibwe to use wage work in the fisheries and lumber camps as a seasonal supplement to subsistence hunting and fishing inhibited this goal. Fisheries experts regarded the Ojibwe practice of spearing for walleye—a prized sport fish—as a significant threat to the resources they hoped to protect. One state official labeled the "nefarious practice" as most "destructive to the finny tribe."[16] Spearing killed fish at their most vulnerable—as they headed to the shallows to spawn—thus threatening the reproduction of a species considered essential for the lucrative tourist trade. Beginning in the 1880s state conservation officials forced Ojibwe fishermen to obey a growing list of hunting and fishing regulations, among them a prohibition on the use of spears to catch game fish. Activities that the Ojibwe had pursued without interference for generations were criminalized.[17]

The Ojibwe had a different interpretation of their hunting and fishing. The right to fish, they believed, had been guaranteed to them by the treaties that they had signed with the US government in the mid-nineteenth century. Two Ojibwe arrested in 1889 claimed "that it has been customary from time immemorial for many of the Chippewas to obtain the major part of their subsistence from that source." One federal agent reported on the Indian reaction to an arrest for violating game laws in 1894: "The Indians all feel that they are entitled to hunt and fish as they may choose and that the stipulation of the treaty with the Government granting this privilege has never been changed." These disputes eventually moved into the courts, which consistently ruled that the state had the right to manage its wildlife, and that federal treaties had been made obsolete when Wisconsin entered the union in 1848. A 1907 ruling known as the Morrin Decision extended the state's regulatory authority over Indian fishing and hunting both on and off the reservations and restricted Ojibwe treaty rights for the next seventy-five years. Judicial rulings did not necessarily change behavior, and the intermittent court cases concerning Indian violations of game laws throughout the twentieth century testify to Ojibwe resistance to state authority and to the maintenance of culturally significant practices. Indeed, the flouting of state game laws—often called "violating"—became an important Ojibwe cultural tradition in its own right.[18]

The use of conservation laws to make the subsistence activities of Native Americans and other marginalized groups illegal was not unique to the Apostles. In places as diverse as Yellowstone National Park, Minnesota's Superior National Forest, western Pennsylvania, and the rural South, environmental historians have traced how the last decades of the nineteenth century brought the restriction of access to resources that had once been used as a commons. Those who utilized resources for reasons other than sport or market production, or who produced at small scales, often found their uses of nature prescribed or criminalized. Game laws prevented the hunting of birds and wildlife, grazing permits and fencing restricted the common use of pastures, and trespass laws prevented the gathering of firewood on public land. Often, the effect of these laws—and sometimes their explicit motivation—was to force wage laborers into the job market. A labor supply more dependent on the market and less on subsistence meant a labor supply more inclined to work at terms favorable to the corporations that dominated extractive industries like fishing, mining, and logging. In other words, conservation had winners and losers. Those with social, economic, and political power used the ideology of conservation to secure for themselves control of resources or advantages in the marketplace. Those able to use the state's managerial authority for their own ends won access to limited resources at the expense of those who could not. Social and ecological relations intersected to determine who could access nature, and how and when they could do so.[19]

These changes coincided with an important shift in the national and regional economy away from subsistence toward the market. This transition relied on treating both natural resources and human labor as factors of production, factors that could be most efficiently utilized through the application of corporate capital and state managerial authority. Different sectors of the American economy and different regions of the nation embraced the market at different times. In some areas, market production—a focus on the accumulation of wealth by reliance on a single cash crop or specialized activity—occurred in the early nineteenth century; elsewhere this transition did not occur until the twentieth century. Bayfield and the other Chequamegon Bay communities had been established in the mid-nineteenth century, and as the region became more connected to national transportation networks, its economy became ever more focused on the market. The arrival of the railroad at the Chequamegon Bay in 1877 accelerated this transition. Frozen fish, finished lumber, and agricultural produce could now be transported quickly and cheaply to urban centers throughout the Midwest and the nation. State authority—in the form of conservation laws, tax codes, and development subsidies—further encouraged the shift to market production. State regulation privileged the kinds of activities that meshed with the emerging national market—resource extraction and the wage economy of the tourist trade—while making it difficult, and even illegal, for anyone to pursue subsistence activities.[20]

It can be very difficult for modern visitors to places such as the Apostles to trace the social and ecological relations that combined to create these dynamics. No one lives in these places any more, and those who visit come for recreation, not for subsistence. In the Apostle Islands, the National Park Service maintains and interprets a restored itinerant fish camp—the kind of place once frequented by the smaller, poorly capitalized fishermen who drifted in and out of the industry. A handful of archaeological sites buried deep in the woods provide a few additional clues to a history—a way of interacting with nature—that has largely vanished.

Recreation, Extraction, and Wilderness

A second economic shift in the mid-twentieth century brought a parallel situation, as changing economic patterns again prompted the use of state authority in the name of nature protection in ways that privileged some uses of nature over others. In the 1950s the United States pivoted from two decades of depression and war into a period of unprecedented economic growth. Armed with disposable income, leisure time, and a pent-up consumer demand, middle-class Americans headed indoors to shopping malls and outdoors to beaches, hiking trails, and campgrounds. Consumerism emerged as a defining feature of American society—people placed more value on the meaning of goods than on their use. This development had a particular impact on the relationships among tourism, recreation, and nature. Nature itself became a consumer good, at least for those who no longer depended on resource extraction to make a living.[21]

The shift toward a consumer economy had important ramifications for the Apostle Islands. From the 1870s to the 1950s, resource production had anchored the economy of the Chequamegon Bay. Farming, logging, and quarrying joined fishing and tourism as economic engines. But to consider these industries in isolation misses an essential component of economic life in the islands: these industries overlapped and reinforced each other. Farmers depended on summer residents and resorts as a market for their produce. Fishermen worked in logging camps in the winter and ferried tourists during the summer. The railroads that promoted the region and brought the tourists also carried lumber, fish, and stone harvested from the islands. The overlapping nature of these different industries provided an important safety net against the boom-and-bust cycles that marked economic life in a resource-producing hinterland. Only in the twentieth century did tourism come to stand apart from these other uses of nature, the result of a growing separation between the acts of production and consumption, the emergence of the consumer economy, and a new way of valuing places like the Apostle Islands—as a wilderness.

In the mid-twentieth century the intersecting economic structures of the Chequamegon Bay economy began to fall apart. Exhaustion of the resources played a role in this transition: lumber mills shut down for lack of raw materials and fisheries crashed from overfishing and the arrival of invasive species. More significant, however, was a change in the way that people viewed the tourist and recreational potential of the Apostles and other natural landscapes. As people from outside the region came to view the islands as a wilderness and a site for primitive outdoor recreation, they segregated tourism from the other, more extractive ways of using nature.

This segregation brought two markedly different ways of viewing and using nature into conflict.

In the prosperous years that followed World War II, the nation as a whole and Wisconsin in particular experienced a boom in outdoor recreation. Since the days of railroad tourism, the state's lakes, resorts, and sporting opportunities had earned it a reputation as the playground of the Midwest. Pressure on state parks and forests increased significantly in the 1950s. Visits to state campgrounds exploded by 243 percent during the decade, and total visits to state parks jumped from 3 million in 1951 to over 5 million in 1956. Funding for the parks, meanwhile, remained constant.[22]

State officials viewed the growing demand for outdoor recreation as an opportunity to ameliorate the economic depression that settled on the northern part of the state as the extractive economy dwindled. If the recreationally starved urbanites of Chicago, Milwaukee, and other cities could be connected to the resources of northern Wisconsin, two problems could be solved at once. Many state planners believed that the recreation industry offered the only escape from the economic stagnation faced by the region. To accomplish these twin goals, they recommended the creation, expansion, and improvement of parks, roads, and forests throughout the area. Governor Gaylord Nelson—later the founder of Earth Day and one of the environmental movement's political champions—built his political career in part on the recognition that recreational tourism and nature protection could help solve northern Wisconsin's economic ills.[23]

The movement for state acquisition of the Apostles began in 1950. That year, the Milwaukee County Conservation Alliance—an affiliation of sportsmen's clubs—requested that the Wisconsin Conservation Department (WCD) investigate state acquisition of the islands "for recreational purposes." In 1952 state officials toured the islands and liked what they saw: a forest recovering after the destructive logging of previous generations, a landscape seemingly tailor-made for scientific experiments in ecology and game management, and a wonderland for the increasingly popular forms of wilderness recreation.[24] One official described Stockton Island as "almost in its natural condition; no fires have destroyed the forests. It has not been logged since 1915." By "natural condition," he did not mean the absence of human activity, but rather that people had not directly shaped forest regeneration. The island had no roads, no buildings save a few ruins, and no active forest management. As plans for public acquisition of the islands developed, their naturalness—or wildness—became their most important attribute. The prevailing ecological belief that forests inevitably and predictably matured from disturbance to a climax ecosystem increased the islands' ecological value. The WCD adopted a "Policy on Acquisition of an Apostle Islands Wilderness Area" in 1955 and singled out Stockton, Oak, and Basswood Islands for state acquisition.[25]

WCD officials believed that the islands' greatest value lay in the opportunity they provided for wilderness recreation. Visitors to the islands had long noted their beauty, their cliffs and beaches, and the plentiful fish and game. But as the outdoor recreation boom intensified, the Apostles took on a new value. They could provide a type of recreation not possible in most places. WCD ecologist Burton Dahlberg wrote to the director of the WCD in 1955: "The value of an undeveloped area where it is possible to get away from the hustle and bustle of modern living cannot be overestimated. There are very few places left in the Middle West that offer an opportunity to establish a natural area, where future generations may know the value of natural things. . . . One of Stockton Island's greatest assets is its inaccessibility. The fact that a vacation on the island requires some planning and the possibility that one may be stranded for a few extra days makes it all the more desirable." Although Dahlberg did not use the term *wilderness*, he employed wilderness rhetoric in calling for public acquisition of the islands. Dahlberg and others worried that logging and development would soon rob the islands of their wilderness value.[26]

As WCD officials toured the islands, the national wilderness movement gathered momentum. In the 1950s wilderness advocates rallied around the defense of Echo Park in Colorado's Dinosaur National Monument, a wild and beautiful canyon at the confluence of the Green and Yampa Rivers threatened by a federal dam proposal. Wilderness advocates strategically appealed to the growing demand for outdoor recreation to build a national coalition against the dam project. The momentum generated by stopping the dam at Echo Park led to the passage of the Wilderness Act of 1964. The wilderness ideal that emerged in the 1950s and 1960s valued seemingly pristine nature—wilderness untouched by human hands—despite the fact that many of the places the wilderness movement sought to protect had in fact been shaped and reshaped by Native American and Euro American inhabitance. The rhetoric of the national wilderness movement informed the developing WCD policy on the acquisition of the Apostles.[27]

But not everyone in the area approved of the WCD's plans for wilderness management in the islands. When discussions on state acquisition of the Apostles began in the early 1950s, residents of the region supported the project. The Ashland and Bayfield County Boards and local chambers of commerce promised to work with WCD officials, who agreed to develop their plans in conjunction with local governments. But as prospects for acquiring the islands solidified, residents of the Chequamegon Bay expressed their displeasure with the WCD's vision of wilderness in the islands. When WCD officials approached the Ashland County Board to purchase land on Oak, Basswood, and Stockton islands, the board declined, and retained a real estate agent to sell its island property to private developers.[28]

Locals disapproved of the WCD's plans for wilderness management, demanding a state park instead.[29] A park, many believed, would bring in more tourists, as well as the roads, hotels, restaurants, and services they needed; it would connect to other industries in the area and stimulate the economy. "[The] people in the Ashland area want something made of the islands so that they will be an attraction for tourists," explained Kenneth Todd, chair of the Ashland County Board. Wilderness would not provide these benefits. Todd believed "it would not help the state, the county, or the islands if they are established as a pure wilderness area . . . [and] there is already enough wilderness area in the north and that the need is for well-developed state parks." For Todd and other local residents, the Apostle Islands had always been a source of income and a place to work. These uses seemed incompatible with the WCD's plans for wilderness.[30]

The two alternatives for development represented strikingly different ways of using and valuing nature. A state park followed traditional local patterns of resource use and extraction. Utilized in this way, the island environments had supported fishermen, farmers, loggers, and tourist operators for over a century. The desire to treat the Apostles as a wilderness originated outside the Chequamegon Bay, with sportsmen who viewed the islands as a retreat, not as a workplace. Valuing the islands as a wilderness had come to stand in opposition to the resource extraction that had anchored past economies in the islands. Wilderness depended on minimizing signs of past extractive use—evidence of the logging, fishing, and farming that had sustained local economies for over a century—and would prohibit such use in the future. It would also mean an end to those extractive activities that still persisted in the islands.

Despite local opposition, the state forged ahead with its plans for the Apostles, formally creating Apostle Islands State Forest in 1959 and purchasing Stockton Island from its private owner. The creation of the state forest did not necessarily mean that the WCD would acquire other islands. Ashland County Board members resolved not to sell county lands on Oak and Basswood Islands to the WCD until it demonstrated an acceptable development program for Stockton. These demands did not dissuade the WCD from managing Stockton Island as a wilderness. The WCD crafted guidelines for this purpose: "General development will be kept to a minimum in order to preserve the Apostle Islands as a primitive, wilderness area." The limited facilities provided by the WCD included a pier, a small office, pit toilets, and a handful of campsites. This did not satisfy the requests of the Ashland County Board.[31]

WCD officials responded to local demands for development by creating Big Bay State Park on Madeline Island, where they again found themselves in the middle of a dispute between locals and outsiders, one with conflict lines more clearly drawn by social class. The WCD established Big Bay State Park in 1963, with plans for a 2,700-acre park with full recreational facilities featuring the expansive beach on the northeastern end of the island. Madeline had been a summer destination for wealthy Midwesterners since the late nineteenth century, and many of the island's well-to-do summer residents opposed the state park. As the state deliberated, the National Park Service proposed a national lakeshore in the islands, one that would be far more extensive than either the state forest or the state park at Big Bay. As the national lakeshore moved closer to designation and the exclusion of Madeline from the proposal became clear, the prospects for private development of the island rose. This strengthened the demands that the WCD scale back on its plans for the state park. Summer resident Theodore Gary led this opposition, and he capitalized on the rising land values with a series of lucrative real estate deals, including the construction of a marina, a golf course, and a lodge. The WCD did create Big Bay State Park, but reduced the size of the park and the extent of its facilities.[32]

Residents of Bayfield and Ashland resented the interference from people they regarded as outsiders—even though the Gary family had first started using Madeline Island as a summer retreat in the early twentieth century. Supporters of Big Bay State Park charged that the Garys and their allies wanted to keep Madeline Island as a retreat for the rich and well-heeled.

The *Bayfield County Press* ran a blistering editorial on the issue: "It seems that the general run-of-the-mill family groups which would frequent such a park, would not be in keeping with the high caliber of people THEY are interested in having on their island." Patricia Gary's comment that the "type of people who frequent a state park would not be good for the island" did not help matters. In fact, many year-round islanders—a presumably less-wealthy crowd—also opposed the expansion of the state park. But most people around Chequamegon Bay supported the state park, much as they wanted a similar development on Stockton Island.[33]

The series of disputes over the creation of state parks and forests in the Apostles reveals once again how some people are able to turn the power of the state to their own advantage. The planners at the WCD responded to the political pressure applied by Gaylord Nelson and sportsmen from outside the region, and created a wilderness area against the wishes of the residents of Chequamegon Bay. Theodore Gary profited from the use of his economic and political connections in minimizing the size of Big Bay State Park. Residents of the region—clinging to economic patterns of the past that required a broader perspective on the uses of natural resources—saw their own uses of the islands prescribed. The results of this process both shaped the material reality of nature—the islands became more wild as the state managed some islands for primitive outdoor recreation and scientific study—and also the ways that people used and understood that material reality.

Remnants of the landscape of production that once defined the island economy are far easier to locate in the modern landscape than are signs of the subsistence economy that it replaced. The paths that once carried tracks for the logging railroads now serve as hiking trails on Michigan and Outer Islands, and rusted logging equipment lies in the woods amidst the resurgent forest on several other islands. The square stone blocks at the quarry sites on Basswood, Hermit, and Stockton Islands sit perched near the lakeshore as if still awaiting transport to a distant market—even though eighty-year-old trees now grow amongst them. Those familiar with the patterns of ecological succession in the North Woods will recognize that second-growth forests carpet the islands—evidence of the widespread disturbances of logging and farming in the past. Yet most of these signs remain hard to find, curious relics that seem out of place in today's wilderness landscape.

The Making of Wilderness and the Importance of Place

Episodes such as the debates over the creation of parks and forests in the Apostles reinforce the perspective that wilderness is a concern of the wealthy, and that nature protection comes at the expense of the working class. This characterization fueled such high-profile controversies as the preservation of the spotted owl in the Pacific Northwest in the 1990s and drilling in the Arctic National Wildlife Refuge in the first decade of the twenty-first century. In these cases, nature protection was portrayed as against the interests of working people and their families. But lines drawn by class and region are not absolute. The disputes over state management of the Apostles faded in the late 1960s as a new controversy arose over the creation of Apostle Islands National Lakeshore. Gaylord Nelson—by this time Wisconsin's senator—spearheaded this campaign. Although Nelson continued to urge that the islands be managed as a wilderness, the vast majority of residents of the region supported the proposal. Even the previously recalcitrant members of the Ashland County Board passed a resolution in favor of the project. Kenneth Todd, a vigorous opponent of state wilderness management, had a very different reaction to the national lakeshore. He determined that the gas stations, motels, and marinas promised by the creation of the park would provide revenue to the county. It would be foolish, Todd believed, to pass on "a proposal as major as this one, with a bonanza of island development, booming tourism, and financial gain." The national lakeshore would provide the jobs and economic incentives to revitalize the economy in a way that a state-managed wilderness would not.[34]

Opposition to the proposal was confined primarily to a coalition of landowners who faced the prospect of losing their property to the new park. This coalition cut across lines drawn by class, race, and region. The Red Cliff Ojibwe opposed the park because of a legacy of distrust in their dealings with the federal government and the government's unwillingness to recognize their treaty-guaranteed rights to hunt and fish within the boundaries of the new lakeshore.[35] Those who owned land within the proposed lakeshore portrayed the project as an attempt by outsiders to use the federal government to take something away from the communities of the Chequamegon Bay. "It seems to me that the southern half of the State should take care of its own responsibilities and let the northerners do likewise," complained one property owner. "All you people in Washington have to do is leave us alone," stated another.[36]

But just who could be considered local in this dispute? Some property owners and their families had been spending their summers in the islands since the early twentieth century, but had never identified them as a permanent home. Others were the children and grandchildren of island settlers—the descendants of fishermen and lumberjacks. The families of some park opponents had lived in the area for generations, and others had just arrived in the region. The prospect of losing access to treasured resources united these disparate interests into a small but vocal group steadfastly opposed to the park. "As for fair market value, how do you figure sentiment footage and your buildings?" wondered Robert Hokenson, a fisherman with ties in the region dating several generations. "Money can't buy what I think of what I own. That goes for all the others along the shoreline."[37]

Sand Island demonstrates how complicated attachments to place can cut across social divides. The island had been home for a community of immigrant fishermen and farmers since the 1880s. The descendants of the island's settlers and summer residents employed their family histories as an argument against the park. "For three generations my ancestors lived and made their living on the island as commercial fishermen and farmers," explained Constance Durham, a fisherman's daughter who no longer lived in the area. The Jensch family had used the island for six decades of summers, but had never made a permanent home there. They wondered why they did not receive the same treatment as Madeline Island property owners whose lands were not being considered for the national lakeshore. "Now Madeline Island has a lot of estates, and fine roads . . . but to us, Sand Island is just as important," explained Samuel Jensch. Some of the Sand Island families had the same level of political connections and economic power as the Garys and other Madeline Island families. They united with the descendants of fishermen and farmers to fight against the park proposal. Race and class associations shape the way that people value and use nature, but so do histories of use and connections to place.[38]

Despite the opposition, Congress established Apostle Islands National Lakeshore in 1970. Wilderness advocates claimed an important victory. They had protected a significant portion of the Great Lakes shoreline from development, securing the islands for outdoor recreation, ecological study, and natural habitat. Thirty-five years later, Congress formally designated

80 percent of the lakeshore a part of the National Wilderness Preservation System.

Since assuming control of the Apostles in 1970, the National Park Service has applied its own wilderness management policies to the islands. This has meant removing the evidence of past subsistence and resource extraction—razing fishing cabins and farmsteads, revegetating disturbed landscapes, and removing docks—to make the islands seem more pristine. These actions have helped protect the healthy and vibrant environments that make the Apostle Islands so valuable today. But in pursuit of a wilderness ideal that prioritizes seemingly pristine nature, the Park Service has erased the evidence of the lives of the men and women who saw the islands as a home and workplace, and who shaped their landscapes accordingly. The wilderness characteristics that visitors have so enjoyed in the Apostles are in part the result of management policies instituted by the WCD and the National Park Service. The intersecting social and ecological relations of past conflicts have shaped the material reality of today's islands. They have created a landscape we today call wilderness.[39]

The patterns of resource use, nature protection, and social change evident in the environmental history of the Apostle Islands have been repeated across time and place. The creation of Apostle Islands National Lakeshore mirrors the dislocation of inhabitants of protected landscapes that marked the creation of national parks such as Yellowstone, the Grand Canyon, and Shenandoah. As American ideas about wilderness and national parks traveled around the globe, this pattern of dislocation has often been repeated, with disastrous consequences for indigenous peoples with long traditions of resource use and inhabitance of landscapes valued today for their wildness and biodiversity. Many scholars have analyzed the tension between national parks and indigenous rights in developing nations as a modern-day counterpart to the creation of American national parks a century ago. The history of the Apostle Islands demonstrates that tensions created by conflicting ways of using and valuing nature are not confined to the distant past or to the developing world.[40]

Analyzing these stories will not compromise the value of the Grand Canyon or the Apostle Islands as wild places, or as wilderness. Rather, these stories help to explain the way that visitors to wilderness encounter and understand such places. Most of the campgrounds that I have used while kayaking or sailing in the islands lie in clearings once inhabited by fishermen, loggers, or farmers. The National Park Service repurposed these sites to meet the needs of wilderness tourism—a fitting commentary on how different ways of valuing and using nature have been layered upon one another to create the modern landscape. Overlapping and often conflicting sets of ecological and social relations have shaped and reshaped these places. Recognizing these layers allows us to better understand the world we inhabit and better protect the wild places that we cherish.

NOTES

1. Jonathan B. Tourtellot, "National Park Destinations Rated," *National Geographic Traveler* (July/August 2005); National Geographic Traveler, "National Park Destinations Rated: Central US and Canada," http://traveler.nationalgeographic.com/2005/07/destinations-rated/central-text; "In good shape" and "No man-made lights," 82; "Visitation to the" and "The aesthetic appeal," Web page.

2. Bob Krumenaker, "An Ecological Disaster in the Making," *Around the Archipelago* (2009), "some of the islands," 2; Emmet J. Judziewicz and Rudy G. Koch, "Flora and Vegetation of the Apostle Islands National Lakeshore and Madeline Island, Ashland and Bayfield Counties, Wisconsin," *The Michigan Botanist* 32 (March 1993): 43–189.

3. *Wilderness* is a loaded and controversial term with no set meaning. Since the 1990s academics and wilderness advocates have engaged in a critical rethinking of the meaning of wilderness and its usefulness as a conservation strategy, raising questions about its historical and scientific accuracy. Many of these critiques point out that Native Americans everywhere directly and consciously shaped their environments—debunking the concept of "pristine wilderness." Other scholars have critiqued wilderness as a cultural construct, as an idea created in opposition to modern industrial society, not a real, physical place that avoided the influence of human activity. Wilderness advocates worry that academic concerns with terminology will undermine a vital conservation strategy essential for protecting biodiversity and wildness. Multiple perspectives on the wilderness debate are included in J. Baird Callicott and Michael P. Nelson, eds., *The Great New Wilderness Debate: An Expansive Collection of Writings Defining Wilderness from John Muir to Gary Snyder* (Athens: University of Georgia Press, 1998).

4. Karl Jacoby, "Class and Environmental History," *Environmental History* 2 (July 1997), "By analyzing the," 326.

5. On the relationship between social and environmental history, see Jacoby, "Class and Environmental History"; Jacoby, "Classifying Nature: In Search of a Common Ground Between Social and Environmental History," in *Situating Environmental History,* ed. Ranjan Chakrabarti (Delhi: Manohar, 2007), 45–58; Thomas G. Andrews,

Killing for Coal: America's Deadliest Labor War (Cambridge, MA: Harvard University Press, 2010); Gunther W. Peck, "The Nature of Labor: Fault Lines and Common Ground in Environmental and Labor History," *Environmental History* 11, no. 2 (April, 2006): 212–38; Benjamin Heber Johnson, "Subsistence, Class, and Conservation at the Birth of Superior National Forest," *Environmental History* 4 (January 1999): 80–99; Louis Warren, *The Hunters' Game: Poachers and Conservationists in Twentieth-Century America* (New Haven, CT: Yale University Press, 1999); and Steven Hahn, "Hunting, Fishing, and Foraging: Common Rights and Class Relations in the Postbellum South," *Radical History Review* 26 (October 1982): 37–64.

6. On the emergence of conservation, see John D. Buenker, *The Progressive Era: 1893–1914*, vol. 4, *The History of Wisconsin Series*, ed. William Fletcher Thompson (Madison: State Historical Society of Wisconsin Press, 1998); Robert H. Wiebe, *The Search for Order, 1877–1920* (New York: Hill & Wang, 1967); Samuel P. Hays, *Conservation and the Gospel of Efficiency: The Progressive Conservation Movement, 1890–1920* (Cambridge, MA: Harvard University Press, 1959); David Stradling, *Smokestacks and Progressives: Environmentalists, Engineers, and Air Quality in America, 1881–1951* (Baltimore: Johns Hopkins University Press, 1999).

7. Walter E. Scott and Thomas Reitz, *The Wisconsin Warden: Wisconsin Conservation Law Enforcement, A Centennial Chronology (1879–1979)* (Madison: Wisconsin Department of Natural Resources, 1979), i, 1–5; Wisconsin Conservation Commission, *Biennial Report of the State Conservation Commission of Wisconsin for the Years 1915–1916* (Madison, WI: State Conservation Commission, 1917), 18; "Conservation does not," 18.

8. James Nevin, "Artificial Propagation versus a Close Season for the Great Lakes," *Transactions of the American Fisheries Society* 27 (1898), "What we need," 25. See also Scott and Reitz, *The Wisconsin Warden*, i, 1–5.

9. Nevin, "Artificial Propagation versus a Close Season," 25; Samuel Quinn, Notes and Files of the Joint Commission Relative to the Preservation of the Fisheries in Waters Contiguous to Canada and the United States, Box 8, vol. 3, RG 22, National Archives, College Park, Maryland, Notes by Subject, Lake Superior, 1894, Box 11, vol. D, 145; "detrimental to a great," 145.

10. *Annual Report of the Fish Commissioners of the State of Wisconsin 1881*, "Hundreds of sportsmen," 8; *Annual Report of the Fish Commissioners of the State of Wisconsin 1889–1890*, "These summer dwellers," 4. See also Fish Commissioners of the State of Wisconsin, *Annual Report of the Fish Commissioners of the State of Wisconsin for the Year Ending December 31, 1879* (Madison, WI: David Atwood, 1879), 11; ibid., 1884, 6; ibid., 1889–1890, 4.

11. No. Wisconsin Central Railroad, *Famous Resorts of the Northwest, Summer of 1887* (Chicago: Poole Bros., 1887), "literally swarming with," 9; see also 7, 9; *Bayfield County Press*, May 26, 1900, "Parties who have"; Cindy S. Aron, *Working at Play: A History of*

Vacations in the United States (New York: Oxford University Press, 1999); Island View Hotel Company, *Bayfield Wisconsin: The Most Famous Health and Pleasure Resort in Northern Wisconsin* (Bayfield, WI: Bayfield County Press, 1890).

12. *Bayfield Press,* August 21, 1878, "aid in consuming."

13. *Annual Report of the Fish Commissioners of the State of Wisconsin 1907–1908,* "While these inland," 13. See also Fish Commissioners *Annual Report,* 1880, 8; ibid., 1907–1908, 13; Ron Poff, *From Milk Can to Ecosystem Management: A Historical Perspective on Wisconsin's Fisheries Management Program, 1830s–1990s* (Madison, WI: Bureau of Fisheries Management and Habitat Protection, Wisconsin Department of Natural Resources, 1996), 3–5.

14. Most historical documents, including the reports of the state conservation officials and federal Indian agents, use the name "Lake Superior Chippewa." Today, the indigenous people of northern Wisconsin are more frequently known as the Ojibwe or Anishanaabe. I will use the term *Ojibwe* throughout this essay.

15. M. B. Johnson, interview by Richard Rathbun, Bayfield, WI, July 10, 1894. See also Irving Chafe, interview by Richard Rathbun, Bayfield, WI, July 10, 1894, IJC Notes, Box 8, vol. 3, "Considerable many half-breeds"; Grace Lee Nute, "American Fur Company's Fishing Enterprises on Lake Superior," *Mississippi Valley Historical Review* 12 (March 1926): 483–503; Patricia A. Shifferd, "A Study in Economic Change: The Chippewa of Northern Wisconsin: 1854–1900," *Western Canadian Journal of Anthropology* 6, no. 4 (1976): 16–41.

16. *Annual Report, Fish Commissioners of the State of Wisconsin,* 1878, "nefarious practice," 24.

17. *Annual Report of the Fish Commissioners of the State of Wisconsin,* 1884–1901.

18. D. M. Browning, Commissioner, to Lieut. W. A. Mercer, June 25, 1894, Wisconsin Department of Justice, Closed Case Files, Series 644, Box 2, Folder 5 (36), "that it has been"; Lieut. W. A. Mercer to Commissioner of IA [Indian Affairs], June 12, 1894, Records of the Bureau of Indian Affairs, NARG [National Archives Record Group] 75, Box 1096, LR [Letters Received] 1894, 22633, "The Indians all feel"; Larry Nesper, *The Walleye War: The Struggle for Ojibwe Spearfishing and Treaty Rights* (Lincoln: University of Nebraska Press, 2002).

19. Karl Jacoby, *Crimes against Nature: Squatters, Poachers, Thieves, and the Hidden History of American Conservation* (Berkeley: University of California Press, 2001); Johnson, "Subsistence, Class, and Conservation"; Warren, *The Hunters' Game;* Hahn, "Hunting, Fishing, and Foraging."

20. Steven Hahn and Jonathan Prude, eds., *The Countryside in the Age of Capitalist Transformation* (Chapel Hill: University of North Carolina Press, 1985).

21. On tourism and the emergence of consumer society and class identity, see Marguerite S. Shaffer, *See America First: Tourism and National Identity, 1880–1940* (Washington, DC: Smithsonian Institution Press, 2001); and Orvar Löfgren, *On Holiday: A*

History of Vacationing (Berkeley: University of California Press, 1999). On tourism and changing ideas of wilderness, see David Louter, *Windshield Wilderness: Cars, Roads, and Nature in Washington's National Parks* (Seattle: University of Washington Press, 2006); and Paul S. Sutter, *Driven Wild: How the Fight against Automobiles Launched the Modern Wilderness Movement* (Seattle: University of Washington Press, 2002).

22. E. J. Vanderwall, "Historical Background of the Wisconsin State Park System" (Madison: Wisconsin Conservation Department, 1953); Roman H. Koenings, "The Status of the State Parks in Wisconsin," delivered at the National Conference on State Parks, September 1960, Box 815, Folder 6, found in Wisconsin Conservation Department Files, Wisconsin Historical Society, Madison, WI [hereafter, WCD Files].

23. I. V. Fine, Ralph B. Hovind, and Philip H. Lewis Jr., *The Lake Superior Region Recreational Potential: Preliminary Report* (Madison: Wisconsin Department of Resource Development, 1962; Thomas R. Huffman, *Protectors of the Land and Water: Environmentalism in Wisconsin, 1961–1968* (Chapel Hill: University of North Carolina Press, 1994), 9–35.

24. Wisconsin Conservation Commission, Minutes, May 12 and November 10, 1950, July 11, 1952, April 1, 1955 (Committee on Land), in Wisconsin Natural Resources Board, Wisconsin Historical Society, "for recreational purposes," 11; Harold C. Jordahl, Jr., *A Unique Collection of Islands: The Influence of History, Politics, Policy and Planning on the Establishment of Apostle Islands National Lakeshore* (Madison: Department of Urban and Regional Planning, University of Wisconsin-Extension, 1994), 101–3.

25. Wisconsin Legislative Council, Conservation Committee, Minutes, January 9, 1956, Box 453, Folder 39, WCD Files, "almost in its." On climax theory, see Donald Worster, *Nature's Economy: A History of Ecological Ideas,* 2nd ed. (New York: Cambridge University Press, 1994), 235–52.

26. Burton L. Dahlberg to L. P. Voigt, May 17, 1955, Box 453, Folder 39, WCD Files, "The value of."

27. Mark W. T. Harvey, *A Symbol of Wilderness: Echo Park and the American Conservation Movement* (Albuquerque: University of New Mexico Press, 1994).

28. G. E. Sprecher to L. P. Voigt, July 6, 1954; Merv Clough to Victor Wallin, October 13, 1954; Ludwig Trammal to Vic C. Wallin, January 6, 1955; all in Folder 39, Box 453, WCD Files; Wisconsin Conservation Commission Minutes, April 1, 1955 (Committee on Land) and December 14, 1956; Jordahl, *A Unique Collection of Islands,* 121–22, 131; Minutes of February 12, 1956 Meeting of the County Board, Box 9, and Minutes of November 13, 14, 1956, Meeting of the County Board, Box 10, Ashland County Board of Supervisors, County Board Proceedings, 1914–1964, [Wisconsin Historical Society Archives, Madison] WHS.

29. The issue was one of classification. The WCD had three land classifications: state forest, state park, or state forest designated as wilderness. Timber production served as the primary function of state forests. State parks were developed recreational sites with

roads, flush toilets, concession stands, and other amenities. *Wilderness,* in Wisconsin state terms, meant areas with little formal management and a primarily natural character. Parks typically had too much development to qualify as wilderness. Jordahl, *A Unique Collection of Islands,* 91–101.

30. Wisconsin Legislative Council, Conservation Committee, Minutes, August 24, 1956, in Folder 39, Box 453, WCD Files, "[The] people in" and "it would not help"; Jordahl, *A Unique Collection of Islands,* 108, 119.

31. Wisconsin Conservation Commission Minutes, January 9 and March 12, 1959; *Proceedings of the Ashland County Board of Supervisors, 1959–1960,* April 19, 1960, 50–51; "Apostle Islands State Forest Guidelines for Development and Management, ca. 1966, Box B, Folder "State of Wis: Re: APIS Proposal—1960s," Harold C. Jordahl Papers, Apostle Islands National Lakeshore, Bayfield, WI, "General development will."

32. L. P. Voigt to Bernard Gehrmann, November 1, 1966, Box 633, Folder 9, WCD Files; John O. Holzheuter, *Madeline Island and the Chequamegon Region* (Madison: State Historical Society of Wisconsin, 1974), 59; Madeline Island Historical Preservation Association, Inc., *On The Rock: The History of Madeline Island Told Through Its Families* (Friendship, WI: New Past Press, 1997), 79–80; Jordahl, *A Unique Collection of Islands,* 319–20.

33. Editorial in *Bayfield County Press,* September 29, 1966, clipping in Folder 9, Box 633, WCD Files, "It seems that"; Robert J. Sneed to L. P. Voigt, December 9, 1966; and L. P. Voigt to Bernard Gehrmann, November 1, 1966, both in Folder 9, Box 633, WCD Files, "type of people."

34. Ken Todd to Gaylord Nelson, September 9, 1965, Box 89 folder 8, Gaylord Nelson Papers, Wisconsin Historical Society, Madison, WI, "a proposal as major."

35. Ojibwe opposition to the proposed lakeshore grew their long-running dispute with the state of Wisconsin over hunting and fishing rights. Initial plans for the lakeshore included large units in the Bad River and Red Cliff Reservations. At first the Ojibwe supported the proposal—they had even helped to initiate it—because they hoped the federal government would protect their treaty rights in the new park and overrule the WCD's authority in the state of Wisconsin. When the federal government refused to take a position in this conflict, most Ojibwe opposed the designation of the new park and lobbied successfully to have Indian lands removed from the proposal.

36. Some of the property owners within the boundaries did support the park proposal, but they were very much in the minority. US Congress, Senate Committee on Interior and Insular Affairs, May 9, June 1–2, 1967, 45–59, 83–87, 158, 168, 171, "It seems to me," 171; Robert Hokenson to Gaylord Nelson, April 10, 1965, Folder 28, Box 123, Gaylord Nelson Papers, Wisconsin Historical Society, Madison, WI, "All you people."

37. US Congress, Senate Committee on Interior and Insular Affairs, May 9, June 1–2, 1967, 156, "As for fair," and "Money can't buy," 156.

38. NPS planners had made the decision to exclude Madeline Island from the

proposal due to its more extensive development and higher land values. Long after the creation of Apostle Islands National Lakeshore, Sand Island landowners continued to try to use their political influence to arrange buy-backs or land trades to regain owner-ship of their island property. US Congress, Senate, Committee on Interior and Insular Affairs, *Apostle Islands National Lakeshore: Hearings before the Subcommittee on Parks and Recreation,* 91st Cong., 1st sess., March 17, 1969, 129, 133, "For three generations," 129; US Congress, Senate Committee on Interior and Insular Affairs, May 9, June 1–2, 1967, 39, "Now Madeline Island," 39.

39. For a more detailed discussion of these issues, see James W. Feldman, *A Storied Wilderness: Rewilding the Apostle Islands* (Seattle: University of Washington Press, 2011).

40. For examples of the dislocation of indigenous peoples as a consequence of the American model of national park protection, see Ramachandra Guha, "Radical Ameri-can Environmentalism and Wilderness Preservation: A Third World Critique," *Environmental Ethics* 11 (Spring 1989): 71–83; David Harmon, "Cultural Diversity, Human Subsistence, and the National Park Ideal," *Environmental Ethics* 9 (Summer 1987): 71–83; Roderick P. Neumann, *Imposing Wilderness: Struggles over Livelihood and Nature Preservation in Africa* (Berkeley: University of California Press, 1998); Michael P. Lewis, *Inventing Global Ecology: Tracking the Biodiversity Ideal in India, 1947–1989* (Athens: Ohio University Press, 2004).

3

"The Rich Go Higher"

The Geography of Rural Development, Fire Management, and Environmental Justice in Utah's Wildland Urban Interface

JASON ROBERTS

We ate our bagged lunches along the freshly paved two-lane road leading up the mountain to the Colony, a gated skiing community in Park City, Utah. We were taking our lunch break in a muddy area near a drainage culvert between the road and a steep snowy stand of blown-over aspen and firs. We had been working that morning to protect the community from wildfire by mechanically cutting and removing these hazardous fuels.[1] The juxtaposition of Red Mountain Fuels Mitigation crew members in hardhats and work clothes and the professional, business-casual community residents driving by in their new suvs, trucks, and Mercedes could not have been more dramatic. In between bites of a bologna sandwich, Rat Face asked, "Where are all the homes?" Medina dragged hard on his cigarette and then replied, "They're up at the top of the mountain. . . . The rich go higher."[2]

Park City is about a thirty-minute drive east of Salt Lake City along I-80. The drive to Park City takes you along a winding ascent into the mountains to skiing and outdoor recreation areas. Narrow canyons with reddish-pink rocky soil, abundant sagebrush, serviceberry, and gambel oak initially surround you on your way to Park City. It is a dry, often flammable landscape consisting of numerous rocky peaks and sparse valleys. The only significant human development in the area appears to be the occasional dusty mineral mine visible from the highway. Urban sprawl seems to have leapfrogged this location, leaving only the highway behind to connect Park City to Salt Lake. It is a hard and uninviting landscape.

However, the view changes and the temperature drops as the elevation increases. The vegetation becomes a greener, yet similarly flammable, mixture of lodgepole pine, subalpine fir, Engelmann spruce, and aspen. The soil and rock are now dark gray in color and snow is visible on the mountaintops. The views must be what have inspired so much settlement and development in this fire-adapted landscape. Small communities such as Parley's Summit reveal brick, stucco, and log homes at the foot of the hills, behind the large granite walls that line the freeway. These are precursors to the upcoming city. Human development increases, becoming denser as you approach Park City and its various residential and commercial enclaves. Homes become bigger and more spread out as you climb the mountain. The transition starts with small, attractive new houses and condominiums packed together at the bottom of the mountain and ends with behemoth estates spread across spacious mountaintop lots. As an area Utah resident explained to me after the crew's first job in Park City, "Anything in that place . . . is going to be expensive. The real-estate values up there are crazy; every ten blocks up the prices go up like $50,000. In Utah, the most valuable properties either have a view of the mountain or the valley. People in this state often introduce themselves by asking what part of the valley are you from, to see whether you have money or not."

Most of the buildings in Park City try to capture a certain woodsy quality, with many structures made of beautiful golden pine logs—the houses, shopping centers, signs, even the car wash. The simulated rustic flavor in Park City attempts to portray this developing locale as anything but developed. Even the Mountain Dew machine at the local plant nursery has a picture of a waterfall pasted on the front. It is an enchanting scene, but as my coworkers' comments illustrate, it is defined by contradiction: "Are those log homes? Because they look plastic, they're so shiny." "Yeah, my grandfather has a *real* cabin, it doesn't look like that." Similar to Blakely and Snyder's discussion of the history of the suburbs, the creators of Park City have done "everything they could to dissociate their developments from the city." Subdivisions in Park City boast nature inspired names such as Jeremy Ranch, Bear Hollow Village, Deer Park, Red Pine Adventures, White Pine, and The Canyons. The names are "meant to conjure up bucolic rural imagery and only coincidentally to reflect the actual landscape."[3] Slowly ascending the mountain in the old crew buggy, it is as if we have wandered into a nature-inspired theme park—a commoditized romanticism of what the rural experience must have been like long ago. When we pull up in sight of an old-fashioned wooden fence surrounding a grassy field in the Colony, my coworker Cymbals rants, "Rich people, man, gotta put up a fake fence to make it look like they're in the country even though everybody knows they're fuckin' rich." Park City has all of the charm and beauty of a backwoods-hunting lodge with none of the associated inconveniences.

This is the urban wilderness, exurbia. This luxury class of residential and recreational development constitutes a re-capitalized nature within the wildland urban interface. This recapitalized interface zone is part of what some scholars have recently called the New West, and it is predicated on a socioeconomic transition from utilitarian, extractive resource industries to amenity migration, aesthetic consumption, and service sector expansion. It is here that consumption has largely replaced production as many of the more-affluent members of American society appear to have come looking for a symbolic reconciliation with the material estrangement from undomesticated nature that characterizes our modern existence. Significantly, this mottled transition between livelihood and lifestyle landscapes in the recapitalized interface of the rural American West has only further complicated already challenging efforts at fire management and forest conservation in the region. Both capitalist development and environmental management continue to be based on the same principles of order, stability, and hierarchy for which fire has been considered inimical for at least a century. On a symbolic and material level, then, fire still represents matter out of place in this highly aestheticized and highly valued landscape. Consequently, institutional fuels and fire management, particularly in the recapitalized interface, were never designed to solve an environmental problem or promote environmental sustainability. It is not the environment that is actually being protected here because the romanticized environment is the basis for consumption. What is truly being protected is the ideological division between nature and culture, and the possibility that one can live in a wild but never dangerous nature. In the ensuing discussion, I will assess the development of the recapitalized interface within the materially and symbolically produced space we call nature. Considering the tenets of environmental justice, I will analyze how cultural valuations of nature have informed recent development and land management practices. Faber and McCarthy contend that the "environmental justice movement is critical to the larger effort to build a more inclusive, democratic and effective ecology movement in the United States—one which can challenge and transform the structures of power and profit which lie at the root of the ecological crisis." Conservation efforts in the recapitalized interface must better address the dialectic between cultural values and the structures of power and profit that shape and are shaped by them in order to promote more-sustainable and more-equitable resource management in the future. Significantly, as Agyeman and colleagues have argued, sustainability and equitability are two sides of the same coin.[4]

Searching for the Interface of Environmental Justice and Sustainability

> *Workin' in rich people's backyards again.*
>   —Dan

Federal wildland fire literature defines the wildland urban interface as "the line, area, or zone where structures and other human development meet or intermingle with undeveloped wildland or vegetative fuels." Unfortunately, this definition understates the complexity of this geographic zone. By conflating industrial, agricultural, and native lands with upscale residential and resort-inspired development, the wildland fire institution has created a misleading administrative concept. The wildland urban interface is not simply one nebulous landmass lying in a highly fueled, liminal space between the city and the country. The focus of current fire policy discussions, funding initiatives, and protection programs on the more economically valuable residential and recreational areas of the interface illuminates the deficiency of this simplified definition. Furthermore, the biased concentration of programmatic support in what I call the recapitalized interface has produced only limited results because this valuable area of residential and recreational development is more than just a technical constraint to efficient, rationalized fire management. It is a microcosm of America's ever-evolving symbolic and material relationship with nature, and it is a poignant example of uneven geographical development—how socioecological systems are consistently reshaped according to the desires of people and the needs of capital as new sources of surplus value and viable investment are sought in order to overcome recurring crises of overaccumulation and stagnation inherent to the system. As Harvey argues, "The accumulation of capital works through ecosystemic processes, reshaping them and disturbing them as it goes . . . the social side cannot be evaded as somehow radically different from its ecological integument. . . . The circulation of money and capital have to be construed as ecological variables every bit as important as the circulation of air and water."[5]

The recapitalized interface is a place where entrenched cultural beliefs about natural settings intersect with the material realities of a consumer culture to form a space in which the aesthetics of nature are bought and sold primarily for the type of lifestyle they have come to represent. As Descola and Palsson argue, "Nature is a social construct and conceptualizations of the environment are the products of ever-changing historical contexts and cultural specificities." In this particular instance, the recapitalized interface represents the mottled transition of nature from the external and exploitable domain of modern economics to a post-modern stock of capital valuable in and of itself. Yet, it is still being managed as a commodity, not as an ecosystem.[6]

Current federally subsidized mechanical fuels mitigation programs in the recapitalized interface merely help to perpetuate a system of economic development and stratification under the guise of improved technology and managerial reform in a situation O'Connor would call "the 'conservation' game." The fundamental, yet inherently problematic, goal of these operations remains market protection through the facilitation of more-efficient fire suppression. It is this mission that my coworkers and I became closely acquainted with during our season in the interface as we consistently performed aesthetically pleasing, yet minimally functional, fuels mitigation projects in an apparent effort to maintain privileged lifestyles in beautiful landscapes. Essentially, we were protecting the upper classes, their property, and a particular idea of nature at the expense of all taxpayers. The opportunity cost for this mission was sustainability and equitability. Unfortunately, this is not an entirely new story for forest and fire management in the American West.[7]

Forestry, Fire, and the Re-Production of Nature

*Up in there is where the guy lives that created the debit card. There's a house up
there it costs $2,800 just to wash the windows.* —Medina

The history of the transformation and commoditization of nature in the
American West has been characterized by relentless expansion and the
palimpsest of rural landscapes and livelihoods by urban landscapes:

> The modern North American West is one of the most contested landscapes in
> the world. . . . Since World War II, the West has been transformed from an over-
> whelmingly rural society dominated by extractive industries such as mining,
> grazing, logging, and agriculture to an overwhelmingly urban one character-
> ized by explosive growth. As cities such as Phoenix, Denver, and Salt Lake City
> relentlessly expand, spawning bedroom communities in relentlessly radiating
> circles all around them, they destroy wildlife habitat, fragment the West's famed
> open spaces, and convert farm and ranch lands into subdivisions. They also cre-
> ate powerful urban political constituencies.

The evolving political economy of forest and fire management and the
development of the recapitalized interface are emblematic of this process.
The production of the recapitalized interface is only an extension of a mar-
ket-based relationship to nature that began much earlier.[8]

The contemporary production of nature in the United States began with
the arrival of European colonists, whose values drove a powerful discourse
used to redefine and separate nature from culture, thereby gaining domi-
nance over the land, its uses, and its values. Under the new regime, nature
was re-produced as a commodity. Through the commodification of nature,
"the forest as a habitat disappeared and was replaced by the forest as an
economic resource to be managed efficiently and profitably." This changing
conception of nature significantly affected attitudes toward and uses of fire
in the West, effecting a transition from fire use to fire suppression. At the
heart of fire suppression has been the idea that suppression is an effective
tool for protecting economic interests in the United States. Fire suppression began in earnest with industrial timber production and has endured
over time in the name of various other interests, such as tourism, recreation, suburbanization, and scenic real estate development. While its ecological soundness has been discredited and the economic motivations have

been subject to change, the management prescription has remained much the same. The United States still "suppresses about 97% of all fire starts."[9]

Consequently, "the history of the forestry movement in the United States from its beginnings in the early twentieth century to the present is in large part the story of a relentless struggle against fire in the woods," advancing as a result of the industrial counterreclamation. The industrial counterreclamation was characterized by "the abandonment of marginal farm land from the mid-nineteenth century on [as a result of] national concern with conservation, prospects of timber famine, water shortages, alarm over the closing frontier, new industrial uses for wood products, and new fuels to replace firewood." The industrial counter-reclamation signaled the coming of a class-defined conservation movement that emerged in the early twentieth century as a "development strategy linked to government action based upon the principles of efficiency, scientific management, centralized control, and organized economic development." The conservation movement of the early twentieth century provided the impetus for a federally directed professionalization of forestry, effectively demonstrating Sivaramakrishnan's argument about forestry as a tool for development: "In forestry, development operates chiefly to enhance common or national goods and values focusing on public lands. This structural distinction mobilizes different cultural hierarchies in the establishment and maintenance of work relations, within the limited field of possibilities generated within a historically formed regional culture."[10]

Professional forestry would be guided by "a resource-based capitalism" in which "unauthorized disturbances" like fire were seen as threats to resource revenues. Indeed, the attempt to suppress fire in most forested lands would legitimize the discipline because fire suppression "distinguished modern forest management from the primitive techniques it claimed to supersede."[11]

Following the transfer of federal forests from the Department of the Interior to the Department of Agriculture in 1905, the US Forest Service assumed management of national forests; the first forest fire management plan was developed by then–Forest Service Chief Gifford Pinchot. González-Cabán explains: "The establishment of the National Forests was a direct result of the active conservation movement of the times. The newly established agency and its Chief wanted to promote an efficient use of the natural resources under the agency's supervision through coordinated, centrally directed decisions made by forestry professionals."[12]

Significant to early Forest Service management policies was the influence of Pinchot's training in German forestry, emphasizing the economic gains to be made through scientific forest management. The purpose of early Forest Service mandates was to "ensure future productivity of forest lands and to prevent forest devastation." The need for forest regeneration after harvest and protection from fire during the intervening years of growth was of foremost importance. Stephen Pyne writes, "In the early years of the century, foresters declared that industrial forestry and the protection of reserved watersheds would be impossible unless surface fires were eliminated." Previous practices of surface burning made common by indigenous Americans in the West and early colonial settlers came to be seen as a threat to professional authority and economic efficiency. Significantly, burning of any kind was considered detrimental to timber production. As Henry Graves, the second chief of the US Forest Service would argue,

> It is not only in shortening life and in reducing growth that fires injure trees; the quality of the *product* is also affected [emphasis added]. Even where there is no infection by insects or fungous disease, a fire that has killed one side of a tree usually leaves its scar. In time the wound may entirely heal over, but there is nearly always a point of weakness, which may ultimately cause a seam or windshake and unfit the butt log for lumber. If rot sets in, it may spread throughout the trunk and make the tree worthless, even if it does not kill it.

The interests of a burgeoning timber industry therefore would shape forest management agendas and drive a dogmatic ethic of fire suppression that would remain nearly unchanged until the 1970s, when the Forest Service's involvement in timber production began to wane.[13]

From the 1960s to the 1970s increasing popular and political interest in wildlife conservation, tourism, and recreation led to the passage of legislative acts that made federal timber production much more difficult as a primary pursuit. These acts compelled the Forest Service to improve long-term planning, analyze potential effects of proposed environmental actions, and make more-concerted efforts to manage forests for multiple purposes beyond timber. These changes underlined an emerging multiplicity of ecological capitals.[14] Significantly, nature was no longer simply valued as an extrinsic domain from which to draw utilitarian resources; it now also represented a more intrinsic, surplus value that would facilitate private exploitation in new markets.

The movement away from utilitarian economics inspired attempts to change Forest Service fire management policies. There was less incentive for full-scale suppression as forest service management objectives changed and federal timber production decreased. Furthermore, it became obvious that exclusive fire suppression at current fuel load levels was ineffective no matter how much money was spent in the effort. From 1968 to 1978, federal land management agencies adopted a policy "that allowed certain fires to burn, especially in designated wilderness areas." While fires of human origin were still suppressed, so-called natural fires were allowed to burn and were considered to be under prescription as long as they did not "jeopardize human life, park facilities, personal property, or endangered or threatened species."[15]

The wildfire dilemma gained momentum through the 1980s and 1990s as fuel loads increased due to continued fire suppression and declines in domestic timber production. Wildland fire issues were further exacerbated during this period by increasing private development in previously open spaces, prompting the creation of the National Wildland Urban Interface Fire Protection Initiative in 1986 to respond to the difficulties of fire management on increasingly fragmented, private lands. More specifically, the area of wildland urban interface in the western United States expanded by 61 percent from 1970 to 2000, with the state of Utah exhibiting one of the greatest proportions of wildland urban interface expansion nationwide. In 1994 these developments combined to produce a fire season with suppression expenses reaching almost $1 billion, thirty-four firefighters lost, and significant damages to natural resources and private property. Efforts to "achieve a balance between [fire] suppression to protect life, property, and resources, and fire use to regulate fuels and maintain healthy ecosystems" were failing. Once again, forests proved too valuable a commodity to burn. Fire still remained antithetical to the growth and maintenance of a transitioning economy, and efforts to selectively reintegrate fire proved inadequate for creating the significant fuels reductions necessary to improve a highly fueled environment. As a result, "full fire suppression continued to be the dominant strategy" for managing fire in the landscape.[16]

Expansion of residential communities and private property in the wild-land urban interface, therefore, "shaped national forest policy in the western United States" from the mid–1980s to the present. Real estate, recreation, and service sector development augmented timber production as leading economic interests in need of protection and federal fire suppression expenditures continued to increase, averaging in excess of half a billion dollars per year from 1997 to 2000. The cost of the suppression effort needed to protect the growing interface would lead to another revision in fire policy with the development of the National Fire Plan in 2001.[17]

The objective of the National Fire Plan within the wildland urban interface was "to reduce fuels around homes, communities, and resources to slow or stop wildland fires from threatening *high-value areas*" [emphasis added]. Again, policy makers authorized substantive fire use by declaring, "Fire, as a critical natural process, will be integrated into land and to resource management plans and activities on a landscape scale, and across agency boundaries." Still, this integration of fire was only practical on large tracts of public lands. Implementation of fire on private lands in the growing interface zone, where it was arguably most needed, presented numerous logistical, jurisdictional, and ideological barriers in an area where nature is consumed for its aesthetic value. As a result, mechanical fuels mitigation became a primary method for dealing with fire risks on private lands as shaded fuel breaks and other fuels treatments were implemented in an effort to facilitate more-efficient fire suppression. The Healthy Forests Initiative and the passage of the Healthy Forests Restoration Act in 2003 only strengthened this strategy. Thus, at-risk communities began to receive government subsidies for the mechanical fuels mitigation treatments favored by most homeowners. From 2000 to 2003, a total of $300 million in federal funding was provided to reduce fuel levels in accordance with these revised fire policies. In the state of Utah "millions of dollars have been expended in modifying landscapes through the use of mechanical and labor intensive treatments of over-grown, dying and diseased forests and woodlands" that are the result of over a century of fire suppression. Policy makers believe "a reduction in hazardous fuels [will] bring about a reduction in the number of wildfires and the associated suppression costs" even as the structure of the system remains fundamentally intact.[18]

Working in Nature, Toiling in Culture

So what's the goal of this project? Is it just to make things prettier?

—Cymbals

The preference of policy makers and interface homeowners for mechanical fuels mitigation dictated the work performed by fuels crews such as the one I worked on, the Red Mountain Fuels Mitigation crew. We carried out fuels mitigation projects on private lands in northern Utah, using chainsaws and the occasional wood chipper. It was the same type of hard, manual labor that Utah fire suppression crews performed, but without the associated fire duty perks of overtime, hazard pay, or actual fire experience. As members of this crew, we were never allowed near a fire. It was an entry-level position that reflected the fixity of fire suppression atop the wildland fire hierarchy. The only significant allure of fuels mitigation work was the possibility of being bumped up to a fire crew if one worked hard enough. The mitigation crew was essentially a finishing school for the prospective wildland firefighters who would probably be needed at the end of a three-and-a-half month fuels mitigation season. Yet it was through the work of the Red Mountain crew that I came to understand that the wildland urban interface is more than a problematic fire environment predicated on the expansion of residential development into highly fueled, fire suppressed zones. Week after week and in community after community, I began to realize that the interface we were trying to protect was also a veiled synonym for a gated community.

In *Fortress America,* Blakely and Snyder define gated communities as "residential areas with restricted access in which normally public spaces are privatized." As they put it, this privatization is maintained through deployment of "designated perimeters, usually walls or fences, and controlled entrances that are intended to prevent penetration by nonresidents." The communities that the Red Mountain Fuels Mitigation crew worked in ranged from a members-only wilderness camping and recreation area charging monthly use fees in Sourdough, to upper-middle-class recreation or vacation homes worth $100,000 to $200,000 in Fruitland and Argyle Canyon, to homes worth nearly $4 million in the Colony and Moosehollow. Yet all possessed a common vision of privatized nature. Gates served to demarcate insider from outsider and nature from the majority of culture. From the imposing metal gates with big padlocks protecting upper-middle-class vacation cabins in the woods to the aesthetically pleasing, mechanical gates with guards protecting upper-class homes in suburban oases, all evoked a message of power and privilege, a withdrawal from the public realm, and a "politics of exclusion." Home ownership in an exclusive, natural landscape became a source of symbolic capital because it connoted a particular lifestyle.[19] The setting was the reason for investment. Thus, it became increasingly obvious that the goal of substantive fuels mitigation efforts in these areas was inherently contradictory. Official management goals never matched what we implemented on the ground. Fuels mitigation plans were consistently scaled back, or occasionally canceled, in order to fit the aesthetic ideals of our interface clients who had invested significant money to live closer to a wild, but not dangerous, nature. As one homeowner explained, "I would prefer it if you leave more trees, especially the maples. They are just beautiful in the fall. And, please don't cut the big trees. My wife loves those trees. They attract owls and things. She would probably divorce me over those trees."

We therefore spent the majority of our time cutting down some of the large dead and dying conifers indicative of the senescence-stage insect and disease infestations prevalent in much of the state's woodlands, and symptomatic of long-term fire suppression in a fire-adapted ecosystem. Afterwards we would cut off their limbs and make brush piles to be burned at a nebulous future date in order to construct what management called a shaded fuel break and what Chunk called a "very shaded fuel break." Rarely did we remove the abundant, lively, and attractive surface and ladder fuels that were more likely to become the source of ignition.[20] Deviation from this formula quickly inspired the type of anger visible in the accusations of one homeowner in Forest Glenn: "Are you guys gonna cut down any dead or just green? Are you guys gonna clean up this stuff here?"

For this reason, our work often amounted to what one district forester would characterize as "a great job that wouldn't make a difference if a fire came through." My coworker Keedy explained the dilemma of interface work perfectly when I asked him about a chipping project in Wolf Mountain: "What do I think of this job? This is bullshit. It's bullshit, man. It's pointless. Come cut down some dead stuff and shit I don't want. Come thin the shrubs on the roadside. That shit's not gonna burn. I'm not a fuckin' lawn service!" It was difficult to accept that our work functioned primarily as a symbolic beginning, that we were protecting not really life itself, but merely an idealized way of life, not preventing environmental crises, but just superficially managing their effects in order to maintain business as usual.

Conclusion

The problem isn't fire. The problem is that people want to put their houses in the woods and not take the proper defensive measures to protect them.

—Fuels Program coordinator

The wildland urban interface has received significant attention over the past three decades as fire policy has responded to the influence of increasing private development in previously undeveloped spaces. A number of studies have investigated what the interface actually is, where it is, and whether fuels treatments are being applied appropriately in these areas. Most of these studies have relied on quantitative variables such as vegetation type, housing density, and city buffer distance to determine the best ways to locate and implement interface protection plans. While these studies are certainly useful, they tend to overlook the numerous social and cultural issues inherent in many aspects of the interface phenomenon. The recapitalized interface is a produced space that reflects the cultural values embedded in the practices of its producers. It is the myth of the pristine wilderness packaged and sold to the highest bidders in the form of residential and recreation properties deep in the woods, but not too far from the luxuries of modern life. Consequently, even the best policy and implementation plans are unlikely to produce satisfactory results without a better understanding of the individuals living, vacationing, and working within these interface areas and their motivations for being there. As William Cronon suggests, in order "to protect the nature that is all around us, we must think long and hard about the nature we carry inside our heads."[21]

The recapitalized interface is the materially and symbolically produced space of a society in which consumption forms an important means of identity construction. The development and maintenance of this zone exemplifies the inequities arising from this sort of value system. Under such a system, where we live and what we have projects a certain image of who we are. Producing and buying into places like the recapitalized interface is, as Geertz might say, a story we tell ourselves about ourselves.[22] Amenities and aesthetics connote a lifestyle that both recapitalized interface property owners and the wildland fire institution strive to maintain despite the inequities and lack of sustainability inherent in this way of life. Our relationship to fire has long been shaped by the fictional boundaries of nature, culture, class, and science to protect valuable commodities within a hierarchical landscape. Fire suppression is still the standard operating procedure in the American West because the capitalist ecosystem cannot afford an alternative. Consequently, much of the mechanical fuels mitigation efforts taking place within this system seem to serve the function of legitimizing, but not rectifying, a broader "politics of unsustainability," whereby "capitalist consumer democracies try and manage to sustain what is known to be unsustainable."[23]

Environmental justice, therefore, does not really factor in to discussions of fire management within the wildland urban interface. The unsustainable practices and inequities that problematize much interface development are merely glossed over as technical problems with attainable, technical solutions. Thus, we rarely ask whether mechanical fuels mitigation is a significant, useful departure from the legacy of fire suppression. Few seem to worry about the equitability or the sustainability of dedicating taxpayer money to the privatization of open spaces, the maintenance of poorly planned rural development, and the protection of select individuals who choose to buy dwellings in areas of disproportionate risk. Hardly any seem to wonder whether the homeowners footing the subsidized balance for fuels mitigation efforts actually want or receive what they do pay for—treatments that should significantly reduce the risk of fire damage to their properties. Even fewer worry about the seasonal laborers engaged in the maintenance of these landscapes, using their bodies and technical skills as a form of capital that has a short shelf life in an arduous field.[24]

As Agyeman explains, the production, consumption, and subsidized maintenance of places such as the recapitalized interface are quintessential examples of the American capitalist dream gone wrong.[25] It is a powerful dream that is unsustainable and largely inequitable, but we protect it as a tribute to the possibilities envisioned within a free-market democracy. We protect it at the expense of asking and answering the hard questions that might lead to a more socially and ecologically sustainable future, and it gives one pause to wonder: Do we really want to know the answers?

NOTES

I would like to thank all of the members of the 2008 Red Mountain Fuels Mitigation Crew and the many other State of Utah employees who were so instrumental to this research. Keep "walkin' hard," my friends. Also, thanks so much to my Dad for agreeing to take yet another memorable road trip with me.

1. Fuels modification or mechanical fuels mitigation: "Manipulation or removal of fuels to reduce the likelihood of ignition and/or to lessen potential damage and resistance to control (e.g., lopping, chipping, crushing, piling and burning)." http://www.nwcg.gov/pms/pubs/glossary/f.htm#Fuel_Modification.

2. All personal communications with coworkers and other informants were made in work-related settings between May and August 2008 (hereafter "Personal communications"). I have used pseudonyms to protect the identity of those involved. Any quotes in this essay not cited otherwise are personal communications.

3. Edward J. Blakely and Mary Gail Snyder, *Fortress America: Gated Communities in the United States* (Washington, DC: Brookings Institution Press, 1997), "everything they could" and "meant to conjure," 14.

4. Martin O'Connor, "On the Misadventures of Capitalist Nature," *Capitalism, Nature, Socialism* 4, no. 3 (1993): 7–40; Paul Robbins, Katharine Meehan, Hannah Gosnell, and Susan Gilbertz, "Writing the New West: A Critical Review," *Rural Sociology* 74, no. 3 (2009): 356–82; Hannah Gosnell and Jesse Abrams, "Amenity Migration: Diverse Conceptualizations of Drivers, Socioeconomic Dimensions, and Emerging Challenges," *GeoJournal* 76 (2011): 303–22; John Bellamy Foster, *Marx's Ecology: Materialism and Nature* (New York: Monthly Review Press, 2000); Timothy W. Collins, "The Political Ecology of Hazard Vulnerability: Marginalization, Facilitation, and the Production of Differential Risk to Urban Wildfires in Arizona's White Mountains," *Journal of Political Ecology* 15 (2008): 21–43; Ann F. Bradley, Nonan V. Noste and William C. Fischer, "Fire Ecology of Forests and Woodlands in Utah," USDA [US Department of Agriculture] *General Technical Report INT-287* (1992): 1–135; Mary Douglas, *Purity and Danger: An Analysis of the Concepts of Pollution and Taboo* (London: Ark Paperbacks, 1966); Neil Smith, "The Production of Nature," in *Futurenatural: Nature, Science, Culture,* ed. George Robertson et al. (New York: Routledge, 1996), 35–54; Daniel R. Faber and Deborah McCarthy, "Neoliberalism, Globalization, and the Struggle for Ecological Democracy: Linking Sustainability and Environmental Justice," in *Just Sustainabilities: Development in an Unequal World,* ed. Julian Agyeman, Robert D. Bullard, and Bob Evans (Cambridge, MA: MIT Press, 2003), 38–63, "environmental justice movement," 59; Agyeman, Bullard and Bob Evans, *Just Sustainabilities.*

5. US Department of Agriculture, Forest Service and Department of the Interior 2001. National Fire Plan. A Report to the President in Response to the Wildfires of

2000, September 8, 2000: Managing the Impact of Wildfires on Communities and the Environment. Washington, DC., "the line, area," 21; Tania Schoennagel et al., "Implementation of National Fire Plan Treatments Near the Wildland-urban Interface in the Western United States," *Proceedings of the National Academy of Sciences* 106, no. 26 (2009): 10706–11; Rosa Luxemburg, *The Accumulation of Capital* (New York: Modern Reader Paperbacks, 1968/1951); David Harvey, *Spaces of Neoliberalization: Towards a Theory of Uneven Geographical Development* (Heidelberg, Germany: University of Heidelberg, 2004); David Harvey, *Spaces of Global Capitalism: Towards a Theory of Uneven Geographical Development* (New York: Verso, 2006), "The accumulation of capital," 88. See also Nathan F. Sayre, "Assessing the Effects of the Grundrisse in Anglophone Geography and Anthropology," *Antipode* 40, no. 5 (2008): 898–920.

6. Smith, "The Production of Nature"; Philippe Descola and Gisli Palsson, eds., *Nature and Society: Anthropological Perspectives* (New York: Routledge, 1996), "Nature is a social," 15; O'Connor, "On the Misadventures," 8; Arturo Escobar, *Encountering Development: The Making and Unmaking of the Third World* (Princeton, NJ: Princeton University Press, 1995).

7. O'Connor, "On the Misadventures," "the 'conservation game,'" 9. Fire suppression is "all the work of extinguishing or confining a fire, beginning with its discovery." National Wildfire Coordinating Group (NWCG) Glossary of Wildland Fire Terminology, http://www.nwcg.gov/pms/pubs/glossary/s.htm; Neil Maher, "A New Deal Body Politic: Landscape, Labor, and the Civilian Conservation Corps," *Environmental History* 7, no. 3 (2002): 435–61; Louis Warren, *The Hunters' Game: Poachers and Conservationists in Twentieth-Century America* (New Haven, CT: Yale University Press, 1999); Agyeman, Bullard and Evans, *Just Sustainabilities*.

8. Thomas Sheridan, "Embattled Ranchers, Endangered Species, and Urban Sprawl: the Political Ecology of the New American West," Theme issue, *Annual Review of Anthropology* 36 (2007), "The modern North American," 122.

9. William Cronon, *Changes in the Land: Indians, Colonists, and the Ecology of New England* (New York: Hill and Wang, 2003); James Scott, *Seeing Like a State: How Certain Schemes to Improve the Human Condition Have Failed* (New Haven, CT: Yale University Press, 1998), "the forest as," 13; State of Utah wildland fire and fuels manager, personal communication, July 21, 2008, "suppresses about 97%."

10. George Morgan Jr., "Conflagration as Catalyst: Western Lumbermen and American Forest Policy," *The Pacific Historical Review* 47 (1978), "the history of the," 167; Stephen Pyne, *Fire in America: A Cultural History of Wildland and Rural Fire* (Princeton, NJ: Princeton University Press, 1982), "the abandonment of marginal," 59; Robert Gottlieb, *Forcing the Spring: The Transformation of the American Environmental Movement* (Washington, DC: Island Press, 2005), "development strategy," 57; K. Sivaramakrishnan, "Work, Identity, and Statemaking in the Forests of Southern West Bengal," *Polar* 21 (1998): 26–40; "In forestry," 32.

11. Gottlieb, *Forcing the Spring,* "resource-based capitalism," 60; Scott, *Seeing Like a State,* "unauthorized disturbances," 18; K. Sivaramakrishnan, "The Politics of Fire and Forest Regeneration in Colonial Bengal," *Environment and History* 2 (1996): 145–94, "distinguished modern," 145; Agyeman et al., *Just Sustainabilities;* Charles Zerner, *People, Plants, and Justice: The Politics of Nature Conservation* (New York: Columbia University Press, 2000).

12. Armando González-Cabán, "Wildland Fire Management Policy and Fire Management Economic Efficiency in the USDA Forest Service," Paper presented at the Fourth International Fire Conference, May 13, 2008, in Seville, Spain, "The establishment of," 3.

13. Frederick Cubbage, Jay O'Laughlin, and Charles S. Bullock, *Forest Resource Policy* (New York: John Wiley and Sons, 1993), "Ensure future productivity," 421; Stephen Pyne, "Fire Policy and Fire Research in the US Forest Service," *Journal of Forest History* 25, no. 2 (1981): 64–77, "In the early," 77; Surface fire is the "burning of fuels on the surface, which includes dead branches, leaves, and low vegetation;" NWCG Glossary of Wildland Fire Terminology, http://www.nwcg.gov/pms/pubs/glossary/s.htm; Pyne, "Fire Policy and Fire Research;" Henry S. Graves, *Protection of Forests From Fire* (Washington, DC: Government Printing Office, 1910), "It is not," 15; Morgan, "Conflagration as Catalyst"; Pyne, "Fire Policy and Fire Research".

14. Multiple Use-Sustained Yield Act of 1960, Pub. L. No. 86-517, 86th Congress, 74 Stat. 215, 16 U.S.C. 528 et seq. (1960); Wilderness Act of 1964, Pub. L. No. 88-577, 88th US Congress Second Session, 16 U.S. C. 1131 et seq. (1964); National Environmental Policy Act of 1969, Pub. L. No. 91-190, 83 Stat. 852, 91st US Congress, 42 U.S.C. 4321 et seq. (1969); Endangered Species Act of 1973, Pub. L. No. 93-205, 87 Stat. 884, 16. U.S.C. 1531 et seq. (1973); Forest and Rangeland Renewable Resources Planning Act of 1974, Pub. L. No. 93-378, 16 U.S.C. 1600 et seq.; The National Forest Management Act of 1976 Pub. L. No. 94-588, 90 Stat. 2949, 16 U.S.C. 1600 (note) et seq. (1976); Richard Freeman, "The EcoFactory: The US Forest Service and the Politics of Ecosystem Management;" *Environmental History* 7, no. 4 (2002): 632–58; Cubbage, *Forest Resource Policy;* Escobar, *Encountering Development.*

15. Mary Franke, *Yellowstone in the Afterglow: Lessons From the Fires* (Mammoth Hot Springs, WY: Yellowstone Center for Resources, 2000), "that allowed certain," 11; "jeopardize human life," 11.

16. Ralph J. Alig, Andrew J. Plantinga, SoEun Ahn, and Jeffrey D. Kline, "Land Use Changes Involving Forestry in the United States: 1952 to 1997, With Projections to 2050," Pacific Northwest Research Station-General Technical Report USDA [US Department of Agriculture] *Technical Document PNW-GTR-587* (2000); James L. Howard, "US Timber Production, Trade, Consumption, and Price Statistics 1965–2002," *USDA Research Paper FPL-RP-615,* Forest Products Laboratory–Research Paper (Madison, WI: USDA Forest Service, 2003); Pyne, "Fire Policy and Fire Research"; Robert H. Nelson, *A Burning Issue: A Case for Abolishing the US Forest Service* (New York: Rowman and Littlefield,

2000); Charles Davis, "The West in Flames: The Intergovernmental Politics of Wildfire Suppression and Prevention," *Publius* 31, no. 3 (2001): 97–110; David M. Theobald and William H. Romme, "Expansion of the US Wildland-Urban Interface," *Landscape and Urban Planning* 83 (2007): 340–54; Population in Utah's Wasatch and Summit counties, where fuels crew efforts were primarily targeted during the author's fieldwork, increased by 163 percent and 410 percent respectively from 1970 to 2000 (Statistics calculated from data provide by Population Estimates Program, Population Division, US Census Bureau): González-Cabán, "Wildland Fire Management Policy"; G. Thomas Zimmerman and David Bunnell, "The Federal Wildland Policy: Opportunities for Wilderness Fire Management," in *Wilderness Science in a Time of Change Conference— Volume 5: Wilderness Ecosystems, Threats, and Management.* Missoula, MT, May 23–27, 1999; David N. Cole, Stephen F. McCool, William T. Borrie, and Jennifer O'Loughlin, comps., Proceedings RNRS-P-15Vol-5. Ogden, UT: USDA Forest Service, Rocky Mountain Research Station, "achieve a balance," 289 [2000 Census Data]; González-Cabán, "Wildland Fire Management Policy," "full fire suppression," 5. See also William T. Sommers, "The Emergence of the Wildland–Urban Interface Concept," *Forest History Today* Fall (2008): 12–18, http://www.foresthistory.org/publications/FHT/FHTFall2008/Sommers.pdf

17. Schoennagel et al., "Implementation of National Fire Plan," "Shaped national forest," 4; Gosnell and Abrams, "Amenity Migration"; González-Cabán, "Wildland Fire Management Policy"; US Department of Agriculture, Forest Service and US Department of the Interior [USDA USDI] *National Fire Plan: A Report to the President in Response to the Wildfires of 2000, September 8, 2000: Managing the Impact of Wildfires on Communities and the Environment* (Washington, DC: Forests and Rangelands, 2001), http://www.forestsandrangelands.gov/resources/reports/documents/2001/8-20-en.pdf

18. Schoennagel et al., "Implementation of National Fire Plan," "to reduce fuels," 4; National Wildfire Coordinating Group, "Review and Update of the 1995 Federal Wildland Fire Management Policy," National Interagency Fire Center, Boise, ID, National Wildfire Coordinating Group, Review and Update, 2001, "Fire, as a critical," iv. A shaded fuel break is a "natural or manmade change in fuel characteristics which affects fire behavior so that fires burning into them can be more readily controlled." NWCG Glossary of Wildland Fire Terms, http://www.nwcg.gov/pms/pubs/glossary/f.htm. See James K. Agee et al., "The Use of Shaded Fuelbreaks in Landscape Fire Management," *Forest Ecology and Management* 127 (2000): 55–66; Les Aucoin, "Don't Get Hosed: How Political Framing Influences Fire Policy," in *The Wildfire Reader: A Century of Failed Forest Policy,* ed. George Wuerthner, 67–74 (Washington, DC: Island Press, 2006): 67–74; Mark W. Brunson and Bruce A. Shindler, "Geographic Variation in Social Acceptability of Wildland Fuels Management in the Western United States," *Society and Natural Resources* 17 (2004): 661–78; Utah Division of Forestry, Fire, and State Lands, "Utah Statewide Forest Resource Assessment and Strategy 2010," Salt Lake City (2010): 1–76 ; "millions of

dollars," 13, http://utah.ptfs.com/awweb/main.jsp?flag=browse&smd=1&awdid=1; Bradley et al., "Fire Ecology"; González-Cabán, "Wildland Fire Management Policy," "a reduction in," 5–6. "Wildland fires had affected more than 24 million hectares at a direct suppression cost of 9.642 billion dollars" (González-Cabán, "Wildland Fire Management Policy," 1). From 1985 to 2010 the state of Utah averaged approximately 759 wildfires burning 134,507 acres per year. During the years 1991–2002, the total state costs for these fires averaged more than $4 million per year. Statistics calculated from data provided by the 2010 State of Utah Hazard Mitigation Plan, http://publicsafety.utah.gov /emergencymanagement/UtahHazardMitigationPlan.html; and The National Interagency Fire Center, https://www.nifc.gov/fireInfo/fireInfo_statistics.html.

19. Blakely and Snyder, *Fortress America*, "Residential areas with," "designated perimeters," 2; Douglas, *Purity and Danger;* Didier Fassin, "Compassion and Repression: The Moral Economy of Immigration Policies in France," *Cultural Anthropology* 20, no. 3 (2005): 362–87; Mark-Anthony Falzon, "Paragons of Lifestyle: Gated Communities and the Politics of Space in Bombay," *City and Society* 16, no. 2 (2004): 145–67, "politics of exclusion," 159; Collins, "Political Ecology."

20. Seventy-seven percent of lodgepole pine stands were at moderate or high risk of attack by bark beetles in 1993. Renee A. O'Brien, "Comprehensive Inventory of Utah's Forest Resources, 1993," USDA *Forest Service Research Bulletin* RMRS-RB-1 [Rocky Mountain Research Station-Resource Bulletin] (1999): 1–105. Surface fuels are "fuels lying on or near the surface of the ground, consisting of leaf and needle litter, dead branch material, downed logs, bark, tree cones, and low stature living plants." NWCG Glossary of Wildland Fire Terms, http://www.nwcg.gov/pms/pubs/glossary/s.htm. Ladder fuels are "fuels that provide vertical continuity between strata, thereby allowing fire to carry from surface fuels into the crowns of trees or shrubs with relative ease. They help initiate and assure the continuation of crowning." Ibid., http://www.nwcg.gov/pms/pubs /glossary/l.htm; James K. Agee and Carl N. Skinner, "Basic Principles of Forest Fuel Reduction Treatments," *Forest Ecology and Management* 211 (2005): 83–96.

21. V. C. Radeloff et al., "The Wildland-Urban Interface in the United States," *Ecological Applications* 15, no. 3 (2005): 799–805; Susan I. Stewart et al., "Defining the Wildland-urban Interface," *Journal of Forestry* June (2007): 201–7; Schoennagel et al., "Implementation of National Fire Plan"; Donald R. Field and Dana A. Jensen, "Humans, Fire, and Forests: Expanding the Domain of Wildfire Research," *Society and Natural Resources* 18, no. 4 (2005): 355–62; Smith, "The Production of Nature"; Cronon, *Uncommon Ground*, "to protect the," 22.

22. Smith, "The Production of Nature"; Clifford Geertz, "Deep Play: Notes on the Balinese Cockfight," *Daedalus* 134, no. 4 (2005): 56–86.

23. Ingolfur Bluhdorn and Ian Welsh, "Ecopolitics Beyond the Paradigm of Sustainability: A Conceptual Framework and Research Agenda," in *The Politics of*

Unsustainability: Eco-Politics in the Post-Ecologist Era, eds. Ingolfur Bluhdorn and Ian Welsh (New York: Routledge, 2008), "politics" and "capitalist consumer," 14.

24. Ingolfur Blühdorn and Ian Welsh, "Eco-politics Beyond the Paradigm of Sustainability: A Conceptual Framework and Research Agenda," *Environmental Politics* 16, no. 2 (2007): 198; Stephen Pyne, *Fire on the Rim: A Firefighter's Season at the Grand Canyon* (New York: Weidenfeld & Nicolson, 1989).

25. Julian Agyeman, *Sustainable Communities and the Challenge of Environmental Justice* (New York: New York University Press, 2005), 58.

4

Beyond Boom and Bust

Recovering the Place of Kootenay Working-Class Stories

CHRISTINA ROBERTSON

When I was about seven, we moved down by the Fraser River in a squatter's area. The places were built on pilings outside the dikes of the Fraser River, two-bedroom cabins. They were floating houses and they'd been dragged up on the beach. In the spring, when the tides got high, you had to roll your socks up. There was no electricity, no running water. We carried buckets of water from a mill half a mile away. My grandmother and grandfather lived next door—Charlotte, Al, and Donny, their youngest son. My grandpa worked in one of the mills, down along the river.

—Jack Robertson, in conversation with the author, August 12, 2002

That's him, I think. In the second row, far left, hand on hip, one foot planted on the timber runner, the other propped up on a good-sized board that rests on a sled hitched to a small Cat. Deep snow blankets the steep road, brushy banks, rocks, and trees. The man wears wool pants tucked into wool socks, leather lace-up boots. His cropped, wool coat pulls apart at the buttons. Too small. Twelve more loggers stand on the sled or Cat donning wool overcoats, overalls, work boots. Some wear gloves, others don't. Each wears a wool fedora or engineer's cap pushed back on his forehead, as if in response to the photographer's command: *We want to see faces, not shadows. Tip 'em back, boys.*

Some of these loggers stand stiff and pinched as new boards, hands at their sides. Others look loose-limbed, set to defy the grinding, widow-making work of cutting, skidding, skinning, hauling, and stacking big timber taken from slopes so steep historical accounts recall teams of horses tethered uphill of the loaded sleds to keep the load from barreling down the mountain. Summoned for this company photograph, the crew has spaced itself out evenly, agreeably. The sepia-toned postcard is overexposed and grainy. Still, the upturned faces are easy to see, if not read. The deliberate stance of the stocky man standing in the back with his too-tight jacket matches his gaze. I scan all thirteen faces but come back to his square, asymmetrical jaw, the furrowed brow and broad nose, the mouth set into neither smile nor scowl. *Could that be him?* Along the postcard's lower edge the caption, "B.C. Spruce Mills, Ltd., Lumberton, B.C.," links these loggers to this job site, this town. The postcard has no date, though another image from the same series, identically captioned, bears a postmark—October 27, 1928. This date makes his presence among those thirteen loggers possible, even probable. *For all I will ever know.*

A decade later another company photograph, "circa 1940," pictures thirty-three "staff and crew" in front of a mill building, posing as if for a grade school photograph. The mill will soon close. The image is numbered, but text underneath asks, *"Does anyone know any of these people?"*[1] This same question tags thousands of images of British Columbia's mining, rail, and logging booms, now archived at universities and historical societies. Countless laborers in photographs older than the average lifetime await identification, kinship, reclamation. But by whom?

Many more images of Lumberton survive. One wide-angle shot reveals the town site perched at the base of an imposing peak. Another showcases a section of the mill's elevated flume hugging the curve of a mountainside. A third pictures the company baseball team in full uniform. *Cranbrook Daily Townsman* journalist Jim Cameron describes Lumberton's logging operation as an "impressively large, modern mill utilizing a record setting twelve-mile logging flume to bring the logs down to a pair of very large millponds and into the mill itself." In the 1920s, Cameron notes, Lumberton boasted "nearly 100 houses, a store, a bank, a schoolhouse, a community hall and an international collection of loggers that included French, Swedish, English, Scottish, Irish, and Poles."[2]

Working-Class Stock

I don't know if my great-grandfather Alfred John Robertson is the stocky man pictured in that postcard. Through a family story based on rough dates, my father's childhood memories, and my eldest cousin's tales, full of gaps, I do know Alfred (Al) worked for years among Lumberton's "international collection of loggers." It's likely that he and his wife, Charlotte, along with four of their six sons, lived in one of those one hundred houses. A sawyer in the era of hand saws and laissez-faire logging, Al's occupation would vanish along with the big trees—Western white pine, Douglas fir, cedar, tamarack—that he cut into lumber for railway ties, flumes, buildings, and the maw of foreign markets. In *A Life in the Woods—Oral Histories from West Kootenay Forests*, old-time logger George Lambert tells his interviewer, "At that time, way back in the 1920s, there was 150 sawmills between Grand Forks and Crow's Nest, 150 working sawmills." Winding through southern British Columbia's mountainous terrain, the Crow's Nest Highway takes its name from panoramic Crow's Nest Pass, where the route crosses the Rockies at the Continental Divide. The town of Grand Forks is 466 kilometers (289 miles) west of the Pass. By Lambert's estimation the peak of the Kootenay region's lumber boom supported an average of 3.1 "working sawmills" for each kilometer between these two places.[3]

From roughly 1920 to 1940 my great-grandfather Al worked as a sawyer in half a dozen of these mills, migrating with his family from camp to camp, following the timber boom. Near the end of his career, in the 1940s, he worked as a night watchman at a Vancouver sawmill operating on the banks of the Fraser River. By then he and Charlotte lived along the river in a squatter's area. When he was a child my father lived with his family in the cabin next door. He recalls, "We had oil lamps and gas lamps, and wood stoves, and you got wood right out of the river. I remember helping my grandfather. He'd spot a log going down and I'd jump in the row boat with him and away we'd go, row out there and get out alongside the log, and take and pound a little spike into it, tie a rope onto it, and then turn and row against the current, back up, pulling this log."[4]

My father was seven years old. A boat trip with his grandpa, no matter how wide or deep or swift the water, could only be an adventure. But by then Al would have been well into his sixties. Was rowing against the current of the mighty Fraser—here the river channel spanned a quarter of a mile and carried more water and silt to sea than any other on Canada's west coast—just an outing with his grandson, an afternoon lark? Or was wrestling firewood from the Fraser's muddy deeps the only way he knew, by dint of sinew, muscle, and bone, to make ends meet?

■ On March 15, 1889, the SS *Siberian* set sail from Glasgow carrying emigrants bound for Canada and the United States. The passengers included 129 boys, 69 boys "over 11 years" and 60 boys "eleven and under," all wards of Quarrier's Orphan Homes of Scotland; twelve-year-old Alfred and his older brother were quite likely among them. Likely. Quite possibly.

Canadian Census data from 1916 estimates the year of Alfred's birth as 1877, and family lore has it that he was eleven or twelve when he was sent to Canada. Alfred was, quite possibly, a passenger on that March, 1889 sailing. Yet the same census lists 1885—not 1889—as the year Alfred emigrated. Immigration records likely linking these two Robertson boys with Quarriers and, quite possibly, with the *Siberian,* list both as "John" (Alfred's middle name), each record bearing the comment, "One page almost impossible to read." If, as the census claims, Alfred instead emigrated in 1885, perhaps it was on the SS *Hanoverian.* That April the North American bound ship carried "100 young boys," also from Quarrier's Orphan Homes. On the Hanoverian's passenger list eight of the boys' names are so faded only a few letters appear in the allotted space. The name of the thirty-sixth boy on this list has faded completely, indicated by "[*].[*]."[5]

According to the family story, Alfred was born in Aberdeen, Scotland. He, his brother, and two sisters spent their childhood in Ireland where their father was stationed with the Black Watch. After their parents were killed in a suspicious carriage accident the four children were sent back to Scotland. When relatives willing to take them in could not be found, the four were turned over to an orphanage. What happened to the two girls after this remains, like much of our family history, a mystery.

On March 26, 1889, the *Siberian* landed in Halifax, Nova Scotia. There the boys were put on a train to Brockville, Ontario, where they were received at Fairknowe, William Quarrier's Canadian orphan residence. From here, each boy was handed to the farmer who'd paid his passage. An indentured servant contract made the transaction legal. (I know nothing about the older brother's servitude. Fifty years later Al and three of his sons attempted a reunion—Al's brother too, lived in Vancouver by then—but the elder brother had done well and his sons suspected Alfred's motives. Minutes after Al and his boys stepped into the long-lost brother's living room a fist fight broke out between the younger men, cousins who were, after all, strangers. The two brothers never spoke again.) Young Alfred's contract sold him into four years of hard labor on a remote farm on land then part of the Northwest Territories, now in northern Saskatchewan. In the town of Prince Albert, not far from where Al's first four sons were later born, winter temperatures average 13 degrees below zero Fahrenheit. Yet indentured boys were commonly housed in barns. Assessing this chapter of Canada's history through contemporary eyes, a *Winnipeg Free Press* journalist describes the plight of children like Alfred as "a plot right out of Dickens."[6]

Alfred's story is far from unique. He belongs to the ranks of British Home Children, the many poor and orphaned minors shipped, often against their will, from the United Kingdom to Australia, Canada, and New Zealand. Launched in the early 1860s by religious charities, this child migration movement was widely promoted as "a mission of rescue." Yet, as historian Lori Jones explains, "By the mid- to late nineteenth century, social reformers targeting poor children used the bleak economic and social prospects facing pauper children to justify their emigration." Between 1881 and 1930 alone, for instance, more than thirty thousand Barnardo Children—so called as wards of the orphanage founded by British philanthropist Dr. Thomas Barnardo—were sent to Canada. A 1922 *New York Times* article extols the benefits of child immigration, the unnamed journalist exclaiming, "In the British Isles there are thousands of children, sprung of good working-class stock, and possessed of fine qualities. . . . Many are orphans and others homeless from unfortunate circumstances."[7]

In Britain, welfare laws enabled this child labor movement. The 1850 *Poor Law Amendment Act* enabled the emigration of a "poor orphan or deserted children under the age of sixteen" at public expense. Another law, the 1889 Prevention of Cruelty of Children Act, intended to prevent the return of abandoned children to unfit parents, further empowered so-called guardians to export institutionalized poor children.[8] Both laws were ultimately repealed.

In Canada, meanwhile, according to Jones, the province of Ontario's 1799 Act to Provide for the Education and Support of Orphan Children addressed both a growing population of so-called pauper children and the need for cheap farm labor in the wake of Canada's land grant system, set up to boost farming in the territories west of Ontario. A shortage of family labor on these farms created a corresponding shortage of cheap labor and, Jones says, "It was this labour gap that imported boy labourers would fill." Ontario's 1897 *Act to Regulate the Immigration of Certain Classes of Children* into the province signaled a growing awareness of juvenile immigration, yet one of the law's main intentions was to prevent emigration agencies from importing criminal and so-called defective children.[9]

While the majority of children sent to Canada were, in fact, Barnardo

Children, at the peak of the child emigration movement, around 1900, Jones notes, "more than fifty organizations were engaged in this work." Quarrier Homes of Scotland, the orphanage that quite likely brokered Alfred's fate, ultimately shipped more than 7,200 boys and girls to Canada. The subtitle of the same *New York Times* story touts the movement's success to date, claiming, "Nearly All Brought from the 'Old Country' Made Good." The story insists such "working-class" children are "of the best citizenship material . . . if taken in the pliable and plastic state. Their only salvation is to be taken from their discouraging environment and be permitted to develop their newer qualities in a natural, richer ground. Canada offers them bright prospects, and the Dominion has need of such potential citizens." All told, Canada's post-Confederation economy was fuelled by an estimated 118,000 Home Children. Only the Great Depression quashed the nation's appetite for imported child labor. (By the mid 1930s, for example, Al's son, my grandpa Del, was riding boxcars back and forth between Edmonton and Vancouver looking for any work that could be had. Del's young family—my grandma Iva, my aunt, and my father—stayed behind on Iva's family's drought-stricken farm.)[10]

In 2009 and 2010, respectively, Australia and Britain formally apologized to their Home Children and descendants. To date Canada has not. Instead, the minister of citizenship, immigration, and multiculturalism declared 2010 the "Year of the British Home Children" and Canada Post issued a commemorative first-class stamp with a face value of 57 cents.[11] The stamp's lower quarter features the SS *Sardinian,* a vessel that carried many child immigrants to Canada. Above the ship is a sepia-toned photograph of a farm boy pushing a horse-drawn plow, breaking ground. The photographer stood behind the child to take the shot and so we see what the boy would have seen as he braced against the plow, the prairie spreading out around him, the horizon forever retreating. A third photograph, also sepia-toned, overlaps both prairie and ship's mast, linking the farm boy to his voyage. In this picture a Home Child dressed in an overcoat stands stiffly beside his suitcase.

To keep Alfred in servitude after he'd turned sixteen—and so was legally free—the farmer lied to him about his age. By the time he left, Alfred had worked like a draft horse on his taskmaster's land for seven years. He was nineteen and without a school diploma.

A Fish Story

In *Kokanee: The Red Fish and the Kootenay Bioregion,* ecologist and essayist Don Gayton offers an environmental history of the West Kootenay region of British Columbia. His account presents the "ecological moral tale" of the kokanee—a landlocked salmon endangered by dams, habitat destruction, and the well-intentioned introduction of an invasive shrimp—as evidence of the need for a "regional mythology." For Gayton, a California native who resisted the Vietnam draft and settled in British Columbia, the kokanee salmon is a "pilot fish . . . leading me forward, past mere biology and ecology, into an unexpected Kootenay bioregionalism." European settlement in the forested, mineral-rich Kootenays brought with it what he calls "smash and grab," the "colonial exploitation model" that destroyed the lifeways of the region's First Peoples, the Sinixt and Ktunaxa; decimated beaver populations; and laid waste to mountainsides, creeks, rivers, and lakes as fur trading gave way to mining, then clear-cut logging, and, finally, to the hydroelectric power boom.[12] What is missing in the wake of such boom-and-bust settlement, he contends, is a "bond" with place stemming from the loss of First Nations knowledge and a lack of locally grown narratives. Elsewhere, Gayton claims that the Kootenay region is "a land measured without stories."[13]

My great-grandparents arrived in the Kootenays in the midst of British Columbia's logging boom. True to the claim in the 1922 *New York Times* article, Al "made good," working as a sawyer while industrial forestry crowded out small-scale logging, and timber companies and sawmill operators gained what amounted to unlimited access to old-growth forests on provincial public lands. Al and Charlotte lived in Lumberton for a number of years, until the big trees had been harvested and the mill shut down, the townsite's houses sold, dismantled, and transported by rail to the next mill site, the next watershed. Like many other nineteenth- and twentieth-century Kootenay communities, Lumberton became a ghost town.[14] I can only guess for how long and exactly when Al worked in Lumberton. Dates, letters, almost all legal documents, family photographs—if ever they existed—were lost over years of moves to the next mill, the next job. Al had begun his working life as a displaced child immigrant. Even as he and Charlotte raised six sons, they would remain landless, itinerant laborers.

In "Bioregion," the closing chapter in *Kokanee,* Gayton lauds the Kootenay-Boundary Land Use Plan, forged in the 1990s through meetings uniting "Foresters, miners, ranchers, and guide-outfitters" with "park advocates, environmentalists, small business people, fishers, and trappers," as a victory over the "usual B.C. stalemate" of jobs versus environment. Yet he laments the absence of storytellers—"No poets. No oral historians, no balladeers"—at the table. Gayton contends, "Storytelling and the oral tradition are crucial to the development of a place mythology, but that tradition is weak in the settler cultures of western Canada, and . . . there are few precedents to build on." Returning to his "pilot fish," the kokanee salmon, Gayton offers a new precedent, translating the fish's food chain into a found poem: "This information is not 'owned' by any particular group and it has good narrative and rhythmic potential." Foregrounding the interdependence of the kokanee's spawning channel and hibernating black bears, Gayton sees setting, character, and plot in this ecosystem. He thus envisions a Kootenay narrative tradition grounded in a sense of place that is informed by bioregionalism, which he defines as "the transformation of our lives by local biology, geology, climate." Gayton wisely asserts that such narratives, attuned to forces that shape the land, have a key role to play in regional land use plans and practices.[15]

Yet something is missing from a "mythology of place" that excludes the consequences of boom and bust on working-class people who form, in the Kootenay region, as in most of British Columbia, the majority. As environmental historian Richard White states, "There is no avoiding questions of work and nature. Most people spend their lives in work, and long centuries of human labor have left indelible marks on the natural world." At the same time, generations of working-class people—European settlers among them—have been "indelibly marked" by laboring in extractive industries such as mining and logging, and in agricultural jobs such as farming and ranching. In order to move beyond boom and bust land use policies, we must take into account working-class experiences, tragedies, insights, and lessons. "We cannot come to terms with nature," says White, "without coming to terms with our own work, our own bodies, our own bodily labor." We must, in other words, reckon with the indivisibility of nature, industry, and human labor. Gayton himself urges us to notice that "The steep plunge of mountain toward the lake is interrupted only by a spidery rail line blasted into rock just above the water" and then to "Contemplate the history and impacts the railroad has had on our region." If we do examine the "history and impacts" of the railroad, the mines, the logging, the dams—impacts unfolding to the present day on the landscape and in the lives of local people—a rich Kootenay storytelling tradition swims into view. This narrative tradition connects the more-than-human world to work and to community life.[16]

Working-Class Stories

The Kootenay region's wealth of storytellers includes oral historians, poets, fiction writers, essayists, and memoirists. Reflecting almost two centuries of culturally diverse settlement, these texts illustrate wild variation in style, theme, and purpose. They share in common an understanding, articulated or not, of what working-class literary scholar Janet Zandy calls "labor's stamp on the body." They speak to the impacts of unsustainable land-use practices on the natural world, on community and family life, and on individual lives. Their stories offer a cultural record of people whose lives have been shaped by physical labor, economic and cultural instability, and boom and bust.[17]

For instance, long-time West Kootenay resident Tom Wayman is internationally recognized as a work poet and also writes poetry and fiction that aims to depict, in a realist vein, life in the Kootenays. His short story collection, *Boundary Country* (2007), portrays the everyday lives of local people and casts a keen eye on the environmental and cultural history of the region. In one story, "Ducks in a Row," set in Nelson—which calls itself Queen City of the Kootenays—Wayman takes up the issue of making a living in a fractious environment. A world-weary first-person narrator sets the stage for a community showdown between old-time capitalists, young ecocapitalists, artists, and escapees from Vancouver, offering this profile of his town's history:

> The Main Street mafia are mostly old money, convinced that municipal and personal wealth originates from cutting down and milling every stick of standing timber, damming any river capable of yielding a megawatt, and digging deep into each ridge that promises to surrender a bucket of ore—ore wrested either from veins or from tailing piles by technology unavailable during the mining boom-and-bust of the 1890s that brought white folks to this region of southeastern B.C. in the first place. . . . [A]long came geeks who wished to gawk at

peaks, or to kayak in the parks, or to tramp through the ever-dwindling forest cover.[18]

The story unfolds in a comic pandemonium that includes a celebrity appearance by none other than Sir Paul McCartney—whose presence in the plot is not so far-fetched, given Nelson's self-avowed reincarnation as a world-class destination—and the reader is left mulling over what it means to live in "an actual community, a little town perched on a mountainside by a lake" and to "contribute to that community."[19]

Another Kootenay fiction writer, Ann DeGrace, sets her novel, *Treading Water* (2005) in the fictional Bear Creek, a community very much like the West Kootenay settlement flooded to make way for the Hugh Keenleyside Dam, which was constructed on the Columbia River in the late 1960s. The story is told through multiple narrators, all residents of this doomed, working-class settlement. Luanne Armstrong's *Blue Valley: An Ecological Memoir* (2007), set on the east side of Kootenay Lake, documents her lifelong struggle as a working-class daughter, farmer, mother, and writer to make a living on her family's subsistence farm. I offer this brief list in the spirit of expanding the reach of a Kootenay bioregionalism to include working-class narratives. Two additional examples of regionally grounded, contemporary texts that engage culture, history, nature, and work, and that illustrate how these interrelated forces unfold not just on the land, but also in human lives, are Fred Wah's *Diamond Grill* (1996) and Patrick Lane's *There Is a Season* (2004). Each reflects a dynamic that Gayton characterizes as "the habitat of the human, its event field, the extent of the landscape that affects people and is affected by people."[20] These stories, then, reveal the human and environmental costs of separating who we are from the work we do, and from the land upon which that work depends.

In his "biotext," *Diamond Grill,* Fred Wah maps the contours of place, race, family, and culture, giving us a hybrid work that is part fiction, part poetry, part memoir. The son of the half-Chinese owner of the Diamond Grill restaurant—located in Nelson, Queen City of the Kootenays—Wah contends that despite how far our lives take us from childhood landscapes, "place becomes an island in the blood." Wah's 1940s boyhood landscape is, on one level, a vivid rendition of place. Yet *Diamond Grill* both charts and refutes cultural-geographical space. In the book's opening vignette Wah claims, "Maps don't have beginnings, just edges. Some frayed and hazy margin of possibility, absence, gap." *Diamond Grill* evokes this liminal space, challenging the dominant, European white status quo that calls itself "pure" Canadian and considers everyone else racially tinged. One quarter Chinese, one-half Swedish, one-quarter Scottish, Wah is "white enough to be on the winning team," yet is marked non-white by his name. He recalls filling out a school form and being "confused" by "the blank after Racial Origin." His child self reasons, "this is Canada, I'll put down Canadian." His teacher refutes this logic, says, "no Freddy, you're Chinese, your racial origin is Chinese, that's what your father is." Wah understands he's not "really Chinese," just as his classmates, back then, were not "*real* Italian, Doukhabour, or British." He sees, rather, "Quite a soup. Heinz 57 Varieties. There's a whole bunch of us who've grown up as resident aliens, living in the hyphen." *Diamond Grill* is a topography of that hyphenated space.[21]

Canada touts itself as a cultural mosaic and as a country built by immigrants. Yet even as Wah recounts his understanding of the Chinese immigrant experience, he resists being "inducted into someone else's story." He tells us, "Sorry, but I'm just not interested in this collective enterprise erected from the sacrosanct great railway imagination dedicated to harvesting a dominant white cultural landscape." Wah does not remind his reader, here, that what made the "great" Canadian Pacific Railway a reality, especially in British Columbia, was the Chinese labor that laid track through mountain passes that buried workers under avalanches of mud, rock, and snow. His indictment of a colonial enterprise that is still celebrated as a hallmark of national progress appears five vignettes on, in the form of a two-page, single-sentence pronouncement on the infamously exploitive Chinese Head Tax imposed on Chinese immigrants. This indictment ends simply with the question, "now that you got that head tax, will you collect a heart tax too?" Wah ultimately confronts his own racism, telling us he is "camouflaged by a safety net of class and colourlessness . . . that allows me the sad privilege of being, in this white world, not the target but the gun." Still, Wah suffered racial slurs as a child because of his Chinese last name. He discovered on the playground that "Race makes you different, nationality makes you the same."[22] Wah's biotext thus illustrates that the history of Canada, in large measure, embodies a history of environmental racism.

Part remembrance, part testimony, part how to cook Chinese–Canadian style (the reader finds recipes for ginger beef, steamed pork with bean curd paste, bitter greens, and deep fried whole rock cod), each of *Diamond*

Grill's 132 vignettes draws on Wah's skill as a poet. Measuring the pulse of his father's life in short rushes that invoke what he calls throughout the book as his "dog ghost," Wah merges son's consciousness with father's in language that slices along the edge of narrative and lyric. Once, watching a bear eating cherries off his tree, he feels himself becoming his father, "decanting through my body his ocean . . . all he could ever comprehend in a single view . . . the *deja-vu* of body, skin and fur and eyes, a brief intersection of animal coordinates." In such intersections Wah gives voice not merely to a time and place already *past* in his own life, but to his now-dead father's life, left unspoken because the latter—born in Canada to a white mother and a Chinese father, sent to China as a young boy as payment to his father's first wife, returning to Canada as a young man with no English—was "Chinese-Canadian, Chinese-white, hyphenated tongue-tied." In *Diamond Grill,* just as form straddles two genres—is prose hyphenated with poetry—story, too, is hyphenated. Fred Wah invokes a contact zone where place, race, history, work, culture, and family intersect. Each of us, this working-class story suggests, embodies such a biotext.[23]

Tailings

I grew up in a town claiming to be the home of the world's largest telephone booth, cut from a felled cedar. As kids we swam in the river, hung out in the pool hall, threw bonfire parties in the bush. Many of us grew up with fathers that worked at the smelter, or in the mines, or at whatever sawmill was running then, or at the pulp mill. We lived surrounded by second- or third-growth forests, and rutted logging roads zigzagging up almost every drainage. We knew where old-growth cedars survived, but we could count them on two hands. We sometimes stood under their canopy and joined hands around their huge trunks, craning our necks toward the light and filling our lungs with the scent of resin, bark, the phloem of old growth rings deep inside these trees. We knew we were standing among ghosts. When we recognized our boredom, we hauled out the local acronym for the town nearest ours, six miles away: Ymir—*Why Am I Here?* The answer came down to how all of our parents made a living.

The clear-cut slopes were out of sight, over the ridge. The mill towns—almost every town had a sawmill or a pulp mill—smelled of sawdust and rotten eggs. The taste of wood and that sulphur stench meant local jobs. In the winter, on Saturday afternoons, snowmobiles raced around the oval tailings pile that sits next to the Salmo River. In summertime the whole town came out for demolition derbies and stock car races, held on the same site. The earthen-walled pile rose out of a cattail marsh, full of mill tailings left over after silver, lead, zinc, and ore booms, trailing back to the 1890s.

Canadian Exploration Company Ltd. (Canex) bought the old claim in 1947 and turned the primitive, ghost settlement at Jersey City into a tidy town site of sixty houses, a recreation hall, and an outdoor swimming pool. Locals called the town site Canex. Everything except the pool was painted brown with white trim. Sheep Creek Road, the only way in, was never paved, just graded in the summer and plowed in the winter. One girl in our class, Joyce, lived at Canex and rode the school bus into Salmo. Her father worked in the mine. We town girls took turns sleeping at her house, vying for swim days in that turquoise pool, a jewel in the middle of the town site. For twenty-five years Canex flumed effluent from sixty thousand tons of ore the nine miles downhill to the tailings pile.[24] When the easy ore dried up, Canex closed shop, laying off more than a hundred men. In 1973 the company auctioned off everything from houses to office furniture. Joyce's family moved into Salmo. Before pulling out of town, Canex graveled over the crushed rock and cyanide and sulphuric acid slurry one last time and left the tailings pile to the community.

On race days a dozen souped-up jalopies fishtailed around the track, kicking up thick red spumes of dust to our whoops and cheers. Inside the track a concession stand was open for business. You could buy a hot dog, a burger, soft pretzels, coffee, pop, and juice. The hot, turbid air tasted like nothing more than rust. Years after the races stopped a handful of houses were built on the tailings pile. The land came cheap and level and the view of the Salmo River valley, from up on the rim of that pile, was grand.

■ While Patrick Lane is well known as a logger-turned-poet, in *There Is a Season*, a memoir, Lane sets the story of his life as an alcoholic against the backdrop of four seasons spent recovering in his garden. Born in 1940 in a remote mining camp in the West Kootenays, raised in two small towns, Lane's working-class origins strip away any nostalgia for the British Columbia interior's pre-and post-war booms. Against the reputed splendor of mountains and lakes and rivers, Lane's childhood landscape is marked by violence.

Late in his story Lane recalls a journey he made in the early 1970s with his alcoholic mother back to Sheep Creek, where he was born. "I thought if I could find the beginning, the place, I might understand what had happened there and so, somehow, understand what has happened since." His hard rock miner father had built the family cabin in the 1930s, in the very canyon that later became Jersey City, and then Canex—the mine site where Joyce's father worked, just south of Salmo—and then, finally, a ghost town. "We bickered and argued all the way there," Lane says, "the truck climbing up the mountains to the high passes and then down again into the desolate, isolated valleys of southern British Columbia." When they finally reach Sheep Creek, Lane sees his mother survey all that remains of the cabin, "a few rotted boards and logs, and the base of a stone chimney." Attempting to see this place and the past through her eyes, Lane shifts point of view: "Three sons in four years and a husband who left her each day in the darkness of the morning for his shift at the mine. Winter and summer, spring and fall. She had watched his back walk away from her up the trail that threaded through the other shacks and bunkhouses as he climbed up to the mineshaft and the men who were waiting to descend into the pit."[25]

It's hard to say whether the alcoholism and abuse that seeped like mine slag into Lane's family originated in this canyon, in the struggles of a young wife and mother trapped in a remote, 1930s mining camp. Lane imagines that his mother "remembers many things she doesn't want to remember" about this time and this ghost town, her return made stranger because "All the mine buildings are gone, hauled away by the company to another mine site above Kootenay Lake." The erasure of human settlement makes it "as if she had never lived here." Like the landscape, like the camp itself, her past, her story, has been razed. Only now, as she surfaces in Lane's recovery narrative, do the hardscrabble circumstances of her life as a mining wife, then a war wife, come to light.[26]

The placement of this bitter homecoming near the end of Lane's memoir reads as a climax, as does the intensity of the return, which is so painful the writer admits, at the start of this final chapter, "It's simpler to be a fiction. In a novel I can imagine things that aren't real, and I can make out of them a story and a place where I might exist free from my life." Sheep Creek, born in the fever of the mining boom and killed by its bust, isn't simply Lane's birthplace. Seeking out the camp's old dump, Lane's younger self digs through the garbage, believing, "Each thing he unearths is a clue to the word *was*. He is thinking that if he can only dig deep enough and far enough he will find something that will explain his life to him." What he does find is his old toy car that he leaves in care of his mother, who throws it out, asking him, *"What do you want with an old thing like that?"* This small cruelty must ultimately be understood through the lens of her pain at being forced to revisit a harrowing time and place.[27]

Forty years after this journey to Sheep Creek, Lane's ordered garden becomes that place he learns to "exist free from [his} life." Here, within the confines of the seasonal round he is able to forgive himself, and his mother, and come to terms with an illness that, in no small way, led to a "wandering life." When Lane tells us, in the last pages of the book, "Listen. There is a story the earth has to tell you," he is talking about lessons learned in his garden by watching, tending, waiting. Yet the story of his return to Sheep Creek, woven into reflections on a winter garden, is integral to his nascent understanding of his mother, his past, and his present: "It was in that narrow cut of rock between two mountains that she birthed her first three sons, all writers, all tellers of stories. She was there when her father died, a man she deeply loved despite the physical wreckage and spiritual and emotional chaos of sexual abuse. It was in Sheep Creek her husband joined the army and left us all behind. The journey to that vanished mining town was a burden she took on for me. I thank her for that."[28]

Lane's twelve-month pilgrimage to recoup his past follows a son, husband, father, logger, alcoholic, and gardener from physical and emotional turmoil to a carefully measured peace. *There Is a Season* is one man's recovery and reinhabitation narrative. Yet, in its unflinching look at the wreckage inflicted on people and landscapes by decades of boom and bust, Lane's story contributes to a working-class mythology of place. And perhaps because Lane's observations of the natural world challenge the boundaries of nature writing, *There Is a Season* creates a space where the measure of human life is taken alongside the place and culture that engendered it. In its insistence that British Columbia is culturally violent as well as physically beautiful, and as a record of determination to heal some of the damage, Lane's story is the almanac of a life and place, however small, in recovery.

Pulp and Paper

I remember when boys I'd been in school with since grade five and six started dropping out, one after the other, to go to work at the smelter,

Cominco, or in Sparwood and Elko, where coal was booming. The money couldn't be beat anywhere in the Kootenays and came with benefits. Who needed a high school diploma? This exodus of boys from school rosters began the summer between grades nine and ten, and picked up between grades ten and eleven. By graduation day, girls often outnumbered boys: the night of the procession, it was common for a boy to walk into the gymnasium with a girl on each arm.

In the Salmo Hotel, on any paycheck Friday before the recession hit, you couldn't get a seat and Waylon Jennings cover bands played until 1 A.M. On a good night I made a hundred bucks in tips ferrying trays of draft through smoke, elbows, drunken hugs, dancers, and brawls. Going to work was like going out with my friends, minus the Saturday morning hangover. The only downside was my clothes and hair always smelling of stale beer and cigarettes.

You started hearing about boys who'd gone to work at Cominco two, three years back, "getting leaded." The lead hit a guy's sperm count. Nobody said much about seizures or hearing loss or fatigue. One of these boys lived two doors down from my house. He was plump and baby-faced, a class clown. Of course, these boys got moved out of the lead room and onto the shovel in the yard until their levels settled down.

I ask my brother, Geoff, who has fished Kootenay creeks and rivers and lakes since he was seven years old, and who now works at Celgar, a pulp mill in Castlegar, how he sees the relationship between regional job security and environmental sustainability. He writes,

> As far as having any sense of job security goes, in this resource-based economy, with all of its "Booms and Busts," I haven't missed a single paycheck due to a lay-off for over 14 years, but that's certainly not the story for many of the people I know. Loggers, sawmill workers, teachers, tradesmen, service industry workers, the list goes on. Many families are hurting. The ripple effects being felt from the loss of the forest industry jobs (tens of thousands of them) over the past decade, have had severe impacts on many of the communities whose very existence depends upon these good-paying jobs and the spin-off benefits that they provide for the rest of the community.[29]

Geoff works the night shift. Two of every four twelve-hour shifts he works from 6:00 P.M. to 6:00 A.M. as a control panel operator, monitoring the mix of chemicals that make the slurry that becomes the pulp the mill exports at a tidy profit. The work is mentally and physically challenging: when the operation goes wrong, he shunts between the computer and the digester, working alongside the crew to keep the plant running. After two twelve-hour days, he shifts his internal clock by sleeping as late as he can on the third day so he can stay awake all night. Geoff knows that—like many other blue-collar workers—he's at increased risk of obesity, diabetes, heart disease, even cancer, because he works at night. He hasn't got a choice: he can't afford the switch to steady days. Day shift pays a lot less, and his wife and daughter are struggling to find jobs in the region's resource-based economy. "If I didn't work nights," he says, "we wouldn't be making it."[30]

With over seven thousand residents, Castlegar is one of the largest communities in the West Kootenays. The town grew up on the banks of the Columbia River. Here, the only public airport for hundreds of miles perches between mountains and river, a runway for low cloud and wind shear. Across the highway sits Selkirk College, the region's only enduring post-secondary institution. When I was eight years old and a Brownie, Queen Elizabeth II paid a visit to the people of Castlegar to help them celebrate the centennial of British Columbia's entry into the Commonwealth of Canada. I remember my sister, Barbara, and me lining up with our Brownie troop on the boulevard that runs from the highway to the college. People from every town within a hundred miles had come to see the Queen, whose coronation photograph hung in schools, legions, community halls, the post office. We all stood for two hours in a hard May rain, waiting for her limousine to pass by. Then it did. I remember her face through steamed-up glass, her white-gloved hand waving, a band of pale skin at her wrist. She might have been wearing blue. I know I waved my miniature Canadian flag with gusto.

In my English class at this same college, years later, our instructor taught us about close observation by stacking a dozen Red Delicious apples into a pyramid on a tray on a table at the front of the room. Our assignment was to describe what we saw. Dutifully we did so, from our seats. Twenty minutes later our instructor rotated the tray: each apple was missing a chunk of flesh where someone—no doubt, it was he—had taken a bite. Not one of us had gotten out of our chairs for a closer look at what we thought we were seeing.

■ Douglas fir. Western hemlock. Cedar. Yellow cedar. Bracken. The florescent green lichen that hangs from tree branches that we call grandpa's whiskers. Salmon berries. Huckleberries. Black bears. Grizzlies. Kokanee salmon. Bobcats, moose, coyotes, red fox, gray wolves. Tiger lilies. Ravens. Eagles, ospreys, hummingbirds. In the deepest pools of the big rivers, white sturgeon. Rivers. The Sinixt, following the seasons in canoes. Creeks. A creek for every drainage and too many drainages to count. Mountain slopes thick with trees and underbrush, too many peaks to name, a welter of spines running north–south but also east–west. And down in the valleys the sun is late climbing over the ridge and early dropping away from us, to the west.

I came upon the fragments of my great-grandfather Alfred's story by chance, after asking my cousin—the one who loves to look back on our lost family history and speculate—a simple, geographical question about the squatter's area where his mother and my father once lived. My father never thought to mention his grandfather's hardships, perhaps because his own parents struggled through the Depression and for many years afterward. The gaps and missing pieces of Al's life do tell a story, about Canada's economic development, about the legacy of boom and bust, about what it means to migrate from place to place just to make a living. Like so many people belonging to British Columbia's working-class settler cultures, Al and Charlotte lived unsettled lives. My brother's story, too, reveals the ongoing challenge of settling in a place shaped by this destructive legacy of boom and bust. For now, at least, a century and four generations after Alfred and Charlotte's arrival in the region, my kin still live and work in the Kootenays.

NOTES

1. Columbia Basin Institute of Regional History, "B.C. Spruce Mills, Ltd.: 0040.0020," *Columbia Basin Institute,* http://www.basininstitute.org/search/details.html?id=11154# .Uy217McozJ4.

2. Columbia Basin Institute of Regional History, "Lumberton, B.C.: 0023.0007," *Columbia Basin Institute,* https://basininstitute.org/search/details.html; Jim Cameron, "The Lady of Lumberton," *Cranbrook Daily Townsman* (Cranbrook, BC), October 22, 2010, "impressively large," "nearly 100 houses," http://dailytownsman.com/.

3. Peter Chapman, West Kootenay Forest History Project, "Interview with George Lambert, Sawmill Owner: Transcript for Lambert Sawmill," 5:20–5:35, in *A Life in the Woods—Oral Histories from the West Kootenay Forests* (Nelson, BC: Nelson's

Kootenay Museum Association and Historical Society, 1994), "At that time," http://touchstonesnelson.ca/exhibitions/forest/index.html.

4. Jack Robertson, in conversation with the author, August 12, 2002.

5. Library and Archives Canada, "Home Children (1869–1930)," http://www.bac-lac.gc.ca/eng/discover/immigration/immigration-records/home-children-1869-1930/immigration-records/Pages/immigration-records.aspx; Library and Archives Canada, "About the 1916 Census," http://www.bac-lac.gc.ca/eng/census/1916/Pages/about-census.aspx; "TheShipsList," http://www.theshipslist.com/ships/passengerlists/HANOVERIAN_1885.shtml.

6. Library and Archives Canada, "Home Children (1869–1930)," http://www.bac-lac.gc.ca/eng/discover/immigration/immigration-records/home-children-1869-1930/immigration-records/Pages/immigration-records.aspx; Carol Sanders, "The Barnardo Boys," *Winnipeg Free Press* (Winnipeg, MB), April 28, 2012, "a plot right," http://www.winnipegfreepress.com/special/ourcityourworld/uk/the-barnardo-boys-149343895.html.

7. Lori Oschefski, "British Home Children in Canada," "a mission," "Between 1881–1930," http://canadianbritishhomchildren.weebly.com/index.html; Lori Jones, "Not Here by Choice: Canada's Importation of Child Laborers," *Strata: University of Ottawa Graduate Student Plenary Review* 3 (September 2011), "By the mid- to late," 115; Anonymous, "26,509 Barnardo Children in Canada," *New York Times,* July 9, 1922, "In the British Isles," http://query.nytimes.com/gst/abstract.html?res=F20715F83B5D14738DDDA00894DF405B828EF1D3#.html.

8. Jones, "Not Here by Choice," "poor orphan," 113; Oschefski, "British Home Children," "Another law."

9. Jones, "Not Here by Choice," "In Canada," 119–20; "It was this," 120; "defective," 125.

10. Jones, "Not Here by Choice," "more than fifty," 117; Oschefski, "British Home Children," "more than 7,200 boys and girls," "estimated 118,000 home children;" Anonymous, "26,509 Barnardo Children," "Nearly All Brought."

11. Oschefski, "British Home Children," "commemorative first-class stamp."

12. Don Gayton, *Kokanee: The Redfish and the Kootenay Bioregion,* Transmontanus 9 Series (Vancouver, BC: New Star Books, 2003), "ecological moral tale," 63; "regional mythology," 81; "pilot fish," 80; "smash and grab," "colonial exploitation model," 35. For a detailed account of the Sinixt Nation, see http://sinixtnation.org/content/timeline. See, also, Eileen Delehanty Pearkes, *The Geography of Memory: Recovering Stories of a Landscape's First People* (Nelson, BC: Kutenai House Press, 2002).

13. Gayton, *Kokanee,* "bond," 81; Don Gayton, "A Tale of Two Kootenays," *The Tyee* (Vancouver, BC), September 2004, "a land measured," http://thetyee.ca/Views/2004/09/15/TwoKootenays.

14. A short history of the scores of ghost towns in the West Kootenay region appears in Elsie G. Turnbull's *Ghost Towns and Drowned Towns of West Kootenay* (Surrey, BC: Heritage House Publishing, 1988).

15. Gayton, *Kokanee*, "Foresters, miners . . . fishers, and trappers," 87; "usual B.C. stalemate," 87; "No poets," "Storytelling and the oral tradition," "This information," 88; "the transformation of," 82.

16. Richard White, "'Are You an Environmentalist, or Do You Work for a Living?'": Work and Nature," in *Uncommon Ground: Rethinking the Human Place in Nature*, ed. William Cronon (New York: W. W. Norton, 1996), "There is no," 172; "We cannot come," 173; Gayton, *Kokanee*, "The steep plunge," "Contemplate the history," 81. As social justice activist and literary critic Joshua A. Dolezal points out, "The false dichotomy between the poor and nature has long been under attack, particularly in international contexts where environmental justice is directly linked to colonialism," Josua A. Dolezal, "Literary Activism, Social Justice, and the Future of Bioregionalism," in *Ethics & the Environment* 13, no. 1 (2008): 2.

17. Janet Zandy, *Hands: Physical Labor, Class, and Cultural Work* (New Brunswick, NJ: Rutgers University Press, 2004), "labor's stamp," 5; See also James McCarthy, "Neoliberalism and the Politics of Alternatives: Community Forestry in British Columbia," *Annals of the Association of American Geographers* 96, no. 1 (2006): 84–104.

18. Tom Wayman, "Ducks in a Row," in *Boundary Country* (Saskatoon, SK: Thistledown Press, 2007), "The Main Street," 84–85; See Tom Wayman, *Going for Coffee: Poetry on the Job* (Madeira Park, BC: Harbour Publishing, 1981).

19. Wayman, "Ducks in a Row," "an actual community," "contribute to," 112.

20. Gayton, *Kokanee*, "the habitat of the human," 83. See also Ann DeGrace, *Treading Water* (Toronto, ON: McArthur & Company, 2005); Luanne Armstrong, *Blue Valley: An Ecological Memoir* (Nelson, BC: Maa Press, 2007); Fred Wah, *Diamond Grill* (Edmonton: Ne West Press, 1996); and Patrick Lane, *There Is a Season* (Toronto, ON: McLelland & Stewart, 2004).

21. Fred Wah, *Diamond Grill*, "place becomes," 23; "Maps don't have," 1; "white enough," "the blank after," "this is Canada," "no Freddy," "really Chinese," "*real* Italian," "Quite a soup," 53.

22. Wah, *Diamond Grill*, "inducted into," "Sorry, but," 125; "now that you," 131; "camouflaged by," 138; "Race makes you," 36.

23. Wah, *Diamond Grill*, "decanting through," 12; "Chinese–Canadian," 31.

24. See also Lisa Heinbuch's *Inventory of the Mine Tailings and Ponds in the Salmo Watershed*, ed. Gary Nellestijn (Nelson, BC: Salmo Watershed Streamkeepers Society, November 2000).

25. Patrick Lane, *There Is a Season: A Memoir* (Toronto, ON: McClelland & Steward, 2004), "I thought if I," 287; "We bickered," 293; "a few rotted boards," 289; "Three sons," 290.

26. Ibid., "remembers many things," "All the mine," "as if she had," 291.

27. Ibid., "It's simpler," 287; "Each thing," 289; *What do you want*," 295.

28. Ibid., "exist free," 287; "wandering life," 304; "Listen," 301; "It was in that," 303.

29. Geoff Robertson, pulp mill worker, personal communication with the author, July 20, 2010.

30. Geoff Robertson, personal communication with the author, July 20, 2010.

The Ways We Work

Toxic Consequences

5

Requiem for Landscape

EDIE STEINER

> *If we say only that we have mixed our labor with the earth, our forces with its forces, we are stopping short of the truth that we have done this unequally: that for the miner and the writer the mixing is different, though in both cases real; and that for the laborer and the man who manages his labor, the producer and the dealer in his products, the difference is wider again.*
>
> —Raymond Williams, "Ideas of Nature"

1959. This is the year a National Film Board of Canada camera crew comes to our home in the northwestern Ontario town of Manitouwadge, to interview my parents for the documentary film "The Mine Makers."[1] *They are the principal interview subjects, representing the local working class of this small company-owned mining town.*

A scene showing my father arriving home from his job at the copper mine precedes my parents' interview. We first see him approaching our house with a smile and a lively stride, his metal lunch bucket swinging from his hand. He is a cheerful and dashing worker, wearing a sporty suit jacket, well-pressed pants, and a fedora. This is not his typical costume for a hard day's work at the mine. These gestures, his wardrobe, and his persona are all dramatized by the film's producers. My father is a good performer who takes direction well. The producers pose him as a heroic worker, ready to sacrifice his body for the prosperity of the new nation he wants desperately to embrace as his own. A recent immigrant and a displaced person from East Germany, his former landscape is now forever lost to him. But on this day my father is pleased to be an actor in a fictional moment where he will perform for the camera. The drama of appearing in a film appeals to his artistic nature: he is an avid photographer, loves to draw, and plays several musical instruments. These creative talents form a part of the composition he is struggling to make of our family's life in our new land.

I, too, am placed in this scene but only as a background figure, a timid child hovering behind the front door screen. Although I do not want to be in the film, the director has positioned me here, excluded from the main action because of my gender, while my brother is allowed to strut forward to retrieve my father's lunch bucket. Over the upbeat, generic film score typical of the era's television programming, the film's narrator intones, "The men who work underground in the metal mines are unique. Proud and tough, they do their day's work in clammy darkness, cut off from open air and sunlight."

■ On a visit to my hometown in the summer of 2002 I photographed the vestiges of a trailer park where my mother once lived. As a practicing media artist and cultural agent, I was seeking evocative images as a social investigation, images I would organize into exhibition work. This was also the year when—after years of searching for the film in various public archives—I would finally locate a copy of *The Mine Makers.* My mother was unable to recall the film's producers or its title and had only once seen a special screening of the film, held at the mine's offices. For years, I assumed *The Mine Makers* must have been a promotional tool for the mining companies, as it did not show up in Canada's National Library and Archives in Ottawa. Then one day my mother called me to say a Manitouwadge librarian had found an old production photograph of the film in their files, credited to the National Film Board of Canada. I subsequently learned that the film's negatives had languished in storage vaults for nearly a half century.

The Mine Makers aired on the CBC national television news program *Frontiers,* a program that featured recent Canadian scientific and industrial developments. Our family missed the film's original broadcast because we did not yet own a television set, so I had never seen *The Mine Makers.*

As my young parents appeared on the screen, as real and as present as they once were, I experienced a powerful emotional tide. More than their images, so familiar to me from our many family photographs, it was their young voices that most provoked my heart. They seemed such an innocent couple, so unaware of what was to become of their lives, and I felt a tremendous sorrow. Speaking in broken English, they were among the many post–World War II working-class immigrants starting new lives in Canada.

In the early 1950s, sponsored by a Canadian federal labor program for Europeans displaced by the devastation of World War II, my father, Alfred

Emil Steiner, arrived in Canada to work in the northern mines. A year or so later he sent for my mother, Lottie, whom he'd left, already pregnant, back in Europe while he tried to set up a home for them in Canada. Now in their twenties, both had suffered through their late childhood during the war in Germany. My mother lived in a seaport that had been severely bombed. At sea, my father had twice survived his ship being torpedoed.

Of the few possessions he brought with him to Canada, one of his most treasured was a camera he bought on the black market after the war, when privately owned cameras were for a time confiscated by occupying forces in his town. He wished to document his family in their new life and location. He had a love for useful tools, and for images. Years later, I would consider my father's images as contributions to the histories of places our family lived. I would resurrect his photographs in my films and research projects, and would donate some of his work to local historical societies of the towns where we had lived.

In one of my father's pictures, our family is positioned against a rough neighborhood of uncleared ground, a pile of logs to one side. In the background is the tarpaper shack that was our first Canadian home. My father often included himself in family portraits by using a tripod and self-timer. In this image, he holds my hand while my mother, pregnant with my brother, Robert, holds my baby sister, Renate. Despite the unrefined surroundings, we are all well presented: working-class people wearing their best clothing. My father is in a suit and white shirt, my mother is stylish in a simple, elegant dress and jewelry, and I am a three-year-old child in a crisp white dress with a large white bow in my hair. I wonder if access to a camera altered the self-perception of my working-class parents. Surviving on a poverty-level income, they show themselves to be cultured and poised. They would have considered film and processing to be worthwhile expenditures.

While public photography usually draws on particular contexts for meaning, personal photographs produce stories worth remembering. My father's camera was an instrument of agency that gave a broader social value to our personal family narratives. My future reconstruction of these personal histories in my own cultural productions would return their embedded agency to my father. Following Bourdieu, Scott McQuire has written that the family photograph functions both as "an index of family unity and a tool to achieve that unity," a means of integrating the family or social group. At the same time, it is "a sign of the family's dispersion" in mass global and regional migrations.[2] The photographs my father created hint that he and my mother had larger dreams for their lives in their new country and viewed themselves as more than just working-class subjects.

In "The Mine Makers" the narrator asks my father if his is a dangerous occupation. My father responds, saying danger is increased when it is an "unexpected danger." He is fully aware of the obvious dangers in his occupational environment—the falling rocks and collapsing tunnels—but he notes, "We take responsibility for our fellow workers . . . so that my wife isn't hurt, and other people's families are not hurt." He is in his early thirties and will live less than twenty more years. His time in the underground workplace, with its unseen toxic dangers, will soon take its toll. He will die from this "unexpected danger," and my mother will be severely hurt by her loss.

In 1974, pressured by labor unions alarmed by the increasing numbers of miners in the province with lung cancer and silicosis, the Ontario government appointed a Royal Commission on Health and Safety in Mining. Led by Dr. James Ham of the University of Toronto, it was known as the Ham Commission. This investigation and its resulting reports would lead to new legislation giving Ontario workers the right to know about their workplace hazards and the right to refuse unsafe work without penalty.[3] But the passage of the Occupational Health and Safety Act, a participative model based on the Ham Commission Report, was still four years away. My father would die in 1975, three years before the act was passed.

In 2002, when I received a copy of *The Mine Makers,* I obtained a copy of the film's production notes. Here the notes quote my father: "On a Sunday, when the mine is quiet, you can hear the mountains working, the movement of the rock over your head . . . [and] you learn to recognize the danger sound of a certain kind of rock noise."

"You can hear the mountains working . . . ."

For my father, the rural northern terrain was a refuge from his stressful and hazardous occupation. He often spoke of how the region's topography, with its low hills and endless forests, reminded him of his homeland in Silesia, which he left as a teenager before the war when he joined the German merchant marines. At the outbreak of World War II he was fifteen years old and his ship was stationed in Newfoundland. Perhaps this first encounter with the Canadian landscape influenced his decision to return to Canada after the war, to a place he could call home. He spent his remaining years in the rural Canadian northland, with its evergreen forests, its northern lights washing over the radiant night sky in the pale cold winter, and its wild rivers and lakes that he traveled in his small fishing boat.

The northern bush is a vast and sometimes formidable landscape, a land of dense forests that can rattle the hearts of those who travel its interior spaces. A tangled place, in summer it is thick with swarms of tiny biting black flies. These conditions can make for challenging crossings into its sublime vistas and secret depths, which have been immortalized by a league of Canadian painters, poets, and authors. Canada's cultural artifacts mythologize the northern landscape, inspiring a national ethos of elemental forces emerging from a dramatic wilderness.

A boreal forest of spruce, poplar, balsam fir, tamarack, cedar, and low-lying wild blueberry bushes overlays the oldest rock on the North American continent. This wild space is filled with populations of moose and bears, foxes, wolves, tiny chipmunks, and great black crows, and, in some regions, surviving herds of woodland caribou. Its lakes teem with mostly still-edible fish. The inland sea that is Lake Superior, less than forty miles south as the northern crow flies, pushes its powerful storms and ever-changing, dramatic skies toward Manitouwadge. Mornings on Manitouwadge Lake are often shrouded in a dense mist. Despite all this wonder, my father's spirit fell down with him into the darkness of the mineshaft, where there was no solace from the labor that ravaged his body.

The narrator of "The Mine Makers" now turns to my mother, asking if she worries when my father goes to work at the mine. She glances over at her husband apprehensively, and answers that it's the night shifts that concern her the most: "Day shift and night shift they change so quick. He's tired the first couple of nights so I'm always thinking, I hope nothing happens to him."

My mother spent many sleepless nights waiting for my father's return. Over the years, as his stress increased, he turned to alcohol for relief. Sometimes our small basement room, which he built as a kind of recreation area, was filled with miners who would spend the night drinking, singing, and arguing. When the others left in the dark early hours my father would often remain drinking alone. Sometimes he felt suicidal. Then the hunting rifles he kept to shoot wild partridge, as food for the dinner table, became a real danger. I recall some nights of terror in my bed, as my mother talked him down from his bitter mood and back upstairs so he'd be well and rested for the next shift of work. This is how we remained intact as a family, and did not become, as my brother once remarked years later on one of our road trips back to Manitouwadge, another media statistic. Together, my parents kept it, and kept us, together.

My young onscreen father comments on the perceived social status of the men who work underground in the mines. He notes that some people think miners are the lowest of the low, men who are considered "good for nothing, but good enough for the mine. But I would say it's not like that. Because we break the ore, and the ore makes the metal, and the metal makes the industry run. So we are the first step." His dark eyes gaze into the lens, making sure the viewer gets the point, that he is an intelligent man aware of the relationship between his work and the larger production of culture.

My father's assertion in the film, that miners are the frontline workers of their industry, reflects his insight that while a miner may be considered a lowly worker, it is his capacity to labor that produces the industry's capital accumulation. Capital is created by the labor of many, but only a small number profit from the wealth that is generated by that labor. The rewards gained by a few are countered by a multitude of losses for many others: the workers and their families who endure occupational accidents, work-related injuries and illnesses, and sometimes death. The poverty that can follow unsuccessful compensation claims is one such loss, but the life of a worker can never really be compensated. As Janet Zandy tells us, "Loss cannot be compensated, but it can be answered and understood through finding meaning within cultural and historical contexts." We begin with sharing our stories, what Zandy calls "humble witnessing."[4]

After reviewing the footage of my family in *The Mine Makers,* I appealed to the National Film Board of Canada for rights to reconstruct the personal images—only those of my family and hometown—into a new film. I had no funding, and the Film Board turned down my project, stating it was too small and personal. Eventually I was granted a limited contract, which allowed me to work with the footage until the film became public domain fifty years after its first release, in 2010.

Originally, I intended to make a documentary film about Manitou-wadge rapidly declining as it approached its fiftieth anniversary in 2004.

Manitouwadge was built on deforested land, forming an almost desertlike sign of disfigured tundra deep inside a wide swath of north Ontario boreal forest. A single road leads to Manitouwadge, some fifty kilometers north of Trans Canada Highway 17. In this isolated and wooded location, community members are issued evacuation procedures and a list of emergency provisions to keep on hand in the event of a forest fire. The local mines are closed, but a new mine some sixty kilometers away, at Hemlo, continues to sustain the decreasing local population.

Northern Ontario spans millions of hectares, encasing the Canadian Shield between Lake Superior and the Hudson Bay. The area makes up 90 percent of Ontario's land mass but holds 6 percent of its population. Sometimes called the provincial north, the near north, or even the forgotten north, its rocky depths contain some of the world's richest mineral deposits of copper, nickel, chromite, gold, and diamonds. The small mining towns of northern Ontario inhabit an expansive geography that is commonly referred to as a *hinterland,* a term loaded with social and political meaning. The hinterland's regions are predicated on resource extraction; without a diversified economy those who live there cannot stay once those resources are fully exploited. Its predominantly working-class landscape positions it in bleak contrast to the romanticized far north and the developed metropolitan that comprises most of southern Ontario. A hundred or so kilometers north of Manitouwadge is the southernmost point of an area known as the Ring of Fire, a rapidly growing zone of thousands of mining claims that threaten to disrupt one of the last intact original forests on the planet.[5]

In the 1950s, supported by government sponsorships, the mining companies quickly erected a town to house the workers and their families. Manitouwadge was promoted as a model project, a joint endeavor by the Ontario government and the mining corporations. The building materials used to fabricate the houses have withstood five decades of long, subzero temperature winters, but my mother and I can recall ice on the interior walls of my childhood bedroom.

In 2002 I interviewed several Manitouwadge elders, including my mother, seeking their memories of the town's early days. It became apparent no one wanted to say anything negative about the mining companies. My respondents were eager to emphasize the positive attributes of life in a dying mining town, and hoped my film would promote the region's recreational and wilderness appeal. Tourism might even revive the local economy. It was only my mother who had a troubling tale to tell.

I discovered that my father had received no income during his months of illness. Following his death, my mother's claim for a spousal survivor benefit from the Workmen's Compensation Board, as the Workplace Safety and Insurance Board was then called, was refused. She accepted the outcome of her claim, and then disposed of the documents when the mining company, which owned her house, evicted her. Working-class people living in remote communities have limited access to the means to challenge decisions made by powerful metropolitan authorities. Reviewing footage of my interview with my mother, I returned repeatedly to her testimonial about how she came to live in a trailer park.

When my father died of pulmonary silicosis and related cancers in 1975, my mother was unemployed. She had taken a leave from her former position as the head cashier of the local Hudson Bay Company store, and now there were no positions available. Left with minimal resources after my father's medical costs, she was allowed six months to vacate her company-owned home of nearly two decades. Because my father died in late November, she was given until late spring to leave. As she said in my filmed interview with her, "They can't throw you out in the winter." With no one in the household now employed by the company, her only other option would have been to buy the house outright. This choice would have consumed my father's entire life insurance policy, a mere ten thousand dollars. My parents didn't own the house they lived in because of the transient nature of miners' work. They had plans to move elsewhere upon their retirement. Having already lost one home in another mining town, they couldn't afford to lose another when this mine closed, as all mines eventually do. My mother decided to relocate to Toronto, to live with my sister who had just announced that she was pregnant and would need help as a single parent. This decision gave my mother a renewed sense of purpose, temporarily buffering her against the loss of both her husband and her community in Manitouwadge.

Three years passed. My mother realized she could not survive financially in Toronto. Her savings were diminishing, and she was too young to receive the Canada Pension. Her part-time bakery job would not sustain her, and my sister had found a new partner. On a return visit to Manitouwadge, my mother was offered a used trailer home for five thousand dollars. Even in the 1970s in a remote north Ontario town, this was a deal. She decided to invest most of her remaining savings in the trailer, a real home that would be hers alone. One that the company could not take from her. She supported herself with various part-time jobs: as a cleaning woman, a cashier, and a restaurant helper.

In "The Mine Makers," my young mother regards my father with trust. "He's a good worker," she says. "He knows what he's doing down there in the mine."

Forty years after her first filmed interview, in my new film, my mother says, "It's hard when you work three shifts in the mine, and you come home from the graveyard shift, and the same day you have to go back to work. It's a lot of stress, not only on the man, but also on the family. Some people just couldn't take the stress, and we had a couple of men who shot themselves." But it is not just the grueling work schedule, the appropriately named graveyard shift that begins at midnight and runs into morning, for a sometimes brief turnaround before the worker is back on the job, which creates the stress. In company towns the employer can have a significant influence on the social life of the family.[6] The company usually has a great deal of authority in local institutions and their politics, leaving workers without access to community support should they commit a grievance, perceived or real, against the company. Local solidarity is aligned with the company, which provides most of the community's infrastructure and resources. Workers often live in company-owned houses. If a man is killed or injured on the job, families are left destitute.

By late summer of 1975, my father was very ill. In September he was transferred to a hospital in Thunder Bay, hundreds of miles from Manitouwadge, which had no specialized health care. My mother had to travel to visit him, without a car of her own, thereby depleting the family savings with months of hotel and transportation costs. My father's northern doctors discovered he had silicosis, an often-fatal disease for miners and other workers who inhale silica dust. The northern doctors initiated a compensation claim on my father's behalf. For several months, a trail of correspondence ensued between the physicians in northern Ontario and those advising the Workmen's Compensation Board in Toronto. The Toronto medical officials denied the claim initiated by my father's doctors. Three weeks before his death in late November, Dr. Charles Stewart, representing the

Workmen's Compensation Board as Chest Disease Consultant, stated that my father's case was "most intriguing" in that his recent X-rays indicated "some signs of dust effects, but certainly no sign of silicosis."[7]

My mother had never challenged my father's unsuccessful compensation claim for his work-related illness and subsequent death, or her own denied claim for a spousal survivor benefit. During our filmed interview she told me she sent all the required documents to the Workmen's Compensation Board via a mining company official. Her English literacy skills were still limited, especially in regard to legal and professional rhetoric. She was told that the company's officials would take care of the matter. Without recourse to her own legal support, she could, in her words, "go nowhere." As a working-class woman facing powerful authority figures, she decided, "You just do the best with what you've got left." In the midst of the turmoil of losing her husband and the imminent loss of her home, she accepted the advice of a friend who told her that even if she did have a lawyer, the mining companies and the Workmen's Compensation Board had better ones.

As I studied my interview with my now elderly mother, I began to grasp the scope of the injustice my parents had endured. I knew that workplace toxins cause silicosis, and so my father's occupational disease should have been compensated. I decided to try to locate a copy of the letter of denial sent to my mother. I asked a social justice lawyer who had once purchased some of my artwork to give me some advice. He told me I could access my father's file at the Workmen's Compensation Board, now renamed the Workplace Safety and Insurance Board, by citing the Freedom of Information Act. I convinced my mother to allow me to act on her behalf.

Months later, a large dossier arrived in the mail. It held over one hundred pages of documents related to my father's illness, death, and appeals for compensation. As I sifted through the correspondence, I again grieved the loss of my father. Going through the file devastated me. I would put it aside for days before going back to the documents. The package held my father's autopsy reports, the letters from his physicians, and the final refusal: Reject Claim. The letter of denial to my mother, dated several months after my father's death, states, "Many extensive tests, examinations were carried out to determine the exact diagnosis . . . [but] it is unfortunate this could not be completed until after your husband passed away." Therefore, the letter concludes, "Medical evidence before the Board has confirmed that the cause of your husband's illness and his eventual death was due to an unrelated non-industrial condition and was not related to or characteristic to the type of work your husband performed in the mines."[8] How could this be so? I was referred to two agencies that provide assistance to injured workers and their families, the Occupational Health Clinics for Ontario Workers (OHCOW) and the Office of the Worker Adviser (OWA). Meanwhile, I began to arrange sequences of my mother's 2002 filmed interview against elements of the 1959 historical footage of my parents in *The Mine Makers*.

Now I imagined a new reading of the passing of the lunch bucket from my father to his son, one that reframed this gesture as a symbolic transfer of intergenerational labor practices, a legacy announced in the object of the lunch bucket. Did the film's creators intend this visual metaphor? In Thomas W. Dunk's study of northwestern Ontario working-class men, *It's a Working Man's Town*, one of his respondents remarks, "It's a working man's town. Everybody carries a lunch bucket here. That's what it's like in northwestern Ontario."[9] Dunk notes that this image of the worker with his metal lunch bucket implies a significance that is both economic and cultural in industries based on resource extraction.

During the filming of *The Mine Makers*, according to the film's production notes, the producers asked my five-year-old brother if he, too, would become a miner. My father intervened, saying he would prefer his son not work in the mines. Why would the producers imagine this legacy for this young child? Perhaps because my paternal grandfather was also a miner. After losing his woodworking practice and all his assets in the post–World War I economic crash in Germany, with no other employment available to him, my grandfather resorted to working in a coal mine to support his family. Maybe that was why my father left home at fifteen for a life at sea. Then the war put him deep under water, where he was trained as a sonar operator on a submarine vessel and forced to spend his days and nights monitoring a radar screen, which he hated. My mother told me this was why he refused to buy a television set until well into the 1960s, rather than what he told his three children: because he didn't want television to take us away from our books.

The Mine Makers clearly depicts class divisions between the northern and southern sectors of Ontario's mining industry. Northern footage features industrial production with miners and machinery working underground. There are images of the town of Manitouwadge under construction, with its unpaved roads without sidewalks, rows of identical prefabricated houses, and the local Hudson's Bay Company Store, often the sole retail outlet in northern towns back then. Segments illustrating southern Ontario's control of the industry feature urban scenes: men in business suits consulting in boardrooms, interior shots of the stock market offices, the downtown streets of Toronto and Montreal, and charts depicting capital growth.

Once the companies extract all the ore, they leave the mining towns behind. The miners must move on as well: to another mine, another town. If the miners owned their houses rather than renting them from the mining company, they would vacate their home, often selling them at a bargain price. Many houses stand empty. When a corporate entity abandons the single-industry community that it built, community members must also uproot themselves. Those who choose to stay must shoulder the increasing tax burden necessary to maintain a community infrastructure.

Manitouwadge is isolated from its nearest neighboring community by hundreds of square miles of dense forest. My childhood memories recall a tedious landscape with long, desolate stretches of unremarkable bush. But we loved the bush for its secrets: the spirits that dwell beyond its dark borders, among the wild animals and the ghosts of its first peoples. The boreal forest is filled with thousands of lakes crossed by countless rivers and creeks. To local preservationists, and to the First Nations people to whom this landscape really belongs, these hills, these lakes and rivers, this relatively pristine, rough country, is "a treasure . . . a jewel . . . a gem."[10] Yet they also know this country is no longer pristine.

This land and its waters are filled with contaminants from the mines and the paper mills. Toxic tailings and waste rock from mining are routinely dumped into local lakes and rivers. Acid mine drainage leaves behind high concentrations of liberated iron, polluting nearby streams and the water bodies they flow into. Winds carry contaminated dust from tailings and other mining waste. Hardrock metals continue to release gases, such as carbon monoxide, making the air around old mining sites unsafe to breathe. Even mines abandoned a hundred years ago may continue to release toxins into the local environment.[11] Northern Ontario is filled with old mines, many abandoned before mine waste disposal and the reclamation of mine sites became an environmental and legal issue.

At the Geco Division of Noranda Mines Limited where my father worked, the primary metals extracted were copper and zinc, along with smaller quantities of silver and gold. From 1957 into the early 1990s, the Geco mine milled over 50 million tons of ore, worth over $5 billion in 1994 prices, and these operations produced 50 million tons of mill waste, as well as substantial quantities of sulfide-bearing waste rock. In the early years of the mine's production, the toxic effects of waste sulfide oxidation were not yet fully understood.[12] My father's former workplace is currently in a remediation and land reclamation phase.

Like the body of the worker, the ground where the mine operates is subjugated to corporate profit. To encounter the visual consequences produced by this ecological sublime—as in the awe and a kind of mitigated terror before the grand object—is to witness the postindustrial landscape.[13] We sense the mysteries lingering in the lakes, in the small old mining towns, amid the ghosts of those who gave their lives to build small solidarities to shelter them in remote and often rudimentary living conditions. Workers like my father endured the damages of their labor in order to glimpse the promise of those jewel-like lakes and everlasting trees, the small mountains of hope rising in the clear and brilliant northern sky, while precious metals glittered in the dark hard rock below.

So this is why my plundering of images led me to the remains of a trailer park, where my mother once lived. Her trailer, no longer mobile, was fixed on a foundation with a built-on shed to keep the garden tools. She had a garden. A fence surrounded the trailer. It had a porch. It felt like going into a real home because of that porch. The trailer park was once a community, an anchored arrangement of mobile homes, with street names and numbers and real yards. But now it is only a large, rough lot, with the detritus of its former inhabitants' lives scattered in the rubble. The foundations of the old trailer homes remain, like gravesites, rectangular impressions, evidence of habitat mingled with hardy garden flowers: a blue morning glory, a small rose bush, a stray poppy. Some people, like my mother, took their gardens with them. She replanted hers in a patch outside her new ground floor apartment.

My mother once told me of a miner a few trailers over who was murdered for his money, his identification papers stolen, and his decapitated body hidden away deep in the bush. What demonic struggle ensued in that trailer home? How did my mother feel living alone in the trailer park, with stories like that going around? A working-class woman who spent her childhood dodging bombs in World War II Europe, she was not afraid.

As I roamed through the site with my cameras, I found shards of crockery, children's toys, and many books. An inordinate number of Bibles. I photographed these objects as ephemera from a time and place I hardly knew, but one I was bound to. What chemical compounds now rest in that ground? Decades of disposal. Oil tanks to fuel winter furnaces. Sewage and sludge, metals and rust.

As I worked, I sensed my father's presence, urging me on:

"What whispers amongst the striving new foliage?"

By 2007 I had completed a new film braiding my mother's 2002 testimony, my trailer park images, and other local landscapes with the images and narratives of *The Mine Makers*. This film, *Northland: Long Journey*, illuminates the irony of my father's dramatized performance of the happy miner strolling toward the family home with his spirited stride, jauntily swinging his lunch bucket. *Northland* reveals that my father never returned home from work in such a positive mood. He was always exhausted and depressed, and as children we never ran to greet him; we stayed out of his way. The agony of his underground work and his sense of entrapment in his occupation made him volatile.

Before I completed my project, the Manitouwadge municipality had decided to move the remaining derelict trailers from the trailer park to a new site across town. My mother's trailer was by then too old to be moved, so ever resourceful, she sold it for its appliances and parts, and retired to the local seniors building. My siblings and I were relieved. She would now be less isolated and more secure.

When my father died in 1975, the global scientific community and its literature had not yet achieved consensus that exposure to airborne crystalline silica dust, which causes silicosis and other respiratory diseases, was also carcinogenic. This would take another twenty years of research and ongoing epidemiological studies. Although his death was caused by years of silica dust exposure in his underground work environment, the Workmen's Compensation Board of Ontario was then able to argue that the primary cause of his death was lung cancer, not silicosis. Because my father had also smoked, the medical officials representing the Workmen's

Compensation Board attributed his death in part to his lifestyle. This was not an uncommon judgment in the 1970s, a decade in which a multitude of claims flooded the Compensation Board from ill and dying northern miners.

A 1987 study published by the *British Journal of Industrial Medicine* followed the mortality experience of more than one thousand Ontario miners receiving compensation for silicosis from 1940 to 1985. This study acknowledges that many deaths from silicosis before 1979 were missed from these statistics because they were not reported to the Compensation Board's silicosis registry. The study notes that the workers with silicosis were found to have "a significantly increased mortality from lung cancer" and that smoking did not account for the increases involved. These findings were confirmed by similar studies conducted in Europe, all suggesting that occupational exposure to silica accounted for the increased deaths from lung cancer. The research suggests "that silica itself might be a carcinogen," and that "silicosis might be an intermediate pathological state leading to cancer."[14]

Workers are often blamed for their work-related injuries. Occupational health hazards curtail the workers' ability to work, and corporations often deny these hazards in favor of more cost-effective means of controlling them.[15] The burden of responsibility for safe practices on the job is typically placed on the worker, who is precariously balanced between the poles of internal corporate politics and the politics of external enforcement of safety procedures by government-regulated inspections.

In 'The Mine Makers' my father speaks of breathing through the nose rather than the mouth, as a preventative against inhaling lethal toxins: "A good miner breathes through the nose . . . or he is finished in four or five years."

Initially, I attributed my father's comment to the folk knowledge of old miners. A few years after seeing *The Mine Makers* for the first time, while still working on my own film, I decided to pursue a doctorate in environmental studies at York University in Toronto. I learned about a process known as aluminum prophylaxis, patented in 1936 by the McIntyre Research Foundation in northern Ontario.[16] From the 1940s to the 1980s, all gold and uranium miners in Ontario were required to inhale a mixture of finely ground aluminum powder and aluminum oxide as a prophylactic agent against silicosis. This black dust, known as McIntyre powder, was pumped into the workers' changing rooms as they changed into their underground work uniforms. Each time they inhaled, powdered aluminum coated their lungs. This treatment wasn't optional. If a miner refused, he could lose his job. The corporate literature assured workers that the aluminum dust would protect them and instructed them to inhale the toxic powder through the mouth, but once underground to breathe through the nose. The nose served as nature's filter, they said, while their aluminum powder-coated lungs would handle the rest.[17] Now I understood the source of my father's comment in *The Mine Makers*.

The aluminum prophylaxis program was adopted by underground mining operations in other parts of Canada and abroad, where silica problems resulted in increasing numbers of workers with diseased lungs making claims for compensation. By 1956 the *British Journal of Industrial Medicine* had published a report revealing aluminum prophylaxis to be ineffective against silicosis.[18] But in the years that it was enforced, millions of dosages were administered globally. Research studies of the late 1980s by the Canadian Industrial Disease Standards Panel, which was created under the Workers' Compensation Act of Ontario, linked aluminum prophylaxis to cognitive impairment and possible neurotoxicity. In the mining towns, some called these effects McIntyre syndrome.[19]

Throughout the twentieth century, silicosis was as much a political issue as it was a medical condition, a disease historically informed by social, economic, and scientific discourse. Rosner and Markowitz write that the disease "brought into question one of the central beliefs of the twentieth century—that technological innovation and the growth of industry would produce general improvements in the quality of people's lives." Silicosis challenged the public's faith in the "neutrality and objectivity" of science.[20] As the disease became framed by its origins in industry, silicosis was revealed to be as much a social and political condition as it was a medical problem.

After securing a forensic review of my father's documents at the OHCOW, I learned that in 1997 the International Agency for Research on Cancer (IARC) confirmed crystalline silica dust inhaled from occupational sources as a carcinogenic agent. This scientific verification meant I could now challenge my parents' long-denied right to compensation. My father's lung cancer, cited as the primary cause of his death and thereby disqualifying him from compensation for his silicosis, was in fact caused by toxic agents in his working environment, and not, as the Compensation Board doctors had decreed, by a combination of lifestyle and a random, unrelated illness.

Aided by a representative from the OWA and a letter from the forensic examiner at OHCOW, I undertook a legal appeal. I saw my father's pride in his work as not just a personal attribute, but also a political position confirming his solidarity with his fellow workers. His commitment to the safety of other workers is reflected in his testimonial in *The Mine Makers,* when he stresses the importance of individual responsibility for the safety of those who share the underground workplace and the need to protect their families. Employer companies did not share this responsibility.

In 2007, a few months before completing my new film, I interviewed Stephen Lewis, a longtime social activist who was the leader of the left-leaning provincial New Democratic Party for most of the 1970s. In the early 1970s, Lewis made an urgent appeal to the Ontario legislature on behalf of northern Ontario miners, commenting on inadequate health and safety standards in mining and the growing numbers of workers with silicosis and work-related cancers. It was Lewis's activism that urged the provincial government to begin investigations that preceded the 1978 Occupational Health and Safety Act, the first legislation giving workers in Ontario the right to know about their occupational hazards. I also interviewed my representative at the Office of the Worker Adviser, Rick Hamilton, a longtime activist on behalf of injured miners. Shortly before my project was completed, Mr. Hamilton called me to say that my appeal had been successful. My mother would receive a settlement and a new pension for the rest of her life. Widowed while still in her forties, she was now eighty years old. I wondered if the public figures appearing in my film could have influenced this revised judgment.

In the past decade, news of silicosis cases at the Hemlo Gold Mines, a short distance from Manitouwadge, has been featured in national media stories. In 2002 an Ontario member of Parliament, Michael Gravelle, wrote to the federal Ministry of Labour regarding the prevalence of silicosis at Hemlo, and called for a public inquiry. The United Steelworkers union pressured the Ontario government to review the Silica Monitoring Program in mines. Ministry of Labour field tests at Hemlo proved that the workers' exposures to airborne silica dust far exceeded the legislated regulation limits. But even so-called acceptable limits are not set in the workers' favor.[21]

In 2006 MiningWatch Canada, a nonprofit group monitoring impacts of mineral development, reported that silicosis cases in Ontario had increased by 10 percent over ten years. Union health and safety officials stated the companies and the government were again downplaying the problem of workers with silicosis, and the fact that ill and dying workers were still being denied compensation.[22] Even now miners with silicosis struggle to have their claims recognized by the province's Workplace Safety and Insurance Board. By 2009 Michael Gravelle, now Ontario's minister of Northern Development, Mines and Forestry, had changed his position on demanding a public inquiry into current silicosis issues at Hemlo, stating that the ministry had already pledged to take action on reducing silica dust exposure. Former Ontario New Democratic Party leader, Howard Hampton, responded by noting an inquiry into silicosis at Hemlo was unlikely because government would not want to deal with what he called the awful evidence coming from former miners or their widows.[23]

The many outstanding cases of occupational disease involving northern Ontario miners grind their way through provincial legislation that obliges each case to be dealt with individually. Appeals can drag on for years. The appeals of many of these workers and their families will remain unanswered.

In my father's documents, I found a copy of his handwritten plea to the Workmen's Compensation Board, asking for help with expenses incurred while traveling to the Board for interviews and medical examinations. The Compensation Board's main offices are located in Toronto, more than one thousand kilometers from Manitouwadge. For several months, my father had no income, something he underlined in his letter. He asked only for reimbursement of his travel expenses: gas for the pickup truck he had himself that year converted into a camper, camping fees, and food. He had built the camper so that he and my mother could begin travelling on his vacation time. The only journey he would take in it would be to Toronto, for his appointments with the Workmen's Compensation Board doctors. In the letter, dated October 9, 1975, the month preceding his death, my father writes that his illness "was not identified as silicosis until I went to Toronto for examination, <u>on my own initiative</u>." He underlines the words "<u>on my own initiative</u>."[24]

Tuesday, November 19, 1975, was the last day of my father's life. The family gathered at his hospital bedside. A week earlier, my mother had called me and my two siblings, telling us not to wait until Christmas to visit. "Come now," she said. "Your father is not well." He was sent back to the Manitouwadge hospital from Thunder Bay, his case deemed hopeless.

On this final day my father constantly asks us to open the windows so that he can breathe. We fill the room with the subzero degree air from outside. Death by silicosis is a slow suffocation. Then, he gives each of us a blessing. His last words to me are, "You have your work."

My father moves through the dark tunnel toward the camera. He is in full mining gear: coveralls, work boots, hard hat, miner's lamp glowing. We cut to a dramatic close-up as his face fills the screen. He gazes intently ahead and slightly upward with searching eyes. A delicate coating of mineral dust feathers his brow, almost as though he were wearing makeup. Transcending the limitations of his job in this cinematic moment, he presents a perfect performance of a skilled and intelligent miner. This is who I am, says his bearing. I am a dynamic human being, a strong worker perhaps, but also a man of talents. I believe in what I do and I embrace all accountability for my actions in this place.

I am a writer descended from a miner, one who was able to advocate for a worker through the power of language, social networks, and possession of the means of cultural production. The production of my 2007 film *Northland: Long Journey,* about my father's death and denial of compensation, led me to research new scientific evidence that ultimately proved the original medical and legal judgments of my father's case wrong. My creative process became a forensic investigation and an appeal for justice. In 1997, more than twenty years after my father died from occupational exposure to crystalline silica dust, the International Agency for Research on Cancer (IARC) finally classified occupational silica dust exposure as carcinogenic to humans.[25] During those two decades of epidemiological research, and for a decade beyond this ruling, my mother lived in poverty, without the benefits she was owed by those who exploited the bodies of so many workers.

The town of Manitouwadge slowly dwindles in population now that its primary economic resources are gone; my mother hopes to live out her remaining days there, in a familiar community, within the constrained solidarity of a working-class town where everyone shops at the same shops and lives in mostly identical houses. She is happy to be retired amongst irreplaceable friends, neighbors, and memories acquired over half a century. Like others who could not simply relocate if the town were to die, she persists with the hope that this community will somehow continue to maintain enough infrastructure to not die out completely, fueled by ongoing speculation and circulating rumors of new ore prospects in this region of the Canadian Shield. The Shield will not protect its hidden riches for long from growing mineral needs, and it won't protect those who bring them into the light above ground.

In "The Mine Makers" my father says, "I've been cutting wood and doing things around my house, working twelve hours, fourteen hours a day, and I'm still feeling fine. But when I do eight hours of hard work in the mine, I need a rest. I need a rest, and I will take my rest."

What I now know is that the miner is telling the camera and the viewer of this film that his body is being abused by his labor. Outside the mine he can work all day long with energy to spare but underground shift work is nothing but exhausting. He demands a rest from this deadly labor, in a time when due rest was not awarded to a worker by the company and the social economy. Capital's indifference to the living bodies of workers has ravaged many human landscapes. These losses are final. We honor them by remembering their stories.

NOTES

1. Epigraph from Raymond Williams, "Ideas of Nature," in *Problems in Materialism and Culture* (London: Verso, 1980), 84; *The Mine Makers*, directed by George Bloomfield (Montreal, QC: National Film Board of Canada, 1959), 16mm film. Unless indicated otherwise, quotes from *The Mine Makers* in this essay are from the film's audio, transcribed by the author. Quotes from my film *Northland: Long Journey* are from the film's audio, transcribed by the author.

2. Scott McQuire, *Visions of Modernity: Representation, Memory, Time and Space in*

the Age of the Camera (London and New York: SAGE, 1998), "an index of family," 60; "sign of the," 60. For discussion of personal photographs, see McQuire, 58.

3. "Ontario's Work Laws," *WorkSmartOntario,* as modified April 8, 2011, http://www .worksmartontario.gov.on.ca/scripts/default.asp?contentID=5-1-1-1.

4. Janet Zandy, *Hands: Physical Labor, Class, and Cultural Work* (New Brunswick, NJ: Rutgers University Press, 2004), "Loss cannot be," 2–3; "humble witnessing," 2.

5. "Ring of Fire Mining," *Ontario Nature,* http://www.ontarionature.org/protect /campaigns/ring_of_fire.php.

6. Barbara Neis, "Social Effects of One-Industry Fishing Villages," in *Encyclopedia of Occupational Health and Safety,* ed. Jeanne Mager Stellman (Geneva: International Labour Organization, 1998), 6613–14; *Northand* "It's hard when you work three shifts."

7. Dr. Charles Stewart, chest disease consultant, Workmen's Compensation Board, October 29, 1975, letter to Dr. H. J. Smith, The General Hospital of Port Arthur, Thunder Bay, Ontario.

8. N. C. MacLeod, Claims Review Branch, Workmen's Compensation Board, April 8, 1976, letter to Mrs. A. Steiner.

9. Thomas W. Dunk, *It's a Working Man's Town,* 2nd ed. (Montreal, QC: McGill-Queens University Press, 2003), 45.

10. Joan Skelton, author, in discussion with the author, August 2008.

11. Scott Fields, "The Earth's Open Wounds: Abandoned and Orphaned Mines," *Environmental Health Perspectives* 111, no. 3 (March 2003): A154–A161.

12. Heather E. Jamieson, Shannon C. Shaw, and Alan H. Clark, "Mineralogical Factors Controlling Metal Release from Tailings at Geco, Manitouwadge, Ontario," presentation, Sudbury '95 Conference on Mining and the Environment, Sudbury, Ontario (May 28–June 1, 1995).

13. Edmund Burke, "A Philosophical Enquiry into the Origin of Our Ideas of the Sublime and Beautiful (1757: second edition, 1759)."*A Philosophical Enquiry into the Origins of the Sublime and Beautiful: And Other Pre-Revolutionary Writings,* ed. David Womersley (London: Penguin Books, 1998), 86.

14. M. Finklestein et al., "Mortality among Workers Receiving Compensation Awards for Silicosis in Ontario 1940–85," *British Journal of Industrial Medicine* 44 (1987), "a significantly increased," "that silica itself," 593, "silicosis might be," 588.

15. Vivian Walters, "The Politics of Occupational Health and Safety: Interviews with Workers Health and Safety Representatives and Company Doctors," *Canadian Review of Sociology and Anthropology* 22, no. 1 (1985): 57–79.

16. McIntyre powder (finely ground aluminum and aluminum oxide) was used as a prophylactic agent against silicotic lung disease between 1944 and 1979 in northern Ontario mines. To find out whether the practice produced neurotoxic effects, S. L. Rifat and colleagues conducted a morbidity prevalence study between 1988 and 1989. There were no significant differences between exposed and nonexposed miners in reported

diagnoses of neurological disorder; however, exposed miners performed less well than did unexposed workers on cognitive state examinations; also, the proportion of men with scores in the impaired range was greater in the exposed than nonexposed group. Likelihood of scores in the impaired range increased with duration of exposure. The findings are consistent with putative neurotoxicity of chronic aluminum exposure. S. L. Rifat et al., "Effect of Exposure of Miners to Aluminum Powder," *Lancet* [Toronto] 336 (1990): 1162–65, PubMed, US National Library of Medicine, http://www.ncbi.nlm.nih .gov/pubmed/?term=Effect+of+Exposure+of+Miners+to+Aluminum+Powder.

17. Lloyd Tataryn, *Dying For a Living: The Politics of Industrial Death* Ottawa, ON: Deneau & Greenberg, 1979): 202–17.

18. M.C.S. Kennedy. "Aluminum Powder Inhalations in the Treatment of Silicosis of Pottery Workers and Pneumoconiosis of Coal-Miners," *British Journal of Industrial Medicine* 13 (1956), 98.

19. Rifat et al., "Effect of Exposure"; Charlie Angus, "Dust to Dust: Gold Miners and Their Families Await Answers on the Link between Aluminum Dust and Alzheimer's Disease," *This Magazine* 27, no. 4 (November 1993): 22–26.

20. David Rosner and Gerald Markowitz, *Deadly Dust: Silicosis and the Politics of Occupational Disease in Twentieth-Century America* (Princeton, NJ: Princeton University Press, 1991), "brought into question," "neutrality," 8.

21. A report, "Occupational Exposure Limits (OELs)" by the Ontario Public Service Employees Union (OPSEU), submitted to the Ontario Ministry of Labour on November 19, 2004, cites several scientific studies (Castleman and Ziem; Roach and Rappaport) confirming that Threshold Value Limits (TLVs) "were set to protect the interests of employers" rather than the workers' health. This report follows a March 2000 report by The Ontario Federation of Labour (OFL), defining TLVs as "what the average healthy white male worker could acutely tolerate." Both reports agree that these Threshold Limit Values are set to protect the interests of industry, not the health of the worker.

22. *Urgent Need to Investigate Respiratory Impairment of Hemlo Miners,* Mining-Watch Canada/Mines Alerte, last modified April 8, 2006, http://www.miningwatch.ca /urgent-need-investigate-respiratory-impairment-hemlo-miners.

23. Carl Clutchey, "MPP Backtracks on need for Silicosis Inquiry," *The Chronicle-Journal* (Thunder Bay, ON), July 3, 2009.

24. Alfred Steiner, October, 1975, letter to Workmen's Compensation Board.

25. "Silica," IARC *Monographs on the Evaluation of Carcinogenic Risks to Humans* 68 (1997), World Health Organization, International Agency for Research on Cancer, http://monographs.iarc.fr/ENG/Monographs/vol68/index.php.

6

"Clean Air, Clean Water, and Jobs Forever"

Filming Mountaintop Removal Coal Mining

TERRE RYAN

"There's a little union saying that's survived from the 1930s from down in Harlan County that says, 'Which side are you on? Which side are you on?'" Cecil E. Roberts, president of the United Mine Workers of America, strides across a stage in a West Virginia auditorium, where coal miners and their families have gathered for a pro–coal industry rally. "There are no neutrals here," Roberts continues, working the crowd with the cadence and energy of a televangelist. "Are you for the people that live, and work and make a livin', and energize this nation, and give you the cheapest electric rates in the whole country?" Balloons printed with the message, "Save Our Jobs," nod as if in agreement. "Or are you for somebody else? I say, which side are you *on*?" Some members of the crowd cheer; others shift in their seats. "The governor of this state wants you to keep your job," Roberts declares to applause. "Senator Byrd wants you to keep your job. Senator Rockefeller wants you to keep your job. Congressman Rahall wants you to keep your job. So my question is, who is it that don't want you to keep your job?"

Roberts's rhetoric in this scene from David Novack's 2008 documentary film, *Burning the Future: Coal in America*, encapsulates the arguments typically posed in response to challenges to mountaintop removal, a form of strip (or surface) coal mining.[1] Roberts borrows the phrase "which side are you on" from Florence Reese's pro-union anthem, penned during the Appalachian coal wars of the 1930s.[2] Although the two sides in Reese's song are workers and their abusive coal industry employers, in the context of Roberts's speech the sides have shifted, aligning miners with their employers and pitting them against anyone who questions the way that coal companies operate. With his references to jobs ("people that . . . work and make a livin'"), energy security ("energize this nation"), and consumer appetites ("[cheap] electric rates") in *Burning the Future,* Roberts echoes a coal industry refrain that is often repeated by the nation's coal-backed politicians. His final question—"Who is it that don't want you to keep your job?"—is a touchy one to pose anywhere, but particularly in one of the nation's poorest states, where the coal industry has long dominated the job market and where the destructive practices of mountaintop removal coal mining and coal slurry storage are hotly contested. The implicit answer casts those who seek to protect their communities from the environmental hazards posed by mountaintop removal—people whom coal industry executives and industry-backed politicians often label as greeniacs and environmental extremists—as direct threats to their neighbors' livelihoods.

Yet "coal, in its extraction process, is killing people," counters West Virginia waitress-turned-activist Maria Gunnoe in *Burning the Future.* She adds, "America does not care." Arguably, much of America does not know. Coal supplies roughly 40 percent of the electricity consumed in the United States. Appalachia is the nation's second most productive coal region. More than twenty states use coal mined in West Virginia, the nation's second-most-productive coal state.[3] Vital as they are to the American lifestyle, the coalfield communities of Virginia, Kentucky, Tennessee, and West Virginia seldom make national headlines unless they are the site of a disaster, such as the 2008 collapse of the Tennessee Valley Authority's Kingston Fossil coal slurry impoundment in Harriman, Tennessee, or Massey Energy's 2010 Upper Big Branch explosion that killed twenty-nine West Virginia workers in the worst coal mining disaster in decades. (The notoriously anti-union Massey Energy was acquired by Alpha Natural Resources in June 2011.)[4] Yet parts of the region look—and to some residents, feel—like disaster zones, and mountaintop removal mining has riven some coalfield communities with conflict so fierce that the late West Virginia activist, Judy Bonds, once described it as a "civil war."[5]

The for-mountaintop-removal-or-against-jobs/energy security/American consumerism platform of coal corporations and the politicians they support pits neighbors against one another and depicts a complicated set of problems in two colors: coal black and tree-hugging-green. Novack's film and four other twenty-first century documentaries—Sasha Waters's 2003 *Razing Appalachia,* Catherine Pancake's 2006 *Black Diamonds: Mountaintop Removal and the Fight for Coalfield Justice,* Mari-Lynn Evans and Phylis Geller's 2009 *Coal Country,* and Bill Haney's 2011 *The Last Mountain*—disrupt this discourse by exploring the shades in between. These five films partake in *toxic discourse,* ecocritic Lawrence Buell's term for activist works of art that consider how people cope with living in an environment altered by technology and that recognize environmental problems as social justice problems.[6] Literary artists have produced a considerable body of work addressing mountaintop removal mining. While Soledad O'Brien's August 2011 CNN program, "Battle for Blair Mountain: Working in America," examined mountaintop removal conflicts, mainstream media typically overlook these stories.[7] By giving voice to local activists and other citizens who typically lack a national platform, these five films reveal that the comforts that all American energy consumers enjoy come at great cost to some of our fellow citizens.

As Chad Montrie has observed of earlier generations of strip mining opponents, "By the early 1970s [some activists had begun] to understand that stripping was only one part of a larger, unjust system and, more importantly, that the part could not be changed without transforming the whole."[8] These documentaries expose mountaintop removal mining as an injustice perpetuated by a system of global capitalism that favors powerful corporations and our consumer economy over working-class communities. Collectively, they reveal that mountaintop removal mining imposes extreme hardships on some coalfield Appalachians—who are among the nation's poorest people—for the benefit of the rest of the nation. In *Burning the Future,* West Virginia activist Larry Gibson reports that he was told (it is not clear by whom) at a public meeting that it was "acceptable" for some people and places to serve as "collateral damage" so that everyone else might benefit. Americans do not like to talk about class, but *Razing Appalachia, Black Diamonds, Burning the Future, Coal Country,* and *The Last Mountain* challenge viewers to consider why such aggressive industrial practices are permitted in Appalachia but would never be tolerated in wealthier regions of the country.[9]

The Appalachian Mountains are "home to one of the highest concentrations of biodiversity" in the nation, but since 2000 nearly half of the region's coal has come from mountaintop removal mining, a form of extraction that requires what the name suggests. After coal companies clear cut the forests, they blow up the denuded mountaintops with heavy explosives. One area hydrologist "determined that 314,000 tons of explosives were being set off in West Virginia each year, [subjecting the state to roughly] one thousand Oklahoma City–sized blasts per southern county per year." John Saddler of Dorothy, West Virginia, clad in baseball cap, T-shirt, and jeans, describes standing four hundred yards from a mountaintop removal blast. "I could feel the concussion in my chest—a visceral concussion," he states in *Black Diamonds*, adding, "You know, they got guys that think you literally have to set off an H-bomb or somethin' to bust that rock up. . . . You just can't do it, not without some sort of ramifications in the communities what suffer."[10]

Massive machines then dump the blasted rock into adjacent valleys, or valley fills, often choking streams and fouling groundwater. To date, five hundred Appalachian mountains have been blasted and close to two thousand miles of streams destroyed.[11] Furthermore, processing coal generates toxic refuse, or slurry. More than one hundred of the nation's 676 slurry impoundments (and what the Environmental Protection Agency calls "similar management units") are located in West Virginia.[12]

West Virginia's nickname is the Mountain State and West Virginians call themselves mountaineers, but according to Appalachian historian Ronald Eller, mountaintop removal "[leaves] communities with miles of deserted, treeless plateaus, poisoned water tables, and a permanently altered landscape" that is vulnerable to erosion and flooding.[13] Coal companies contend that mountaintop removal is a cost-effective way to mine coal, but as retired underground miner Chuck Nelson remarks in *Coal Country*, "It's not so cheap for the people living under these sites." Communities near mountaintop removal operations endure daily nerve-rattling explosions that sometimes damage personal property; floods that take lives and destroy property; loss of habitat for fish, wildlife, and plants on which subsistence hunters and gatherers may depend; compromised air quality; and contaminated drinking water.

"We want what everybody else wants, we *deserve* what everybody else wants, or has, as far as peace and contentment," Larry Gibson, known to friends and colleagues as Keeper of the Mountain, states in *Burning the Future*. A former autoworker who died of a heart attack in 2012, Gibson began fighting mountaintop removal mining in the 1980s, after it began engulfing the mountains surrounding the fifty-acre parcel of land that had belonged to his family for more than two hundred years.[14] The peace and contentment and clean air and water that Gibson enjoyed growing up— what legal scholar Jedediah Purdy, who was born and raised on a farm in West Virginia, calls "the clean landscape"—have long underlain American pastoral mythology. Widespread desire for that clean landscape gave rise to the post–World War II suburban pastoral, idealized in all its variations as "unpolluted, free of rank smells and waste, [and] safe for children to run in." But American landscape mythology teaches us to regard some places as worthy of protection and some as "cultural trashlands." Purdy observes that "[s]ince the mid-1990s, central Appalachia has become the country's purest sacrifice zone."[15] These five films demonstrate that what gets sacrificed are the clean landscapes of some of America's poorest communities, the industries that these landscapes could support if not for mountaintop removal mining, and the life-sustaining labor of what Maria Gunnoe describes in *Burning the Future* as a "culture of survival" that includes hunting, gathering, gardening, and fishing. As a shirtless man standing beside a pickup truck asserts in *Black Diamonds*, "You kill the mountain, you're killin' the people."

Documenting the Toxic Discourse of Appalachian Coal

Lawrence Buell traces contemporary American toxic discourse to Rachel Carson's 1962 *Silent Spring*, which exposed the clean landscape as an illusion by featuring a small American town contaminated by pollutants that sicken or kill both wildlife and people. Contemporary toxic discourse, Buell writes, maintains "that the biological environment . . . ought to be a healthy, soul-nurturing habitat." He notes that toxic discourse typically features several overlapping themes, beginning with "pastoral disruption" (the realization that toxins have infiltrated the landscape), which leads to a sense of "entrapment." This "pastoral betrayal" prompts some to engage in community activism. Buell observes that such works of art frequently feature a David versus Goliath motif, pitting the activist(s) against more powerful forces, a trope that is also typical of environmental films.[16] Many of the people in these five films occupy land that has belonged to their families for generations; others, such as descendants of Native Americans and early settlers, trace their regional roots back hundreds of years. They describe their exploited landscape as a treasured homeland under attack by powerful corporations and a political system that favors business over people.

For example, in *Burning the Future* Maria Gunnoe, whose roots in the area go back to the eighteenth century, describes her deep ties to her home-place. Gunnoe's children are the fourth generation of her family to live on land that her grandfather purchased in the 1950s with money he earned working in underground coal mines. Her brothers were also deep miners, and she is proud of her family's coal mining heritage and wishes the indus-try would focus on underground mining. The mountains around her home, she says, were rich in flora and fauna before mountaintop removal mining. Gunnoe says that she is unable to pass on to her children her knowledge of local plants and gathering traditions. "What I knew is on the mountaintops and in the hollers," she says, "and they're being blown away and covered up." She describes a flood—caused, she believes, by runoff from the moun-taintop removal operation above her house—that washed away five acres of her property in less than three hours and came within a few feet of her door. Her eyes fill with tears as she recalls falling to her knees and praying that her house would be spared. Since mountaintop removal mining began above her property, she says, the stream that runs through her land has become "a pollution spillway."

In *Black Diamonds,* when Russell Elkins of Rawl, West Virginia, tells Catherine Pancake about a mining blast that broke one of his windows, he points out that his neighbors are afraid to complain about the blasting that affects their homes. "There's a lot of people up and down this holler got damages," he says. "The ones that work for Massey ain't gonna say nothin' about it 'cause they know they won't have a job to work no more if they do. Basically, Massey runs the place."

Buell writes that nineteenth-century social justice works typically fea-tured a privileged narrator who spoke for the disadvantaged.[17] Each film features experts in science, law, or public health, some of whom argue from elsewhere on behalf of their fellow citizens. Bill Haney's *The Last Mountain* adheres most closely to this format by devoting considerable screen time to author and environmental activist Robert F. Kennedy Jr., who visits West Virginia to speak against mountaintop removal coal mining. Bo Webb, a West Virginia native and Vietnam veteran who spent much of his adult life in Ohio and returned to West Virginia to settle on his family's ancestral land, explains in *The Last Mountain* that outsiders come to protest because the local economy is so heavily dependent on coal jobs. Webb says that some locals who object to mountaintop removal mining (and not all West Virginians do, as these five films make clear) cannot speak out because they fear for their jobs. "You do whatever the coal man says or you don't have a job," Webb asserts.

The mountains-or-jobs angle is perhaps the coal industry's most persuasive rhetorical tool. Yet coal mining employment has declined dramatically over the past three decades, from 175,642 nationwide in 1983 to 89,838 nationwide in 2012. Of the 57,629 employees working in Appalachian coal mining jobs in 2012, 22,786 were working in West Virginia, with 5,701 of these employed at surface mines.[18] Machines have rendered many of those former jobs obsolete. Each film features scenes of colossal earth-moving equipment, such as dragline rigs, which can be twenty stories high but are run by a single worker. When Sasha Waters asks several miners in *Razing Appalachia* what other jobs are available in the area, they answer in unison, "Minimum wage."

A man identified as Butch S. of Boone County, West Virginia, a United Mine Workers of America member who works in an underground mine, tells Catherine Pancake in *Black Diamonds* that he objects to mountaintop removal. The coal companies "do it in little parcels," he explains, building to an operation that may devour ten thousand acres of mountains and streams. "States let them get away with it," Butch says. "Both Democrat and Republican, it's not one party. It's both of them. Money gets them all."

The Vanishing Pastoral

Documentary films expand toxic discourse with the powerfully persuasive component of visual rhetoric. These five films show the clean landscape of wild and country places by drawing on traditional American landscape iconography popularized during the mid-nineteenth century by the Hudson River school of painters. Hudson River school images of the American landscape offered scenic glimpses of wild and domesticated places at a time when American terrain became widely associated with American identity.[19] Mountains, lakes, and farms, for example, became totems of American national narratives. While pastoral traditions are ancient in origin, many Americans would associate them with Thomas Jefferson; images of farms, rural landscapes, and suburban neighborhoods resonate with American pastoral mythology. The filmmakers plumb the American pastoral by shooting country lifeways, farmsteads, and rural towns, offering glimpses of backyard gatherings and footage of children fishing, swimming, and playing in creeks.

Cultural anthropologist Luis Vivanco observes that environmental films have often focused on preserving vanishing wilderness and/or endangered species.[20] These mountaintop removal coal mining films give viewers glimpses of both vanishing wildness and a *vanishing pastoral*—landscapes literally blown out by industrialism, lifeways disrupted by nearby mining, and people sickened or otherwise harmed by mountaintop removal mining. The filmmakers pair American pastoral scenes with images of the *raw industrial*—shots of mountains exploding, depictions of slurry impoundments filled with toxic muck, scenes of massive machines operated by only a handful of workers moving blasted rubble. Drawing heavily on American landscape mythology, this visual rhetoric ensures that arguments against mountaintop removal and on behalf of Appalachian people and their environment will reverberate beyond the region.

All of the films include flyover scenes. Because mountaintop removal takes place at elevations higher than most public roads, much of the mining process remains hidden from valley vantage points. Flyovers expose the scale of mountaintop removal mining operations by revealing industrial wastelands that look like deserts among the lushly forested terrain of the Appalachian range. In *The Last Mountain,* West Virginia Coal Association president William Raney points out that people have an "emotional" reaction "when they see a picture of an active [mountaintop removal mining] operation, which is nothing more than a construction site that is unfinished." (A finished, or reclaimed, surface operation is remolded and planted with grass, but the biodiversity of the original forest is irrecoverable.) Flyover shots reveal the sharp contrast between reclaimed mountains and the mixed hardwood forests of the rugged terrain around them. The juxtaposition of wild mountain scenery and American Arcadian imagery with the raw industrial and the reclaimed reveals that both the wild and the pastoral are fast disappearing, that what looks like a clean landscape may already be (or soon could be) contaminated by toxins, and that whatever one has—land, other personal property, health, even life—may easily be destroyed.

For example, *Razing Appalachia* frames the narrative of mountaintop removal in the story of Jim and Sibby Weekley, residents of Blair, West

Virginia. Married nearly forty years, the Weekleys were childhood sweethearts who raised their six children on land that had belonged to Jim's father. Their traditions included hunting and fishing, and the camera shows the couple and their granddaughters searching for crawdads in a creek bed. What looks like an idyllic existence has been destroyed by a neighboring mountaintop removal operation that so harassed Blair with explosions and dust that the town's longtime residents began to flee.

Black Diamonds opens with Hudson River school–style shots of the Appalachian Mountains, accompanied by a voiceover that travels from pastoral ideal to warzone horror. "Go to the most peaceful place that you can imagine, and let yourself feel like you've spent your life there." Maria Gunnoe's voice seems to drift on a breeze over visuals of leafy mountains and rushing streams. Gunnoe adds, "And then watch somebody drop a bomb on it." Catherine Pancake maintains the sense of "pastoral betrayal" throughout the film by contrasting scenes of vibrant local culture—folk festivals, prayer meetings, shots of people fishing, locals recounting tales of gathering plants—with images of blasted mountains.[21] Pancake interviews men and women who learned the science of gathering roots and herbs from their parents and grandparents, but who can no longer access terrain they once combed for plants. For example, an unidentified man in Boone County, West Virginia, wearing a camouflage T-shirt, baseball cap, and jeans, says that when he was only six years old his grandfather began teaching him and a friend how to identify and gather roots in the woods above their home. That forest has been destroyed by Massey Energy's Black Castle mine. "My grandpa, he knowed every inch of these woods," the man says. "He's 94 years old now, and if he could just go and see what they've done to the mountains—it's terrible."

Coal Country intertwines the stories of clusters of activists protesting the impact of energy development on their communities. Pauline Canterberry and Mary Miller, whose Sylvester, West Virginia, community rubs shoulders with a coal processing plant that peppers the town with dust so thick that residents are unable to open their windows, take *Coal Country* viewers on a walk through their charming neighborhood. It looks like a scene of an American pastoral promised land, with lovely homes (from one of which waves an American flag), perfect lawns, and flower gardens. As they stroll, Canterberry points out house after house where neighbors have died of cancer. By underscoring talk of cancer with suburban pastoral imagery, the filmmakers expose the fraudulence of the clean landscape in contemporary industrialized society. Mary Miller's house, a handsome brick structure once appraised at $144,000, is now blackened with coal dust and worth only $12,000. In these scenes, pastoral illusions collapse, exposing injustices visited on communities by powerful industrial neighbors.

Toxic discourse is "most lurid," Buell writes, "when the victim has no choice."[22] The threat of a flood, heightened by heavy erosion caused by mountaintop removal, looms like the coal slurry impoundments that sit above these communities, where residents live uneasily with their region's history of catastrophic impoundment failures. When West Virginia's Buffalo Creek slurry impoundment broke in 1972, 138 million gallons of black sludge pounded through a nearby valley; the flood killed 125 people, injured a thousand others, and leveled five hundred homes.[23] In 2000 a slurry impoundment collapsed near Inez, Kentucky, dumping 300 million gallons of coal sludge into nearby creeks, contaminating "100 miles of waterways," damaging property, and piling toxic muck as high as six feet in some yards.[24] The 2008 impoundment failure at the Tennessee Valley Authority's Kingston Fossil coal plant discharged 1 billion gallons of coal ash sludge. This spill—the largest of its kind in US history—caused extensive property damage on public and private lands and contaminated rivers and groundwater with heavy metals. Environmental justice theorists Michele Morrone and Geoffrey Buckley write that "[f]or every major incident that has taken place over the past four decades, dozens of minor ones have occurred," contaminating groundwater. Morrone and Buckley contend that our emphasis on short-term gains and our appetite for cheap electricity "create the conditions that make another [such] spill . . . almost inevitable."[25] *Coal Country*'s Canterberry and Miller hold up pictures of a massive slurry impoundment that sits directly above their town. "If that breaks," they say, "we're not going to have a chance to get out."

Black Diamonds includes a scene of a community protest staged following the 2004 death of three-year-old West Virginian Jeremy Davidson, who died when a thousand-pound boulder, dislodged by mountaintop mining, barreled downhill, smashed through a wall of his family's home, and crushed him as he slept in his bed. The film shows community members marching together and holding up pictures of a smiling Jeremy. The camera pans the faces of the marchers, many of whom are children. In another scene, Pancake records a public meeting where a man, whose wife was killed by a flash flood, breaks down as he speaks against a proposed mining project. By lingering on the agony of coalfield communities whose families have been devastated by the environmental impacts of mountaintop removal and coal slurry storage, Pancake exposes the gross injustices posed by coal extraction and processing.

Burning the Future's most horrifying scene takes place in a modest trailer home, where a man afflicted with a tumor turns on his kitchen sink. "This is my tap water," the man says, raising a glass of brown swill toward the camera. "I'm unemployed. I can't afford to buy any bottled water," he says, adding urgently, "I *can't afford* it." Another man, a former miner whose skin is raw from bathing in tainted water, recognized what was coming out of the tap the day his water first turned black and gritty. "I looked at it and I said, 'My God, what's wrong? That's refuge,' " he says, using the colloquial term for coal slurry. Other community members hold up blackened household water filters.

Burning the Future also features an interview with Williamson, West Virginia, physician Diane Shafer, who has worked in regional coal communities for "parts of four decades." As Rachel Carson, in *Silent Spring*, linked pesticides to illnesses and deaths among wildlife and people, Dr. Shafer lists the ways that she believes local water quality impacts the health of her patients: "Gastrointestinal disorders, gastroesophageal reflux disease, diarrhea, ulcers, and then neurologic disorders—dementia, numbness, forgetfulness, and generalized demise of the quality of life." A 2008 study by the environmental organizations Green Cross Switzerland and the Blacksmith Institute revealed that "localized pollution is the leading contributing factor to disability and disease in communities across the world."[26] In *Coal Country*, Michael Hendryx, Director of Research at the West Virginia Institute for Health Policy Research, states that since 1979, "the [annual] mortality rates [have been] significantly higher in coal mining areas of Appalachia compared to other areas of Appalachia where there's no coal mining, as well as compared to the nation at large." These insidious health problems are what postcolonial critic Rob Nixon calls the "slow violence" of "turbo-capitalism" inflicted on communities disrupted by industrial development.[27] The respondents in these films offer their own testimonials. For example, *The Last Mountain* follows Prenter, West Virginia, activist Jennifer Hall-Massey on a walk around her neighborhood. Hall-Massey's brother died of a brain tumor at age twenty-nine. Five other neighbors are also afflicted with—or have already died from—brain tumors. Hall-Massey blames contamination of their water supply.

Coal Country suggests the pervasiveness of toxic infiltration of the pastoral by detouring to Meigs County, Ohio, where Elisa Young farms land that her ancestor, George Rousche, earned as payment for his military service in the Revolutionary War. Young's farm is surrounded by coal-fired power plants, with additional power plants in the planning stages. The farmer tends to her dogs and chickens, then sits on the grass in an early nineteenth-century cemetery on the property and plants flowers at Rousche's grave. Young says she needs clean water, soil, and air to keep farming, but the film shows a clean landscape threatened by surrounding industry. With the headstones beside her and a power plant behind her, the angle of the camera frames Young directly between two smokestacks that appear to be squeezing her, showing a small farmer whose work and way of life are being crushed.

Throughout the Meigs County episode, the filmmakers show neighboring agrarian and industrial landscapes. In one scene, the camera frames abutting pastoral and industrial icons: a cross atop a church steeple, the branches of trees, and plumes of steam drifting from a cooling tower. Because her work is threatened by industry, Young may have to give up the land of her ancestors. By conveying the relationship among Young's occupation, her land, and the founding of the nation, Evans and Geller present pollution-heavy energy development as the ultimate "pastoral betrayal," an environmental injustice that strikes at the roots of national mythology.[28]

Confronting Goliath

The most haunting scenes in these films juxtapose people, their land, and lifeways against the trope of an industrial behemoth. *Coal Country* follows Elisa Young as she walks along a road that appears to run beside a massive power plant. The persistent roar of nearby highway traffic suggests an ocean of industrial might that could easily obliterate this lone farmer and her ancestral farm. Similarly, the camera of *Razing Appalachia* follows the diminutive Larry Gibson (he stood at 5 feet 2 inches) around his property, past old cabins. The cabins are relics of Gibson's family history, but they are also American icons evocative of frontier settler culture; they serve as totems that identify Gibson with the self-reliant individual of frontier mythology. Gibson's property is a green speck encompassed by a twelve-thousand-acre mining operation.

Burning the Future returns repeatedly to an image that signifies the vanishing pastoral and the imbalance of power. A modest home, with toys in the yard, appears to abut the grounds of a power plant; cooling towers dominate the sky directly above the roof of the small house. But *Burning the Future* features three giants: the coal companies, the gargantuan machinery required for mountaintop removal, and the American appetite for electricity. *Burning the Future* suggests that American demand for electricity is the most powerful colossus. Novack illustrates this point during a brief cartoon segment that shows a family caught up in its morning routine—alarm clocks buzzing, toaster popping, television beaming, stovetop sizzling, radio playing, hair dryer blowing. As family members depart for the day, they pocket their freshly charged cellphones, leaving the chargers plugged in to sip electricity all day, while the air conditioner cools the house and the giant-screen TV plays for the amusement of the dog. The exterior of their house glows with the energy it burns, as does every house in the community, and every house is hooked up, via an extension cord, to a distant coal-burning power plant.

Lest viewers fail to see the relationship between their behavior and the hardships that some coalfield Appalachians endure, Novack draws explicit connections between American electricity consumption and mountaintop removal mining toward the end of *Burning the Future,* when Maria Gunnoe and fellow activists stage an impromptu demonstration in New York City's Times Square. Dominated by electrified screens that illuminate the neighborhood day and night, Times Square signifies a capitalist-driven economic system powered by cheap coal. Novack reinforces the activists' toxic discourse with compelling visual rhetoric. Images shuffle between shots of Times Square's electrified billboards, Maria Gunnoe calling out to passers-by in New York City, and images of West Virginia coalfields. The viewer confronts a rapidly shifting panorama interspersing some of the electrified brand names of everyday life—Samsung, HSBC, Coca-Cola, Prudential—with images of coal in an underground mine, coal running along conveyor belts, coal floating on barges, coal piled in freight trains, a mountain exploding, a blasted mountain crumbling, trucks dumping blasted mountaintop into valleys, slurry ponds, coal processing systems, polluted streams, brown water pouring out of the tap of a kitchen sink, and a West Virginia billboard reminding us, "Coal Keeps the Lights On." As the images shift between tokens of our electrified lifestyle and the damage caused by mountaintop removal, Maria Gunnoe shouts in Times Square, "Do people realize that mountains in southern West Virginia are being leveled to keep this street lit up? Do you realize your connection? For the sake of the families in southern West Virginia, turn out the lights!"

By intermixing the electrified urban shots and corporate names with images of industrialized rural places and the people who inhabit them, Novack ties mountaintop removal mining to globalization and puts human faces on the problems caused by profligate consumption of electricity produced by violent extractive methods.

Just Jobs

Labor theorist and film critic Tom Zaniello writes that earlier Appalachian mining films centered on labor.[29] While *Razing Appalachia, Black Diamonds, Burning the Future, Coal Country,* and *The Last Mountain* focus primarily on the impact of mountaintop removal mining on the health and welfare of coalfield communities, they also demonstrate that in the case of mountaintop removal mining, toxic discourse and stories of place are intimately tied to labor. The filmmakers draw heavily on the region's labor justice history by including historical photographs and footage of miners and underground mining operations. As well, many of the activists that viewers encounter in these films come from mining families or have worked in coal mines, and many are proponents of underground coal mining.

Whether they oppose or support mountaintop removal, for many of the people in these films the region's coal mining heritage is a source of pride. In *Burning the Future,* miner Rocky Hackworth speaks glowingly of mountaintop removal and reclamation. "I think it's a shame that people in New York or Pennsylvania or New Jersey don't realize what the coal miner does to provide electricity for them," he says. "I know we're doin' somethin' that's valuable and needed for the industry, for the community, for all the United States." *Coal Country*'s Randall Maggard, who manages environmental compliance for coal concern Argus Energy WV LLC, is proud of his work and depends on his job to support his family. Maggard says he was deeply troubled when one of his children was asked to write a school assignment protesting mountaintop removal mining. His client, Delsie Vance, who leased property to Argus Energy, is pleased with the company's work and reclamation of her land. William Raney insists in *The Last Mountain* that the people in his industry are "practicing environmentalists." Filmmaker Bill Haney follows Raney's statement with a visual counterargument: a shot of a mountain exploding.

Much of the community conflict in these films centers on jobs. For those who have coal industry jobs, a respondent says in *Coal Country*, coal is "the income, it's the food in children's mouths, it's the turkey on the Thanksgiving table." In Appalachia, which is "relatively poor overall," observes epidemiologist Nancy Irwin Maxwell, "[m]anufacturing industry, which generates pollution, also brings much-needed money into a county." However, Maxwell adds, "[t]his dilemma represents a different brand of injustice, a forced choice between pollution and poverty in a disadvantaged region of the American landscape." Environmental justice theorists Julian Agyeman and Bob Evans counsel that cultures should focus on "just sustainability," a view that recognizes sustainability as a fundamental component of justice. "A truly sustainable society," they contend, "is one where wider questions of social needs and welfare, and economic opportunity are integrally related to environmental limits imposed by supporting ecosystems."[30] Joe Lovett, executive director of the Appalachian Center for the Economy and the Environment, says in *Razing Appalachia*, "There is a great problem about how to develop these coalfield communities in the future, and how to allow people to stay there." Mountaintop removal "is clearly not the way," he says, "because this is running them out." Maria Gunnoe observes in *The Last Mountain* that twenty-five regional communities have already "been depopulated" by mountaintop removal.

In June 2013, when President Barack Obama announced a new climate initiative aimed at reducing carbon emissions, the West Virginia Coal Association's William Raney responded that the move would "negatively impact West Virginia coal jobs, result in higher electric bills for consumers and businesses and lead to America's economic disarmament via US manufacturing jobs relocating to other nations." But as *Charleston Gazette* energy reporter Ken Ward notes, "the [natural] gas boom and its low prices—more than tougher federal environmental regulations—are at the heart of the troubles facing the Appalachian coal industry." In 2008 coal accounted for 50 percent of our electrical supply. But by 2012, coal's share of the electric power market had slipped to 40 percent, and some analysts predict that it could drop to 30 percent by 2020.[31]

Like a company that relies primarily on one product or service for its survival, a regional economy that depends too heavily on one industry renders itself vulnerable to shifting market conditions. Without greater economic diversification, coalfield communities will continue to struggle with few options. In an interview with ecocritic Salma Monani, Agyeman argues that "we should be interested in *enhancing human potential* and *protecting environmental potential.* The classical case of this," Agyeman says, "is the *green jobs* idea, which is about jobs *through* the environment, not the tired old binary of jobs *or* the environment" [emphasis in original].[32] A woman who identifies herself as "Patty S., West Virginia citizen activist," argues in *Black Diamonds* for developing her state's other natural resources— resources that are being destroyed by mountaintop removal mining. With the area's rich mountain forests, Patty says, "We could have that timbering, we could have furniture stores, we could have tourism, we could build cabins. With our streams, we could sell bottled water, which is a hot commodity right now everywhere." But because of mountaintop removal, she warns, "We're not going to have any mountains, we're not going to have any clean streams, we're not going to have any wood . . . and when the coal's gone, that either. I want to ask them then: How cheap was that coal? How cheap was our state? Better yet, how cheap are our politicians? They're not very smart. Everybody knows you don't use up everything you have, destroy everything you have. Then what are you going to live on?"

Toward the end of *Coal Country,* demonstrators are calling for green jobs; others are proposing a wind farm to be located atop a mountain that coal companies are eyeing for mountaintop removal. When Judy Bonds addresses a crowd at a sustainable energy rally, she shouts, "We must *fight* for this wind farm and green jobs because our children deserve clean air, clean water, and jobs forever."

Places of American Power

When Jennifer Hall-Massey walks through a West Virginia neighborhood where six people have been stricken with brain tumors, *The Last Mountain*'s camera reveals a community of manufactured homes. *Burning the Future,* with its iconic image of a modest home dominated by cooling towers, also repeats footage of coal trains trundling past Maria Gunnoe's tiny house. By training their cameras on the unpretentious dwellings of their subjects, the filmmakers continually remind viewers that the problems they document are enabled by a system that favors wealthy corporations over people—especially people of modest means.

In *Razing Appalachia,* activist Patricia Bragg says that mountains are "like breath" to West Virginians. Her voice breaking, Bragg insists that "whether we live in a $10,000 camper or . . . a $200,000 home, if that home and that community is being destroyed, then it should be protected, it should be protected by those people in that community, it should be protected by the other workers from West Virginia, and by all means, it should be protected by our government." As Bragg speaks, the camera cuts from her to pastoral scenes: children play with dogs on a lawn and people gather at picnic tables, emphasizing the relationship between these people and the place they call home.

As various environmental justice theorists have pointed out, business practices and government policies that impose excessive burdens on particular groups of people and places are neither just nor sustainable.[33] By covering coalfield stories typically overlooked by mainstream media, these documentary films intervene in the coal industry's for-mountain-top-removal-or-against-jobs/energy security/American consumerism discourse. They demonstrate that under our current system not everyone is entitled to the clean landscape, and that anyone in the United States who uses electricity benefits from this imbalance of power. "Coal Keeps the Lights On," proclaim the billboards. But at what costs? Judy Bonds, who would die of cancer in 2011, provides one answer in *Coal Country:* "We're mountaineers. If they take away our mountains, who are we? Who are we?"

NOTES

For Judy Bonds and Larry Gibson.

1. *Burning the Future: Coal in America,* directed by David Novack (San Francisco, CA: Specialty Studios Entertainment, 2008), DVD. All quotes from *Burning the Future* were transcribed by the author from the DVD.

2. Nick Coles, "'Which Side Are You On?': The Life and Travels of a Working-Class Song," *Working-Class Perspectives* (April 9, 2012), http://workingclassstudies.wordpress.com/tag/which-side-are-you-on/.

3. Associated Press, "US Coal Use Falling Fast; Utilities Switch to Gas," Fox News. com, June 12, 2012, http://www.foxnews.com/us/2012/06/12/us-coal-use-falling-fast -utilities-switch-to-gas/; US Department of Energy, Energy Information Adminis- tration, "Figure 8.2a Electricity Net Generation, Total (All Sectors)," Annual Energy Review 2011, DOE/EIA-0384 (2011), September 2012, http://www.eia.gov/totalenergy /data/annual/pdf/aer.pdf; US Department of Energy, Energy Information Administra- tion, "Table 1. Coal Production and Number of Mines by State and Mine Type, 2012 and 2011," Annual Coal Report 2012, December 2013, http://www.eia.gov/coal/annual/pdf /acr.pdf; US Department of Energy, Energy Information Administration, "Profile Anal- ysis," West Virginia State Profile and Energy Estimates, last updated December 18, 2013, http://www.eia.gov/beta/state/analysis.cfm?sid=WV.

4. Alpha Natural Resources, "Alpha Natural Resources Acquires Massey Energy, Creating a Global Leader in Metallurgical Coal Supply," June 1, 2011, http://alnr.client .shareholder.com/releasedetail.cfm?ReleaseID=582243.

5. Coal Country, directed by Phylis Geller (Akron, OH: Evening Star Productions, 2009), DVD. All quotations from this film were transcribed by the author from the DVD.

6. Lawrence Buell, "Toxic Discourse," Critical Inquiry 24, no. 3 (Spring 1998): 639, 657, 643, http://nrs.harvard.edu/urn-3:HUL.InstRepos:2637816; Razing Appalachia, directed by Sasha Waters (Oley, PA: Bullfrog Films, 2009), DVD; Black Diamonds: Mountaintop Removal and the Fight for Coalfield Justice, directed by Catherine Pancake (Oley, PA: Bullfrog Films, 2006), DVD; Coal Country directed by Phylis Geller (Akron, OH: Evening Star Productions, 2009), DVD; The Last Mountain, directed by Bill Haney (Los Angeles, CA: Uncommon Productions, 2011), DVD. All quotes from the films dis- cussed in this essay were transcribed by the author from the DVDs.

7. "Steady Job or Healthy Environment: What Would You Choose?," In America, CNN, August 14, 2011, http://www.cnn.com/2011/US/08/14/blair.mountain.react/.

8. Chad Montrie, To Save the Land and People: A History of Opposition to Surface Coal Mining in Appalachia (Chapel Hill: University of North Carolina Press, 2003), 205.

9. Patricia Nelson Limerick, "Hoping against History: Environmental Justice in the Twenty-first Century," in Justice and Natural Resources: Concepts, Strategies, and Appli- cations, ed. Kathryn M. Mutz, Gary C. Bryner, and Douglas S. Kenney (Washington, DC: Island Press, 2002), 352.

10. Patrick Reis, "Are Endangered Species Being Sacrificed for Coal in Appalachia?" Scientific American, August 10, 2009, "home to one of," http://www.scientificamerican. com/article.cfm?id=endangered-species-coal-appalachia-mountaintop-removal; Ron- ald Eller, Uneven Ground: Appalachia Since 1945 (Lexington: University Press of Ken- tucky, 2008), 228; Michael Shnayerson, Coal River (New York: Farrar, Straus, and Gir- oux, 2008), "determined that 314,000," 49.

11. Appalachian Voices, "End Mountaintop Removal Coal Mining," 2012, http://

appvoices.org/end-mountaintop-removal/; David C. Holzman, "Mountaintop Removal Mining: Digging into Community Health Concerns," US National Institutes of Health, *Environmental Health Perspectives* 119, no. 11 (November 1, 2011), http://www.ncbi.nlm .nih.gov/pmc/articles/PMC3226519/.

12. US Environmental Protection Agency, "Information Request Responses from Electric Utilities," Wastes—Non-Hazardous Waste—Industrial Waste, August 3, 2012, http://www.epa.gov/epawaste/nonhaz/industrial/special/fossil/surveys/index.htm; "similar management units"; Coal Impoundment Location & Information System (2009), http://www.coalimpoundment.org/locate/list.asp.

13. Eller, *Uneven Ground*, 227.

14. Jim Witkin, "Larry Gibson, 66, a Foe of Mountaintop Mining, Is Dead," *New York Times*, September 13, 2012, http://green.blogs.nytimes.com/2012/09/13 /recalling-a-foe-of-mountaintop-mining/; Matt Schudel, "Larry Gibson, W. Va. Activist Who Fought Mountaintop Mining, Dies at 66," *Washington Post*, September 13, 2012, http://articles.washingtonpost.com/2012-09-13local/35495135_1_kayford-mountain -mountains-foundation-coal-miners.

15. Jedediah S. Purdy, "An American Sacrifice Zone," in *Mountains of Injustice: Social and Environmental Justice in Appalachia,* ed. Michele Morrone and Geoffrey L. Buckley (Athens: Ohio University Press, 2011), "the clean landscape," "unpolluted, free," 182; Terre Ryan, *This Ecstatic Nation: The American Landscape and the Aesthetics of Patriotism* (Amherst: University of Massachusetts Press, 2011), "cultural trashlands," 4; Purdy, "An American Sacrifice Zone," "since the mid-1990s," 182.

16. Buell, "Toxic Discourse," 645; ibid., "that the biological," 648; ibid., "pastoral disruption," 647. See also ibid. 646, 648, 647, 649, 651; Luis A. Vivanco, "Seeing Green: Knowing and Saving the Environment on Film," *American Anthropologist* 104, no. 1 (December 2002): 1199, http://www.jstor.org/stable/3567107.

17. Buell, "Toxic Discourse," 654.

18. Richard F. Bonskowski, Fred Freme, and William D. Watson, "Coal Production in the US," in *Encyclopedia of Energy Engineering and Technology,* vol. 1, ed. Barney L. Capehart (Boca Raton, Fla.: CRC Press, 2007), 150; US Department of Energy, Energy Information Administration, "Table 18. Average Number of Employees by State and Mine Type, 2012, 2011," Annual Coal Report 2012, December 2013, http://www.eia.gov /coal/annual/pdf/acr.pdf.

19. Angela Miller, *The Empire of the Eye* (Ithaca, NY: Cornell University Press, 1993), 7–8.

20. Vivanco, "Seeing Green," 1195.

21. Buell, "Toxic Discourse," 649.

22. Ibid., 654.

23. Marshall University, "1972 Buffalo Creek Flood," 2002, http://www.marshall.edu /LIBRARY/speccoll/virtual_museum/buffalo_creek/html/default.asp.

24. Dylan Lovan, "After a Decade, Still Signs of Coal Slurry Spill," *Washington Post,* October 17, 2010, http://www.washingtonpost.com/wp-dyn/content/article/2010/10/15/AR2010101507010.html

25. "Inside the Tennessee Coal Ash Spill," *Newsweek,* July 17, 2009, updated March 13, 2010, http://www.thedailybeast.com/newsweek/2009/07/17/toxic-tsunami.html; Shaila Dewan, "Tennessee Ash Flood Larger than Initial Estimate," *New York Times,* December 26, 2008, http://www.nytimes.com/2008/12/27/us/27sludge.html; Michele Morrone and Geoffrey L. Buckley, "Environmental Justice and Appalachia," in Morrone and Buckley, *Mountains of Injustice,* "[f]or every major," "create the conditions," xii.

26. Daniel Stone, "Resolving Environmental Injustice on a Local Level," *Newsweek,* October 20, 2008, updated March 13, 2010, "localized pollution is," http://www.thedailybeast.com/newsweek/2008/10/20/and-justice-for-all.html

27. Rob Nixon, *Slow Violence and the Environmentalism of the Poor* (Cambridge, MA: Harvard University Press, 2011), 4.

28. Buell, "Toxic Discourse," 649.

29. Tom Zaniello, "Filming Class," in *New Working-Class Studies,* ed. John Russo and Sherry Lee Linkon (Ithaca, NY: Cornell University Press, 2005), 154.

30. Nancy Irwin Maxwell, "Pollution or Poverty: The Dilemma of Industry in Appalachia," in Morrone and Buckley, *Mountains of Injustice,* "Relatively poor overall," 76; Julian Agyeman and Bob Evans, "'Just Sustainability': The Emerging Discourse of Environmental Justice in Britain?," *The Geographical Journal* 170, no. 2 (June 2004): 157.

31. West Virginia Coal Association, "Statement by Bill Raney, West Virginia Coal Association, Concerning Today's Climate Speech by President Barack Obama," [June 25, 2013], "negatively impact," http://www.wvcoal.com/latest/statement-by-bill-raney-west-virginia-coal-association-concerning-todays-climate-speech-by-president-barack-obama.html; Ken Ward Jr., "In Attacking Obama on Climate, W.Va. Leaders Ignore Natural Gas," *Charleston Gazette,* June 26, 2013, "the [natural] gas boom," http://www.wvgazette.com/News/201306260129?page=2&build=cache; Associated Press, "US Coal Use Falling Fast."

32. Salma Monani, "An Interview with Julian Agyeman: Just Sustainability and Ecopedagogy," *Green Theory and Praxis: The Journal of Ecopedagogy* 5, no. 1 (2009): 62.

33. David Naguib Pellow and Robert J. Brulle, *Power, Justice, and the Environment: A Critical Appraisal of the Environmental Justice Movement* (Cambridge, MA: MIT Press, 2005), 2–3, 5; Monani, "An Interview with Julian Agyeman," 60, 63.

7

Bright Lights, Big City Ills
Artificial Light and the Night Shift

PAUL BOGARD

Night shift is an entirely different way of life that few people who have not experienced it can understand. On a good day I sleep for about three hours twice a day. We live in a state of fatigue that most people never know, or would want to know.

—Matthew Lawrence, manager of night-shift custodians,
Wake Forest University

For Matthew Lawrence and more than 15 million other Americans—a total that grows every year—the pain of the night shift is a daily reality. The overwhelming majority of these are working-class Americans employed in retail sales, customer service, food service, or—like Lawrence—custodians cleaning workspaces for the rest of us. The World Health Organization now lists night-shift work as a probable carcinogen, and researchers have linked working the night shift with ailments such as diabetes, obesity, depression, and cardiovascular disease. The truth is that nearly every American is now exposed to the effects of artificial light at night, a situation that has scientists increasingly worried as they seek to explain the litany of health problems affecting those who work at night. The difference is that while the rest of us have some control over the life we lead after dark, the same can't be said for those Americans who work the night shift.

During the past two decades as the service industry has exploded in this country, more and more Americans have started to work at night. Most have no choice—their employers (from restaurants to convenience stores to factories) benefit from staying open after dark. Others work in jobs influenced by globalization, and still others work in the safety sector (police, hospitals) that society requires be available 24/7. And it isn't only in the United States that more people are working the night shift: estimates are that in developed countries around the world nearly 20 percent of the working population now works at night. While some of these workers profess to be night owls, studies show that less than 12 percent of night-shift workers choose to work at night because of personal preference. Some (8 percent) choose these shifts because of "better arrangements for family or child care," and 7 percent choose the night shift for the better pay. But the vast majority of night-shift workers take these jobs because they have no other choice, and as a result bear the burden of "high levels of family stress, poor health, and significant fatigue that can negatively impact on-the-job productivity and safety."[1] In other words, night-shift workers enjoy a lower quality of life than those who work during the day, and their work puts them at greater risk for physical, emotional, and mental pain and illness. At times for our safety but more often for our convenience, millions of predominantly working-class Americans pay the price for our addiction to light.

■ Artificial light at night as we know it began in the nineteenth century as cities such as London, Paris, and Berlin created the world's first systems of public lighting, beginning with oil lamps, then gaslights, and finally electricity. Perhaps more than any other technological development, this spread of light has changed human civilization. Suddenly, the hours after dark were made open for activities once rendered impossible by darkness, especially economic activities such as cafés, shops, and factories. Where business once stopped with the end of natural daylight, now it marched forward with artificial light. Working-class populations felt this change as much or more than any other, as hours that had once been theirs for family and private pursuits now became owned by their employers. Increasingly, if you wanted a job you had to be available to work at night. Beginning in the United Kingdom at the turn of the nineteenth century and rapidly expanding alongside the growth of the industrial revolution, night became open for business, and artificial light began to exact its costs on human life.

The situation has only grown worse in the twentieth century and into the twenty-first, as recent decades have seen the levels of electric light expand exponentially. Views of the United States from space from the 1970s, 1990s, and 2000s show a steady spread of electric light across the country, and across Western Europe and in major cities across Asia, South America, and Australia. Two-thirds of Americans now live where they cannot see the

Milky Way because of light pollution, and 99 percent of Americans live in areas considered polluted by light. In our houses and apartments, on our streets, and at our places of work, we bathe in the wash of electric illumination. Human beings evolved over tens of millions of years to be awake during daylight hours and to sleep during dark hours, and now we are confusing that rhythm with our electric lights, extending our days into our nights, not knowing what happens when we so abruptly change our ways.

What seems to be happening isn't good. Recent research shows that night-shift workers have a 41 percent increased risk of heart attack, prediabetes is most likely to blossom into full-blown diabetes in those working at night, and night-shift working women are likely to have an increased rate of breast cancer.[2] These are just the latest findings from researchers who for the past twenty years have increasingly been sounding the alarm about the harmful effects of light at night on human health. And still, because our nights have changed so rapidly, so recently, we are only just beginning to see the results of this ongoing experiment we're conducting on ourselves— and especially on those working the night shift.

■ One spring morning I approach Matthew Lawrence, manager of the night-shift custodians at the university where I work. He immediately invites me to go undercover as a temp worker in order to understand what it's like to join the night shift from 11 P.M. to 7 A.M.

"I would just tell them you were here for a night to try it out," he says. At forty-four years old and nearly bald, with bags under his eyes, he leans back in the office chair I've offered. At 9:30 in the morning it is already "getting late" for him, he says. "I've been here since 10:30 last night, and I've been up since 8:30 yesterday evening." He still has to make the ninety-minute drive back to his home in Chapel Hill before he can get a few hours of sleep, then play with his kids for a while, then try to sleep for a few hours more. "I've been working the night shift for thirteen years now," he explains. "I had a headache constantly for the first five years." I've described for him the book I'm writing about night, darkness, and light pollution, and I think I've spent most of our time together shaking my head as he shares his story. Then he offers his invitation. I know it's a great idea, a true opportunity to get an intimate feel for the graveyard shift. Maybe I would even get to clean my own office during the wee small hours. And I honestly consider the idea for nearly a minute before admitting there is no way I can do it.

"No pressure," he laughs. "Stay as long as you like. They'll be tickled pink to have a professor take an interest in what they're doing."

Lawrence explains that the university has recently moved to a new cleaning system that asks each custodian to do one task repeatedly—that is, the same task again and again and again through the night—rather than be responsible for every cleaning task in a certain building. Thus, for example, an employee becomes "the vacuum specialist" or "the bathroom special-ist." Lawrence says that management is doing what it can to make the new roles "a profession, rather than drudgery. We're trying to make it into a real profession with real skills and documented achievements and a way to progress, to advance yourself." But he admits that custodial work is "the forgotten career, the forgotten industry." And when I ask if doing the same task all night gets boring, he jokes, "Yeah, that's why I'm a manager." But then he pauses. "Not just boring but I would almost say soul destroying, because you go in and put your life's effort into making an area neat and tidy, and you come back and the kids have trashed it again. And the next night they're going to trash it again. Every single day."

My guess is that none of my forty-five first-year students know their classrooms, libraries, and campus are cleaned by working-class men and women toiling through the night. I don't blame them: before I began my research I wasn't aware of the university's night-shift custodians either. My students come primarily from upper-middle-class or even upper-class fam-ilies—the parking lots here tell stories of financial comfort rather than pain from the Great Recession—and it has most likely not occurred to them that people their parents' and grand-parents' age are cleaning up after them for a wage that wouldn't match that of their summer job. I don't mean to criti-cize my students here—many if not all would be entirely sympathetic to the situation of those on the night shift, and would be quick to understand not only their own privilege, but also the way American society has created the situation. But first they would need to become aware of that situation. Because unless you consciously look for them, you won't notice the night-shift employees reaching campus as you're heading back to your dorm, thinking about bed. Unless you consciously look, these men and women will remain invisible, and you will return each morning to find your work-spaces and gathering places cleaned as though by magic. However sympa-thetic my students or any of the students here at this prestigious and very expensive southeastern university are, they will most likely never have to work the night shift. They may choose to work it because the career path they follow—physician, nurse, international stock trader—requires it. But again, they will do so by choice, and with much greater financial reward than any custodian here could ever expect. Perhaps most importantly, they would work the night shift knowing that if they wanted to quit they could, and they would most likely be fine. The ability to choose whether to work the night shift, and in what capacity, seems another issue directly related to class: the vast majority of these middle- and upper-class students here will never have to spend their nights performing such a repetitive and menial task as cleaning up after wealthy teenagers and their teachers.

This is what I'm thinking about as I drive to campus just before 11 P.M. on a Thursday to meet Lawrence. Simply going to campus at that hour feels . . . I wouldn't say soul destroying, yet, but it does feel odd. Shouldn't I be going to bed right about now? On campus, that's exactly where I imagine everyone I see is headed. That is, except for Lawrence and the dozen custodians gathering in the break room. They look weary already—each shuffles into the room as though they've just awoken—and their shifts are just beginning. In fact, they almost certainly have just awoken after perhaps a few hours of sleep. And while Lawrence expresses satisfaction and even pleasure with working all night ("I feel like I own this campus"), what captures my attention is his description of the physical ordeal that is night-shift work.

"I spent five years with a permanent headache," he tells me again. "You can be so fatigued, and you really have to learn how to manage it, even down to how to breathe. People on the day shift they breathe all the time and they don't even think about it. But when you've got to slug it out and keep moving all night long you even begin to manage how you breathe and move your arms and legs. And sometimes you get so fatigued. . . . I would lie down on my bed and immediately hit REM sleep and dream psychedelic fantasies and wake up an hour later sweating and my heart pounding like I had been for a run. That can't be good for you, right?" About the people he supervises, he says, "It's beating them up. One or two say it's the best thing, but for a lot of our people it's just very tough."

I tell Lawrence how this makes me think about my love for night, and how the night I love is a voluntary night—I get to choose when to stay up and when to sleep. But . . .

He interrupts me with a chuckle. "To be bound to it with chains? It's a different story."

I hear a number of those stories as I follow Lawrence on his rounds. The first is Joe's: "I worked for Hanes Brands for ten years, 7 P.M. to 7 A.M. They closed the plant and I was out of work for a couple years. Then I started here. I've worked third shift pretty much for thirteen years." When I ask how he likes it, he sighs. "Like it? It's okay. It's where the job is. I am trained in music, Christian education, and that never paid well enough. It's a mindset pretty much. You either fight it or you say this is what it is and you go with it. See, I work a part-time job also, in the mornings. So I go to bed around 2 and get up around 9. A lot of time when everyone else is enjoying a beautiful afternoon, you can't. I wake up a lot of nights before coming here and think oh, you gotta be kidding me."

A heavy-set woman in her fifties, Susan has done custodial work at the university for eighteen years, but has only worked the night shift for the past two. "It's been a real challenge," she admits. "It's sucked." But then she says—and I will hear this phrase repeatedly tonight, said with varying degrees of resignation—"You get used to it." When I ask what the hardest part is, she doesn't hesitate. "Sleeping in the daytime is the hardest part. My sleep is broke up. Like I go home and try to sleep two or three hours, then I get up, and then I try to lay back down in the afternoon, and that's the hard part. Sundays are really hard because your whole family's together and all of sudden you have to go to bed. I look forward to Friday and Saturday night so I can get my sleep. I look forward to going to bed. It's my best sleep. A lot of people can't sleep on their nights off, but I can really wreck out."

The toughest hours of the night shift, she says, are from 2 A.M. to 4 A.M. "Yeah, that's true," agrees Lawrence. "Because even if you were partying at night that's when the party would be over."

"How do you get through?" I ask her.

Susan says, "Oh, you got so much work that you just can't think about it."

■ That may be true, but as Charles Czeisler, professor of Sleep Medicine at Harvard Medical School explains, "You can't just order people not to be exhausted when they're working at night." No one will know if Joe or Susan or any other custodian crashes a cleaning cart, but in our 24/7 society where train, plane, and automobile traffic continues through the night, other crashes could be catastrophic. In 2011 a tractor-trailer slammed into an Amtrak train in Nevada, killing six passengers and injuring fifteen, and authorities believe the truck driver fell asleep at the wheel. Stories such as this one are in the news regularly. But the stories could easily be worse.[3]

Exhaustion is only one in a long list of health problems suffered by those who work at night. Harvard epidemiologist Eva S. Schernhammer reports that "increases in cardiovascular risk, peptic ulcer disease, a higher abortion and miscarriage rate as well as lower pregnancy rates, higher rates of substance abuse and depression, a greater number of vehicle accidents and higher body weight due to abnormal eating habits . . . have all been reported in shift workers."[4] The culprit is not simply that night-shift work requires people to stay awake when their bodies are craving sleep, but that night-shift work requires working under bright lights, which in turn disrupt the circadian rhythms humans depend on for health.

Humans have evolved to rely on the natural rhythm of bright days and dark nights. Our body's circadian (meaning, essentially, "about a day") rhythms control not only our sleep/wake cycle, but also "the ebb and flow of hormones, the rise and fall of body temperature, and other subtle rhythms."[5] The brain controls these rhythms based on the signals sent by light—for tens of millions of years the signals sent by the presence or absence of the sun. During daylight, when strong light signals hit the photoreceptors in the back of the eye, the body's production of cortisol and other hormones increases and our blood pressure and body temperature rise. At night, in darkness, when the eye receives a weaker light signal, the body produces melatonin, a hormone that lowers blood pressure, drops our body temperature, and—perhaps most striking—seems to inhibit the growth of tumors in the body, especially sex hormone–driven cancers such as ovarian, breast, and testicular tumors. When we stay awake into the night, living and working amid electric light, we disrupt this vital day–night rhythm.

The apparent link between the disruption of the body's production of melatonin and cancer may be the most troubling aspect of light at night and ill health. Significantly, those most at risk seem to be those who work a rotating schedule—working the night shift sometimes, then the dayshift other times—rather than those who maintain a regular night-shift schedule. Researchers believe that switching back and forth between sleeping during the day and sleeping at night prohibits the body from adapting, and thus hinders the body's circadian rhythms from adjusting to a new schedule and melatonin production from returning to normal levels. But the fact is that the vast majority of those who work a steady night shift revert to a normal day–night sleep schedule on their days off, and thus confuse their circadian rhythms.[6] Explains Harvard's Steven Lockley, "You can't adapt the clock quickly enough. It takes about a day to shift an hour, on average. So if you go from a day shift to a night shift, it's a twelve-hour shift, it will take you at least twelve days to adapt to. Then when you go from a night shift back to a day shift, it takes you twelve days to go back. And of course very few people work twelve night shifts in a row. Usually they have days off, and on days off they tend to go back to what they did in daytime." As a result, says Lockley, "Essentially, no shift workers are ever adapted to their night schedule."[7]

■ "The question of 'why do you do this work' is kind of a moot one, isn't it?" I ask Lawrence after we've made our first stops.

"It's true, they don't see that they have an option in this economy," he says. "But most people are doing it for the sake of their family and their home life."

I hear this from several of the night-shift custodians, including Lawrence. ("I love it," he claims of working all night. "It's the only way of life I have found so far that allows me to meet all the needs of my family.") While studies report that slightly more men (16 percent of Americans) than women (14 percent) work the night shift, women report that their main reason for doing so is that they can be with their family during the day. As one woman tells me, "It plays havoc on your body. I lost 30 pounds from the start, and I didn't have it to lose. It makes your body feel run-down, tired, exhausted. But I also have a family, and so I try to get back to a regular schedule on the weekend."

"Have you adjusted?" I ask.

"No, and I don't think I ever will."

Ironically, women who work the night shift "report significantly higher work–family conflict than women who regularly work days."[8] Most people working the night shift have spouses who work the day shift, which dramatically cuts down time spent together. Even when they do spend time together, the spouse working the night shift is often exhausted.

"I worked first shift for sixty-five years," says a gray-haired man Lawrence addresses as Mr. Singletary. "But now I'm supposed to flip this body, make it turn into the graveyard shift—and now I know why they call it the graveyard shift. When everybody's asleep, I'm wide awake. Eating habits, out the window. I don't have breakfast no more—when I'm getting home my wife is already gone to work." Mr. Singletary reminds me of my grandfather, not only his age and appearance (furrowed brow, slight stoop), but also how he chuckles to himself after nearly every phrase. For a moment I find myself lost in thought: He worked first shift for sixty-five years? So, he has to be at least seventy-five, or certainly eighty? How would any of my students feel if their eighty-year-old grandfather were cleaning the bathrooms at the local university nearly every night? Nothing about the scenario seems right. Did he really say sixty-five years? A grandfather cleaning toilets and sinks all night? In this country, in the twenty-first century?

When my focus returns I hear Mr. Singletary wondering aloud—as though Lawrence and I aren't standing just feet away—about how he will find time to mow the church lawn, the local football field, his own yard.

"You're just going to have to give up sleep," I joke.

"I'm going to have to figure out something," he sighs. "I'm not sure how I'm going to do it." And then, quieter, "God will show me a way out of it. He will show me a way."

Like most of the other custodians working the night shift at this well-known southeastern university Mr. Singletary is African American. The custodian who tells me he's "used to it" because he worked from 5 P.M. to 5 A.M. for years at the local peanut factory? African American. The woman who tells me that for eighteen years she's existed on sleeping two or three hours a day? African American. The man who tells me simply, "Some people's not cut out for third shift"? African American. When I ask him what it feels like he pauses. "You ever worked third shift before? Okay, well. Wouldn't do me no good to explain it to you, then."

Here lies another truth about night-shift work: certain segments of our population bear its burdens more than others. Nearly 20 percent of African Americans work the night shift, for example, and more blacks work it than whites, Hispanics, Latinos, or Asians. In addition, poor and minority city neighborhoods are often brightly lit in a mistaken effort to deter crime (studies show little or no correlation between higher lighting levels and reduction of crime rates) and their populations disproportionately fill the increasing number of third shift jobs.[9] As scientists affirm the connections between the flood of electric light at night and a long list of health problems, working the night shift will become another of those issues that certain parts of our population will deal with—and suffer from—more directly than others.

■ Even if we don't work the night shift, however, electric light may be affecting our health. For example, Schernhammer found that it's not only women who work the night shift who have lower levels of melatonin, but also women in general. That is, even if we aren't working the night shift, we are staying up later, exposing ourselves to light at night in ways that our bodies haven't evolved to handle. The blue-white light used in computer screens, for example, is suspected of having a greater negative impact on our health than the older red wavelength lights of incandescent bulbs.[10] Common activities such as staring at a computer screen or watching television before going to bed may be enough to disrupt our circadian rhythms and negatively affect our health. If this link proves true, the ramifications will be huge. "Should TV and computer screens prove to be culprits in cancer," writes Catherine Guthrie, "that may solve, at least in part, the maddening riddle of breast cancer. Last year, 211,000 women were diagnosed with breast cancer and another 40,000 died, yet doctors still have few clues as to what drives the disease."[11] As Dr. George Brainard, another leading expert on the connection between artificial light at night and cancer, explains, "Even if lighting is at the root of only 10% of breast cancer cases, what we learn may help thousands and thousands of women."[12]

We have barely begun to understand the health effects of our living amid the flood of light at night, a flood most of us are so used to we wouldn't even think to question it. But the handful of researchers devoted to the topic caution that even sleeping in a bedroom with artificial light coming through the window or seeping under a closed door might spell trouble. All agree that more research is needed, but as Harvard's Lockley told me, "While we have yet to understand fully the environmental and health impact of being exposed to light at night, the data to date suggest a detrimental effect of prolonged exposure to light at night."[13]

I ask Lockley if he thinks, based on what we know now, that it is fair to say the connection between working at night and cancer exists.

"I think that is fair," he tells me. "As a scientist, I can only report what we find experimentally, and those experiments have not been done. And that's why I use the terms *possible* and *likely*. But the shift-work studies are as close as you can get to proving unequivocally without having done it. The World Health Organization classification as a probable carcinogen is as high as you can get without actually proving, without a shadow of a doubt, that shift work causes cancer."[14]

Lockley explains that an example of a Type One risk of cancer would be asbestos, which we now have no doubt causes mesothelioma. A Type Two risk—the level at which the World Health Organization has placed shift work—is the same level as breathing diesel fumes or UV light causing cancer. Researchers only hesitate to identify shift work as a Type One risk because of the lack of direct evidence—there simply is not a test we can do to prove the connection. And yet we accept the connection between UV light and skin cancer enough to support a sunscreen industry worth some $650 million worldwide, even though, as Lockley says, "No one's done a study, I don't suspect, where they have purposely given people UV light and watched them get cancer."[15]

For those who can choose to sleep in dark bedrooms, dim the bulbs in our other rooms, and keep regular sleeping patterns, it is relatively easy to change our patterns to protect ourselves. But for those increasing numbers of night-shift workers around the world who have little to no control of their exposure to light at night, the situation is far more troubling. In our homes, on our streets, and in our places of work we are using more and more electric light. Ultimately, the question we must ask is if this is really the direction we want our society to grow. We are putting increasing numbers of primarily working-class and minority citizens at risk, simply as they try to make a living.

As we do, of course, we are also endangering the ecosystems on which we all rely. With 60 percent of invertebrates and 30 percent of vertebrates nocturnal, and countless other species crepuscular (active at dawn and dusk), darkness is simply invaluable. Research increasingly shows that ecological light pollution is having a destructive effect on ecosystems, as species that have evolved over billions of years have no chance to adapt to our sudden flood of artificial light. For Lockley, the connections between what researchers are finding out about the human health effects of artificial light at night and what they're finding out about the ecological effects come as no surprise. "Humans are animals as well," he tells me, "and there's no reason to give ourselves any higher level in the rankings than everything else.

And so when light/dark cycles mess up seasonal patterns of trees or breed-ing cycles of amphibians, which I think is quite well established, there's no reason to think it's not doing the same to us."[16]

The simple truth is this: life on Earth evolved with bright days and dark nights, and life needs both for optimal health. Inseparable from the natural world that sustains us, humans are no different in terms of suffering the health effects of artificial light at night. The sooner we realize that what we do to the rest of creation we do to ourselves—and vice versa—the better.

■ By the end of my time with Lawrence, nearly 1:30 A.M. on a day where I woke at 7 A.M. and worked my usual schedule, I've grown so tired I can't concentrate on either my questions or the custodians' answers. I can't keep from yawning, either, and when I do yawn tears fill my eyes. I'm reminded of the nurse I heard of who, when she drives home after working all night, closes her pony-tail in her car's sunroof to jerk her head upright if . . . when . . . she falls asleep at the wheel.

All night as he has made his rounds, Lawrence has ended our conversa-tion with each custodian by asking, "Can you be back at the break-room at 6 A.M. for a meeting?" Each time he does this I think, you mean 6 A.M. tomorrow morning? I'm exhausted, but anytime I want to I can say good-night and head home to my warm, comfortable bed, while everyone I've met still has six more hours of work to do tonight.

And tomorrow night.

And the next night.

And, for many, the hundreds or even thousands of nights in the years to come.

And that, indeed, sounds utterly soul destroying.

NOTES

An earlier form of this essay appeared in Paul Bogard's book, *The End of Night: Searching for Natural Darkness in an Age of Artificial Light* (New York: Little, Brown, 2013).

1. "Opportunities for Policy Leadership on Shift Work," The Sloan Work and Family Research Network, http://workfamily.sas.upenn.edu/sites/workfamily.sas.upenn.edu/files/imported/pdfs/policy_makers6.pdf.

2. Ron Chepesiuk, "Missing the Dark: Health Effects of Light Pollution,"

Environmental Health Perspectives 117 (2009): A20–A27; Richard Stevens, "Light-at-Night, Circadian Disruption and Breast Cancer: Assessment of Existing Evidence," *International Journal of Epidemiology* 38 (2009): 963–70.

3. "You can't just"; *USA Today,* "NTSB: Bad Brakes, Driver at Fault in Reno Amtrak Crash," December, 12, 2012, http://www.usatoday.com/story/news/nation/2012/12/12 /reno-amtrak-truck-crash/1765171/.

4. Eva Schernhammer, "Light at Night and Health: The Perils of Rotating Shift Work," *Occupational and Environmental Medicine* 68, no. 5 (2011: 310–31, published online October 4, 2010, http://www.oem.bmj.com/content/68/5/310.full.

5. Catherine Guthrie, "The Light-Cancer Connection," *Prevention* 58, no. 1 (January 2006), published online November 2011, http://www.prevention.com/health/health -concerns/kick-these-cancer-related-habits.

6. "Considerations of Circadian Impact for Defining 'Shift Work' in Cancer Studies: IARC Working Group Report," *Occupational and Environmental Medicine* 68 (2011): 154–62.

7. Steven Lockley is associate professor of medicine, Harvard Medical School; and neuroscientist, Division of Sleep Medicine, Department of Medicine, Brigham and Women's Hospital. Lockley in phone interview with author, December 2010.

8. Rosalynd Chait Barnett and Karen Gareis, "Mothers' Shiftwork: Effects on Mothers, Fathers, and Children," in *Handbook of Families and Work: Interdisciplinary Perspectives*, ed. D. Russell Crane and Edward Jeffrey Hill, (Lanham, MD: University Press of America), 355–73, "report significantly," 361.

9. The Institute of Justice, in their 1997 report added, "We may speculate that lighting is effective in some places, ineffective in others, and counter-productive in still other circumstances. The problematic relationship between lighting and crime increases when one considers that offenders need lighting to detect potential targets and low-risk situations." Institute of Justice, "Preventing Crime: What Works, What Doesn't, What's Promising," 7–32.

10. Catherine Guthrie, "The Light-Cancer Connection," *Prevention* 58, no. 1 (January 2006).

11. Ibid.

12. Ibid.

13. Lockley, phone interview with author, December 2010.

14. Ibid.

15. Ibid.

16. Ibid.

8

From Orchards to Cubicles

Work and Space in Silicon Valley

DEBRA J. SALAZAR

━━

My grandparents are Mexican immigrants. They settled in San José, California, before World War II. As a child, I spent much time in wild spaces—forests, beaches, ghost towns, abandoned orchards, lonely creeks. As I grew older, I noticed that very few of the people I encountered in those places looked like me. I began to wonder about the absence of brown people from these wild and beautiful spaces. My pondering became a troubling obsession until the emergence of the environmental justice movement during the 1980s. Then it became a research focus, a legitimate obsession.

Environmental injustice takes many forms. Early in the movement, attention focused on illnesses caused by exposure to toxins in poor neighborhoods, communities of color, and in the workplace.[1] Soon activists and scholars identified inequitable access to land and other resources as environmental injustices.[2] It was this form of environmental justice that resonated with the experience of my family in California.

Three years ago I meandered down a road in Palo Alto, twenty miles from where I grew up. While walking I revisited my childhood contemplations about how particular groups of people come to inhabit beautiful spaces while other groups are confined to crowded, treeless slums. I thought about the kinds of environmental injustice visited on my family and others like us. The story of this walk, recounted below, explores how those who control wealth and exercise power have managed the transformation of Silicon Valley. But more importantly, this essay recalls a history and describes a present for a particular set of working people in the Valley who have endured the unjust exercise of power over their lives. These people—workers, dreamers, gardeners, parents, and interpreters of history—have created and re-created places as they have struggled to live rich lives.

High-Tech Medicine in High-Tech Land

My father is having surgery at the Palo Alto Veteran's Administration (VA) Hospital, his shoulder worn out from decades of lifting, pulling, and pushing.[3] The hospital, busy with veterans of more-recent wars, found a space in its schedule for my father, an eighty-year-old veteran of the Korean War. The surgeons anticipate it will take two to three hours for them to scrape and saw out the mess in my father's right shoulder and replace it with a shiny new titanium humerus.

Like my father, I do not sit still well. So as the second hour of the wait begins, I head out for a walk. The VA Hospital sits at the southern edge of Palo Alto at the base of the Los Altos Hills, which rise southwest of the San Francisco Bay in California. Palo Alto defines the northern boundary of the renowned high-technology capital, Silicon Valley. We used to call it the Santa Clara Valley, but by 1970 the priests of high tech had supplanted Spanish colonialism as the source of regional identity.

Amending My Inner Silicon Valley

I grew up twenty miles from Palo Alto but never went there as a child. Still, my parents venerated Stanford University and what it symbolized about education and their daughter's future. I could find Palo Alto on a map and could have given directions to anyone. But we never went there. With its wide, shaded avenues, lined by tile-roofed mansions on large lots, it was a foreign country. The only Mexicans there resided in East Palo Alto, a separate municipality, and they served the people who lived in the mansions. Silicon Valley has changed. Since my childhood, I have ventured into this foreign land on numerous occasions, but not here, not to the southern reaches of Palo Alto, where it edges up against Los Altos Hills, 94022: one of the fifty richest zip codes in the country.[4]

Walking in Silicon Valley is never a straightforward experience for me. The landscape and its transformation over the past four or five decades evoke my childhood and my family's history. Freedom, fruit, injustice, love—rise from the landscape and dance across my path every time I step out onto a Valley sidewalk or stride up a trail. Some days these ghosts are a bit much to bear, but stillness is costly, too.

As I meander south from the VA campus, I sense the wealth and whiteness surrounding me. A familiar discomfort tugs on my chest. But I ignore this tightness as the need to navigate traffic signals and crosswalks draws me back to Palo Alto. I focus on mapping my walk, amending my inner Silicon Valley. My route parallels Highway 280, which traverses foothills along the west side of the Bay to link Silicon Valley to San Francisco. To the west of the highway rise the Santa Cruz Mountains, framing the Valley on the south and west, separating it from the Pacific Ocean. I cannot see the mountains, but I know where they are from any point in the Valley.

The Santa Cruz Mountains and the ocean beyond them make Silicon Valley habitable; they embody hope and hint at infinity, something outside the crawling traffic and the concrete walls separating condo developments from freeways. Coast redwoods rise from the mountains feeding on fog, taunting the sky. Between groves of redwoods, coast live oaks drop acorns and California laurels offer their leaves for the evening marinara. And houses dot these mountains, too. In my youth, it was mostly hippies who squatted in small mountain meadows, cultivating gardens and practicing simplicity. Increasingly, the Santa Cruz Mountains have become a building site for the very rich, who buy exclusive views of redwoods, Santa Cruz cypress, and tick-ridden mule deer. The middling rich have evicted the hippies in the lower valleys, while the extraordinarily rich have enclosed the ridge tops along Skyline Boulevard. From a distance, I imagine the ocean views from decks constructed of sustainably grown tropical hardwoods. The ocean is wild along this section of the California coast; the water is cold, the waves crazed. In contrast to the sea, the Valley landscape is orderly and tamed. I visit my family in Silicon Valley three or four times a year now, and I try on each visit to spend time in these mountains or next to the ocean. On this spring morning of my father's surgery, I cannot see the ocean.

I continue walking by the Stanford Research Park, passing a series of corporate campuses—Varian, SAP, DPIX, VMware.[5] I know nothing of the companies whose campuses I pass, but I commit to memory the names on the signs. Later, back in the north Puget Sound where I live, I will look up

the companies. Driven by curiosity about the Valley and by my first exposure to this part of the landscape, I learn about these companies and the
Stanford Research Park.

Becoming Silicon Valley

Despite their strangeness to me, corporate campuses are not new to Silicon
Valley. International Business Machines (IBM) Corporation has been in the
Valley since 1943, Hewlett-Packard (HP) a few years longer. IBM's punch
card plant in central San José was its first West Coast facility. The one-story,
stucco building filled a city block and initially employed fifty-two people,
most of those workers imported from the East Coast. In the late 1950s, after
IBM engineers had invented the hard disk drive at its San José research laboratory, those drives were manufactured on Cottle Road in San José. More
recently, IBM built an expansive research park at the south end of the Valley, twenty-five miles from Hillview Avenue. Unlike the more urban spaces
adjacent to its manufacturing facilities, IBM's Almaden Research Center
epitomizes green development, allocating 650 of its 691 acres to wildlife
habitat, managed jointly as a county park. Scientists with PhD's and windows look out at the Almaden Valley and, in the distance, the Santa Teresa
Hills. They exchange emails with colleagues at UC Berkeley and Stanford.
They can take lunch walks through valley oak savannah, taking time to
marvel at the arroyo lupine or my own favorite, California poppies.[6]

I like the image of workers on lunchtime walks through meadows and
woodlands. I wonder if the janitors have the time or energy for such walks,
to appreciate the beautiful spaces just steps away from the dark hallways
they travel. Economic development in the Valley has led to increased
demand for janitors. Most are Latino immigrants, and most high-tech
firms contract out janitorial services, avoiding the costs of benefits and
state and federal employment taxes.[7]

But IBM's iconic status does not conjure up the janitor. Rather, IBM and
the Valley itself evoke the promise of electronics and high technology. And
this promise owes much to Stanford University's support of both established electronics firms and newer firms started by young engineers in the
Stanford Research Park.

■ The Stanford Research Park was the prototype for post–World War II
high-technology development. Created by the university in 1951 at the

urging of its engineering dean, Frederick Terman, firms signed leases with the university; in addition to space, they received access to university researchers. Many of the early entrepreneurs who moved into the Stanford Research Park had been Stanford graduate students or scholars. This was true of Varian Associates, its first tenant, which signed a lease with the university in 1951 and moved into its facility in 1953. Like many Silicon Valley high-tech companies, its early success was built on defense contracts.[8] Indeed, before Silicon Valley birthed the high-tech scene symbolized by HP printers and cute Macintosh computers, it was the land of bombs and missiles.

Varian was founded by brothers Russell and Sigurd Varian and a group of their physicist and engineer friends in the late 1940s. The founders had socialist leanings and were drawn to military research and development to combat the Nazi threat during World War II. It seems they tried to build their company and their lives to reflect their political beliefs; Varian Associates was originally set up as a cooperative, with all stock owned by employees. The brothers Varian and their colleagues supported progressive social causes and even lived in a housing cooperative in the hills above Palo Alto. But their political views might seem at odds with the company's early research and development program, which focused on increasing the effectiveness of atomic weapons. The country's Cold War focus on atomic weaponry to combat the communist threat, the company's need to secure government contracts, and the technical challenge of directing and detonating missiles likely led them more deeply into the development of products associated with atomic bombs. Varian developed microwave tubes that were used as fuses for atomic bombs and in defense imaging (e.g., radar, missile guidance, communications). As the Korean War proceeded and the Cold War missile competition developed, Varian grew from 325 employees in 1951 to 1,300 in 1958. Like many Silicon Valley companies, Varian later developed nonmilitary product lines. But the Cold War was good to Varian and military contracts continued to provide revenue for research and development through the 1990s.[9]

■ As I walk through the heart of high-technology land, missiles, radar, and the military industrial complex are far from my view, even though automatic irrigation systems require me to take evasive action at times. Without walking up long driveways (at least one of them guarded), I can see only landscaping, parking lots, and the beige stucco walls of low buildings. A few brown-skinned men tend the sprinklers. On the east side of the avenue, some of the buildings must have views of the Santa Cruz Mountains. To the west, the flatter side, the views undoubtedly offer only other buildings and corporate landscaping—strips of lawn punctuated by lollipop-trimmed evergreen trees and bordered by low shrubs that obscure expanses of parking lots, all aligned in striking uniformity. This order impresses me because when I was a child the edges of the Valley were shaped by the irregularity of wild spaces, orchards, rangelands, and watershed.

A Child's Landscape

I was born in the mid-1950s, after the peak of Santa Clara Valley orchard production, and just as Valley elites began to reap the benefits of the Cold War. IBM had invented the hard disk drive before I could chase the ice cream truck that drove by our metal home at Airport Village, leftover military housing rented to civilians after the war. Varian had made its first public stock offering before I learned to read. The future of the Valley had already been decided in San José bars, Palo Alto conference rooms, and the Pentagon. Even before Stanford's Frederick Terman integrated the university and the Valley into the military industrial complex, collapsed demand for tree fruit during the Great Depression led Valley elites to look away from agriculture and toward defense contracts. Dutch Hamann, the San José city manager from 1950 to 1970, led the city on a path of annexation that would provide the land base for economic growth. San José gobbled up surrounding smaller cities as its population expanded nearly five-fold during Hamann's tenure. The climate and landscape made the Valley attractive to World War II veterans. Those veterans provided a labor force for the missile, electronics, and other manufacturing firms that migrated into the Valley.[10] But orchards still defined the landscape in the 1950s.

■ My first memories of the Valley are of small houses on deep lots along quiet streets. Backyards were livened by fruit trees and clotheslines, where children ate fallen fruit and handed clothespins to their mothers and grandmothers. On the east side of the Valley, hidden in the foothills of the Diablo Range, Alum Rock Park welcomed families like ours onto its lawns and trails. Hundreds of children crammed into the indoor pool. Mexican families picnicked on the lawns shaded by live oaks, roasting wieners and grilling burgers on Sunday afternoons. Parents warned their children to stay out of the poison oak as we rushed off into the woods to play army or hide and seek. Invariably, a cousin would return with a rash and spend the next week slathered in Calamine lotion. At dark we climbed back into the cars for the ride down the hill, first passing the rich people's homes in the hills, then through new subdivisions next to prune orchards, across downtown, and then home on the north side of town. I can only assume that white working-class families also spent Sunday afternoons at Alum Rock Park; they appear in none of our snapshots.

During the mid-1960s my mother and I would hike farther into the Diablo Range. The hills were covered in tall grasses, brown through most of the year, with oak and laurel in the draws on northern and eastern slopes. When we were up high enough, we could see the Valley—green fields to the north and south, but subdivisions were overtaking the orchards in most of the rest of the Valley. By then, electronics companies employed far more people than did orchards and canneries.

Orchards remained only as remnants of an agricultural past by the 1970s. The semiconductor industry was firmly rooted in the Valley. But even then numerous farms remained. I would ride my Peugeot ten-speed from our apartment in the East Bay to my grandmother's home in north San José. My mother had given me money for half of the Peugeot for my sixteenth birthday. Her determination that I would learn fiscal responsibility led to the practice of matching funds for major gifts. Through my twenties, I was required to pay half the cost of such gifts—a guitar, a violin, a pair of boots, the bicycle. The Peugeot transported me through graduate school. But my first long rides were along the eastern edges of Silicon Valley. I rode on Mission Boulevard, past Mission San José, through strawberry and broccoli fields and the very few new housing developments, to my grandmother's house in north San José. In the parts of San José where I roamed, high tech was invisible; corporate campuses did not appear on my map of the Valley.

Settling and Being Unsettled in the Valley

My family predates IBM, HP, and Varian in Silicon Valley (of course in the long narrative of California history, we are relative newcomers).[11] My mother's and father's people have been in California since the 1920s, initially migrating up and down the state with the harvest, later settling in San

José. My paternal grandfather, Emilio Salazar, worked in the fields until his body was spent. I knew him for my first six years. His deeply lined skin was even darker than mine. His thick gray hair gave context to an Indian face that, for me, was all gentleness and mystery. In the early 1940s he and my grandmother purchased a house on San Antonio Street in east San José. Three of their older children commuted forty miles each way to work in an Oakland shipyard during World War II; their earnings, joined with those of the rest of the family, provided a down payment. Seven-day work weeks and thriftiness could still get you a small house in pre–Silicon Valley. But in 1947 their house was condemned to make room for the expansion of Highway 101; economic development trumped the Mexicano neighborhood. My grandparents moved their family a few miles west to a three-bedroom Victorian on Spencer Avenue, a home with no space for a garden, but within walking distance of a small store to buy milk and eggs. I never knew the San Antonio Street house, but I spent many hours entertaining my grandfather in the living room of the Victorian. It was dark and cramped, exhaustion emanating from the walls.

During the 1970s, a decade after my blind and stooped grandfather had died, the Victorian was condemned. Once again the Salazar family stood in the way of freeway expansion. No one asked the Salazars about how the Valley should develop or how to regulate semiconductor manufacturing. My grandmother moved again. The former family home on Spencer Avenue now sits below Highway 280.

My Salazar grandparents were not alone in making way for progress. My maternal grandparents had to move in the 1980s. Their home was condemned to accommodate an expanding airport. I can chart my teen years by the frequency of jets roaring overhead. At some point during the 1970s, city officials decided the noise was excessive for nearby residents and initiated condemnation proceedings. Perhaps my grandparents were accustomed to migration. It did not matter; complex decisions about land use and economic development were made by the Hamanns and the Termans, not by the Lopezes and Salazars. My grandmother Candelaria studied civics, pledged to support the Constitution, and believed in democracy and America. But nobody asked her about how to shape a collective future. Already in their seventies, my grandparents were among the last to leave the neighborhood.

■ My maternal grandfather, Próspero López, was a barber. With his acute sense of right and wrong and generosity that knew few bounds, he was not the kind of man who could work for others. From the 1950s until a stroke felled him in 1970 he ran his own barbershop at the north end of downtown San José. A small community of Mexican families lived near North Market Street, shopping at the Mexican market. Many of the men gathered at my grandfather's barbershop to talk politics and *viejas*. He walked the mile or so to that barbershop every day, edging along the increasingly diminished but still discernable Guadalupe Creek. My cousins and I regularly meandered along the part of the creek that flowed down the street from our grandparents' white stucco Mediterranean.

Work in the Orchards and Canneries

My grandparents had settled in the Valley more than a decade before they bought that house in the early 1950s. During those years my grandmother and oldest aunt, Eva, worked in the fields and orchards while my grandfather cut hair. Eva could map the distribution of agricultural crops in the Valley, with perfect recall of every field they had picked and every campsite my grandmother had sanitized. Eva fondly described those campsites, adjacent to prune orchards and strawberry fields. No complaints from Eva, no recollections of aching joints after bending over all day picking broccoli. She wove the story of her youth as a migrant laborer into the American narrative of camping, adventure, and discovery.

I heard stories about months of missed school from my parents. Equally damaging, the schools mistreated migrant Mexican children when they enrolled. One of my aunts, struggling to learn English and to catch up after missing weeks of class, was designated as mentally retarded. At one school, my father and his brother were assigned to clean the elementary school grounds while the real students sat in classrooms, absorbing lessons about multiplication and the land of the free. But these stories were cautionary tales rather than rants; my parents, aunts, and uncles wanted their children nowhere near the fields. Education was the ultimate goal, something no one could take from us.

Still, some of my cousins picked prunes to earn money for school clothes during the 1960s. One summer I joined them for a few days. With no pressure to fill crates, no children to feed, no anticipation of a life bent over, and a clean apartment to go home to, they were not so bad, those days in the sun.

■ Fortunately, my family left the fields and orchards before the intensification of pesticide use after World War II. The military supported research and development into chemical weapons, which led to the development of very effective chemical pesticides. These were applied to California fields in increasing amounts during the 1940s. Farmworkers were quick to recognize the damage to their own health, and since the 1960s regulation of pesticides has been a focus of farmworker organizing and activism.[12] But my grandparents, parents, aunts, and uncles were lucky; they shared the fields and orchards with organophosphates for only a few years.

■ Once they settled in the Santa Clara Valley, my grandmothers and aunts worked in the canneries during the summers. The grinding gears and roaring motors of the factory deafened them as the fruit flew down the lines, to be cleaned, cut, and pitted before being dropped into cans. The fruit was first soaked in a lye solution to ease peeling; the lye would eat through the gloves worn by the women on the line, reddening their hands. The peaches were my favorite. Sometimes when my mother would take me to pick up my grandmother after her shift, I would be rewarded with fresh peaches that appeared from under her apron.

■ All of our fruit was fresh (if not always organic). One could not wander through the Valley without encountering prune orchards and strawberry fields. Every yard had peach and apricot trees; Mexican yards often included a ragged *nopal*. More ambitious and gifted orchardists, like my grandmother Candelaria, cultivated figs, avocados, loquats, lemons, walnuts, and almonds. My grandmother fed a large extended family with her fruit trees and vegetable garden. She also fed the neighbors with the diverse flower ecosystem she created in her front yard. My cousins and I followed her through that garden in the early mornings as she weeded, laid coffee grounds, and watered, carefully assessing the needs and condition of each plant. Though most of the plants in her garden were exotic, not native to the Valley, she taught her children and grandchildren to appreciate the nature of the Valley, to dig our fingers into the soil of the garden, and to respect the squirrels that dropped nuts on us. Candelaria Arias López felt a kinship with nature and embraced it. She had spent her early years on a ranch in Baja California, and often recalled those years in the country, before her parents' deaths forced her to migrate. As natural foods invaded the American lexicon during the 1970s, she declared her leadership in the movement, asserting the naturalness of the food she grew and the clothes she sewed. Gardening, cooking, cleaning, working in the cannery—my grandmother's life was nature and work. She was constant motion and song. I thought she never ate.

◼ I did not think to ask why the women in aprons and hairnets pouring out of the cannery gates after graveyard shifts were mostly brown skinned, or why only men drove the forklifts, loading crates on trucks. Cannery jobs became available to ethnic Mexican workers as opportunities in military production lured away the Italians and Portuguese who had preceded them as workers in fruit processing.[13] I knew very few white people. Aside from Italian neighbors who looked at us warily, the nuns at St. Elizabeth's, and the very few priests I had seen at close range, my world was mostly brown. It was natural that some questions would not occur to me. Like why all the teachers were white. Or why the police were white and never smiled at us. Or why no one in my family owned an orchard. My life, and the lives of my cousins, was mostly brown and warm. I did not often look outward.

Work in the Defense Industry

Regardless of my limited view, many white people inhabited the valley during the 1960s. Some white women worked in the canneries. It was mostly white men who worked in the manufacturing economy that had emerged in the Valley after World War II. Increasingly, those jobs were open to brown men, but not without injury to their souls. After spending the war years dancing and visiting with soldiers at the VA, my Aunt Eva decided she wanted more than a dance partner. Through his sister she met Mario Méndez, a handsome soldier who did not dance well. They married in 1946. Early in their marriage, Mario struggled to hold a job. He was a hardworking man with bulging muscles who ran his house with military discipline. But he often walked off the job in a burst of anger. He never spoke about what transpired that made him walk away from paychecks that would feed and house his children.

In 1962 Mario settled at the Westinghouse plant in Sunnyvale. I used to think my uncle made refrigerators. I had no idea my uncle's factory made propulsion systems for missiles launched from submarines, or that his factory worked on the Polaris, Poseidon, Trident, Peacekeeper, and Cruise missile projects. I never got the chance to ask my uncle what it was like to be a machinist in that factory, what he thought about those missiles. I never asked if his lingering sadness had anything to do with day after day in that factory, in that giant windowless structure. Perhaps the factory was a place of joy for him, of pride in a job well done. I do not know. But I do know that Mario spent his evenings and weekends alone in his backyard, tending his fruit trees; in his garage, pumping weights he had made from old coffee cans filled with cement and bolted and wired to lengths of steel pipe; or attempting to quell the chaos created by his eight children as they bounced off the walls and each other in their eight-hundred-square-foot house.

My Uncle Mario was one of many Valley workers whose wages originated in Defense contracts. My mother worked on the Polaris project at Lockheed. Polaris, the United States' first submarine-launched, nuclear-armed missile, was built in Sunnyvale just a few miles from the Westinghouse factory where Mario worked. My mother was hired on at Lockheed shortly after it opened its Sunnyvale facility in 1956. Eventually she moved to the Polaris project, leading the Document Control section; she was among very few ethnic Mexicans working at that level.[14] At twenty-four my mother combined beauty, command, and competence. She was a mathematics whiz and an analytical powerhouse. Had she been born a decade later, or with lighter skin, she would have been a lawyer or an accountant. But in 1950s Silicon Valley, Lupe López exploited every opportunity she could find, ran up all the paths she could see.

After filling out pages of forms that asked for every address she had ever had (not easy for a woman from a migrant family), my mother got a secret clearance and managed the flow of Polaris documents. Scientists and engineers could not keep these documents in their offices; the documents had to be stored in a controlled, central repository. My mother and her seven employees worked in a large windowless room, filing, checking out, keeping track of, and sometimes destroying secret documents. They were not allowed to look at the documents but they were too busy to do so in any case. My mom worked through breaks and lunch. She and thousands of other Californians at that Lockheed facility devoted their work hours to ensuring the security of the Polaris project and our country.

The bomb and missile businesses—national security—gave Silicon Valley its start.[15] The war industry built the human infrastructure of Silicon Valley. The Defense contracts that fed Westinghouse and Lockheed required engineers and mathematicians and supported research at Stanford and UC Berkeley. Of course it took more than engineers to build a missile; the lower rungs of the industry were increasingly open to first- and second-generation Mexican Americans. My uncle Mario's oldest daughter, Shirley, also worked at Lockheed, but as a federal employee. Starting in 1966 Shirley worked on the Poseidon missile project for the US Navy while her father worked on the same project at Westinghouse. Having taken the Civil Service test in high school, she got on the federal employment register just as the federal government was becoming more concerned about employment discrimination. But even in the mid-1960s, California high schools were not directing bright young Mexican American girls to college. Shirley worked her way up the ladder of jobs open to her, first as a file clerk, then a secretary, and finally an accounting position.

■ The war and high-technology industries supported my family. These industries also poisoned the groundwater. The South Bay is lousy with Superfund sites; there are more in Santa Clara County than any other county in California.[16] Westinghouse has its very own Superfund site, as do Intel, Fairchild Semiconductor, Raytheon, Advanced Micro Devices . . . and the US Navy. It is not surprising that the bomb and missile industries would generate toxic substances. But the high-tech boosters failed to inform the rest of us that the clean rooms where microchips are manufactured were poisonous. The solvents used to clean microchips and circuit boards have sickened exposed workers and polluted the water.[17]

By the time the semiconductor industry began hiring, mostly immigrant women, my aunts and uncles were settled and most of my cousins had enough education to find other kinds of work. My family was spared the horrible illnesses associated with work in the clean rooms. More-recent immigrant families were not. Those families were hit both at work and at home as they tended to live in the neighborhoods served by the polluted groundwater.[18]

Twenty-First Century Patrones and Space in Silicon Valley

But war and poisoned water seem far from my morning walk. My father was taken into surgery at 6:30 this morning but the sun is high over the valley now; it is time to remove a sweatshirt. As the corporate campuses end, I step onto West Fremont Road and enter a neighborhood unlike any I have ever walked through in the Valley. The houses are expansive, classic, low-slung, stuccoed, Mediterraneans with tile roofs and circular driveways. They are set back far from the road with fifty to seventy-five yards between mailboxes. My pace slows as I take it all in. I see no fruit trees, just an occasional redwood, and the ubiquitous live oaks. Each yard is exquisitely landscaped; instead of lawns, dark green shrubs sit in orderly, but not perfect, rows. I can see openings in the tree canopies behind the houses where, I imagine, tennis courts and swimming pools are hiding. My favorite house sits above me on a hill; the lights around its tennis court are visible and so is the pool house. I wonder if the plants are native; they do not look like any I learned about in college. Still, their placement is intentional, part of a stylistic vision. And then I see how the whole scene evokes Spanish California, and not just any nineteenth-century scene—the classic hacienda. I am walking through haciendaville.

Of course many California subdivisions mimic the hacienda, but their mimicry is transparent when only ten feet separate one house from the next. These twenty-first century *patrones* make decisions that shape the lives of others, that circumscribe possibilities. Under the burden of such power, they are comforted by views of quiet gardens, forested mountains, and space, so much space.

■ My father has always dreamed of building his own house on some land. He is so American in this regard; freedom is a house without curtains, with space, distance from neighbors' noise. My dad transmitted that dream to me during my childhood. From Yosemite to the North Coast, we would drive up dirt roads then hike abandoned trails; he punctuated these trips with history lessons about Indians, agriculture, and industry, his own interpretation of how people and the California landscape had shaped each other. My father's accounts portrayed our Indian ancestors as both heroes and victims, the Spaniards as cruel, and the mestizo descendants of both as hardworking people, the hardest workers. Very few non-Spanish white people inhabit my father's narrative of California history.

My dad's favorite stops were abandoned structures and cemeteries. On educational tours of the buildings, he was careful to monitor my steps, making sure I did not fall through rotten boards as he explained nineteenth- or early twentieth-century construction methods. At night we camped along logging roads. I froze under a blanket in the cab of his '62 Chevy pickup. My dad slept under the stars in the bed of the pickup; I think he had a blanket, too.

Though the cemetery visits may appear morbid, the lessons I learned from our camping trips were about work and space and home. My father always noted the hillsides that would make good building sites for his dream home—nothing as majestic as those on West Fremont Road—but a house on some land. He has all the skills and tools, but he has never had the land. I have neither the skills nor the tools. But by moving away from California, I was able to buy my own house on some land. It is nothing like what I see on this road, but it is a place of space and quiet, no curtains, no neighbors' noise.

The Gentrified Valley and the New Migration

Others in my family also have moved away to find small spaces for themselves. My youngest aunt, Elisabel, lived nearly her whole life in the Santa Clara Valley. In the early 1980s she saved enough money to purchase a small mobile home and lived in it for over a decade. In her mid-fifties, my aunt saw that she would never be able to buy a house anywhere near the garden her mother had tended for thirty years, the prune orchards her older sisters had picked in, or the canneries that had consumed her own teenage summers. Land in Silicon Valley had become too valuable to house middle-aged women earning middling paychecks. Gentrification had overtaken the Valley; as property values increased, middle-class incomes were no longer sufficient to purchase modest homes with space for a garden. So, like her parents had seventy years before, my aunt migrated.

Elisabel López journeyed over the Diablo Range, into the heat of the San Joaquín Valley, where her civil servant salary sufficed to get her name on the title of a house in a Merced subdivision. The last year or so of my aunt's life she spent four to five hours a day on the road, commuting to and from her job in San José. She was not alone on her daily pilgrimage along the

Valley highways. Thousands of Californians who work on the periphery of Silicon Valley economy have moved east, leaving their home to find houses they could afford.

■ Gentrification may be defined as the purchase and occupation of desirable places by affluent people and the consequent displacement of the less well off.[19] Because it reserves the best places for the most privileged, gentrification is a form of environmental injustice. Working people, especially Latinos, have endured and resisted many kinds of injustice in Silicon Valley. Gentrification compounds these injustices, forcing the poor and lower-middle class into polluted neighborhoods with less access to open spaces, often inadequate public services, and situated far from the places they work.

Though many of my family members have left the Valley to find work and housing, four generations of my family still live there. We have done well; my generation was able to live in one place long enough to absorb the lessons of public schools. We do not work in the fields. A few of my cousins and their adult children work for high-tech companies. But they are not engineers or venture capitalists, just creative, hardworking people with little time or space to plant gardens. They do not live in houses like the ones I pass on this walk through haciendaville. They do not work in corner offices with views of the Santa Cruz Mountains. My cousins live in small spaces at the south end of the Valley. They would have to go out of their way to walk on streets like West Fremont Road.

Holding on to Small Spaces

My cousin Sharon works for the county library, managing administrative services. She has her own office, without windows, and lives in a two-bedroom condominium in Campbell, on the west side of the Valley. The recession has turned her mortgage upside down. But she makes her payments and gives the county ten-hour days. Sharon does not talk about it much, but I know she worries: Will she be able to refinance in time to make that balloon payment? Will she be able to retire with her name on the title of this cozy condo? Will she have some small measure of wealth—a home perhaps—to leave to her children? In the evenings she takes classes at the community college. On the weekends, when not working or studying, she takes her bicycle out on the county's trail system.

Parks, especially the linear kind, have proliferated in the Valley as other kinds of open space have disappeared. In the southern part of the Valley, where the working people live, open spaces are especially limited.[20] Sharon takes advantage of every mile; she has seen bobcats, wild boar, and many squirrels on her weekend rides. But she is most animated talking about the plum tree along one of the trails. The free plums are so coveted that the tree is picked bare before the fruit is ripe. Sharon gets excited about free fruit. She picks from trees in the yards of older family members who live in central San José, sharing the tangerines and persimmons with my mother. Sharon can afford to buy organic fruit at Whole Foods. But eating figs shipped from Chile, priced at $6.00 a pound, is a different culinary and economic experience. It does not give Sharon the same kind of joy as standing on a ladder and tossing figs down to a bucket held by her sister. But Sharon never picked for money.

Few people pick for money in the Valley anymore. My mother interviews farmers at her local farmers' market; many drive two hundred miles or more, from the hot and dry San Joaquín Valley, to sell their produce in these outdoor stalls. For our family, orchards, fields, and canneries are the past. During the 1950s my parents and most of my aunts and uncles worked in the canneries, but most were on their way to other kinds of factory and trades work (for the men) and clerical and administrative work (for the women). Thus, while jobs were often difficult to find, and their work may have been tedious, most paid well enough for employees to purchase modest homes in and around San José. The path they took to middle-class backyards is no longer available in Silicon Valley.

■ Continuing along West Fremont Road, I am increasingly aware of being out of place. Yes, I know the Valley has never really been ours. But we had spaces here for fruit trees and gardens. We looked out at open spaces on the hillsides that shaped our American dreams. Those spaces have been taken from us, enclosed.

I walk back to the hospital and see my father, drowsy and weak, but triumphant. He does not look like an icon of high-technology medicine, with his newly fashioned shoulder joint. Rather, I see a man who has always worked, disoriented by his immobility. Despite doctor's orders not to work for six weeks, my father returns to his crane within a week. I return to the North Puget Sound, to rain and cedars.

■   Three generations of immigrant dreamers have followed my grand-parents into the Valley. First in the poisonous clean rooms of semiconductor factories and now in the service sector, cleaning hotels and corporate campuses, they have found work. The latest generation of immigrants marches up and down hallways, hauling cleaning supplies. This generation has come to inhabit a valley that is increasingly paved, where the most beautiful spaces are reserved for the wealthy, where Latino immigrants are largely confined to overcrowded and underserved neighborhoods in east San José. As I contemplate the spaces in which they live, work, and play, I wonder what landscapes will shape their American dreams.[21]

NOTES

1. Robert J. Brulle and David N. Pellow, "Environmental Justice: Human Health and Environmental Inequalities," *Annual Review of Public Health* 27 (2006): 103–23.

2. Laura Pulido, *Environmentalism and Economic Injustice: Two Chicano Struggles in the Southwest* (Tucson: University of Arizona Press, 1996), 125–90.

3. See Palo Alto Healthcare System, US Department of Veterans Affairs, http://www.paltoalto.va.gov/.

4. Wealth in the United States, http://wealth.mongabay.com/tables/100_wealthiest_zip_codes-1000.html.

5. Margaret O'Mara, "Landscapes of Knowledge and High Technology," *Places* 19, no. 1 (2007), 50. Also see "History of Varian," http://www.varian.com/us/corporate/our_company/company_facts_history.html.

6. San José card plant, http://www-03.ibm.com/ibm/history/exhibits/supplies/supplies_5404PH06.html; "The History of the Almaden Research Site," http://www.almaden.ibm.com/almaden20/history.shtml; Robin M Grossinger et al., "Historical Landscape Ecology of an Urbanized California Valley: Wetlands and Woodlands in the Santa Clara Valley," *Landscape Ecology* 22 (2007), 105; Almaden Wildflowers, http://www.almaden.ibm.com/almaden/almaden/environs/wildflowers/; Wild Almaden, http://www.almaden.ibm.com/almaden/almaden/environs/.

7. Christian Zlolniski, *Janitors, Street Vendors, and Activists: The Lives of Mexican Immigrants in Silicon Valley* (Berkeley: University of California Press, 2007), 48–50; Christian Zlolniski, "The Informal Economy in Advanced Industrial Society: Mexican Immigrant Labor in Silicon Valley," *The Yale Law Journal* 103 (1994): 2309–10.

8. Aaron Sachs, "Virtual Ecology: A Brief Environmental History of the Silicon Valley," *World-Watch Journal* (January–February 1999), 15; Christophe Lecuyer, *Making Silicon Valley: Innovation and the Growth of High-Tech, 1930–1970* (Cambridge, MA: MIT

Press 2006), 91–128; "History of Varian"; Stuart W. Leslie, "The Biggest Angel of Them All: The Military and the Making of Silicon Valley," in *Understanding Silicon Valley: The Anatomy of an Entrepreneurial Region*, ed. Martin Kenney (Stanford, CA: Stanford University Press, 2000): 48–67; Lecuyer, *Making Silicon Valley*, 5–8; Mia Gray et al., "New Industrial Cities? The Four Faces of Silicon Valley," in *Readings in Urban Theory* (2nd ed.), ed. Susan Fainstein and Scott Campbel (Malden, MA: Blackwell Publishers, 2002), 57–79.

9. "History of Varian"; Lecuyer, *Making Silicon Valley*, 93–95, 103–4, 92, 102; Gray et al., "New Industrial Cities?" Varian Associates divided into three different firms with different product focuses in 1999. Varian, Inc., http://www.fundinguniverse.com/company-histories/Varian-Inc-Company-History.html

10. Sachs, "Virtual Ecology," 15; Glenna Matthews, "The Los Angeles of the North": San José's Transition from Fruit Capital to High-Tech Metropolis," *Journal of Urban History* 25, no. 4: (May 1999): 461; Lecuyer, *Making Silicon Valley*, 124; Matthews, "The Los Angeles of the North," 460–461; Sachs, 15–17; Matthews, "The Los Angeles of the North," 461; Stephen J. Pitti, *The Devil in Silicon Valley: Northern California, Race, and Mexican Americans* (Princeton, NJ: Princeton University Press, 2003), 129.

11. David Naguib Pellow and Lisa Sun-Hee Park, *The Silicon Valley of Dreams* (New York: New York University Press, 2002), 23–45.

12. Linda Nash, *Inescapable Ecologies: A History of Environment, Disease, and Knowledge* (Berkeley: University of California Press, 2006), 129–134; Pulido, *Environmentalism and Economic Injustice*, 72–86.

13. Pitti, *The Devil in Silicon Valley*, 87.

14. Leslie, "The Biggest Angel of Them All"; Pitti, *The Devil in Silicon Valley*, 131.

15. Pellow and Park, *The Silicon Valley*, 59–62; Joan Dideon, *Where I Was From* (New York: Vintage Books, 2003), 102–127.

16. Rank Counties by Superfund Sites, http://scorecard.goodguide.com/envreleases/land/rank-counties.tcl?fips_state_code=06.

17. Pellow and Park, *The Silicon Valley*, 112–13; Amanda Hawes and David D. Pellow, "The Struggle for Occupational Health in Silicon Valley," in *Challenging the Chip: Labor Rights and Environmental Justice in the Global Electronics Industry*, ed. Ted Smith, David A. Sonnenfeld, and Davi Naguib Pellow (Philadelphia: Temple University Press, 2006), 120–28; Pellow and Park, *The Silicon Valley*, 73–79.

18. Hawes, "The Struggle for Occupational Health"; Pellow and Park, *The Silicon Valley*, 59–62; Andrew Szasz and Michael Meuser, "Unintended, Inexorable: The Production of Environmental Inequalities in Santa Clara, California," *American Behavioral Scientist* 43, no. 4 (January 2000): 602–32.

19. Robert Bullard, ed., *Growing Smarter: Planning for Regional Equity and Environmental Justice* (Cambridge, MA: MIT Press, 2006); Debra J. Salazar, "Gentrifying Ecotopia: A Brown Girl Looks at Home, Landscape, and Power," in *Starker Lecture Series*

2001: Visions of Natural Resources: Peeking into the Neighbor's Yard, comp. Bo Shelby and Sandy Arbogast (Corvallis: College of Forestry, Oregon State University, 2001), 18–35, http://ir.library.oregonstate.edu/xmlui/bitstream/handle/1957/22721/PeekingIntoTheNeighborsYard.pdf?sequence=5.

20. Sachs, "Virtual Ecology," 16.

21. *Proceedings: The First National People of Color Environmental Leadership Summit* (October 24–27, 1991), United Church of Christ, Commission for Racial Justice, Washington, DC.

The Workers and the Land

Toward a Just and Sustainable Future

9

"It's a Different World"
Using Oral Histories to Explore Working-Class Perceptions of Environmental Change

PETER FRIEDERICI

You can see a lot from atop a horse, and Doy Reidhead has seen it all. He is the iconic Marlboro cowboy forty years past his youthful prime, slim as a whip, hands calloused and leathered by the sun, eyes narrowed to a permanent squint. Part of his jaw is gone from the decades of holding tobacco chaw—he switched the plug to the other side so he could keep up the habit. He's rode horse, he says, about as far as anybody could in this day and age, and from that swaying vantage he's seen some things.

The landscape he looks out on is the arid grasslands of high-elevation Arizona, between the dried-up sand bed of the Little Colorado River and the overgrown pine woodlands of the Mogollon Rim. To the casual observer it might seem a perfect example of the wild and untrammeled West: widely scattered ranch houses looking over broad vistas of red-tinged plains, scrubby piñon-juniper thickets, sandstone draws that hold much of the best cattle feed. To the aficionado of a certain Western mythos it *is* Marlboro Country, a place where rugged, plainspoken individualists live or die by their own wits. To the historian, it might be a place where the long conflict between Anglo settlers and Native inhabitants, or between the settlers and nature itself, has played out. All these portraits of the arid West have been painted before. But what does the place look like to a lifelong resident? The answer is that in Reidhead's eyes the land has become something that is at once familiar and dramatically new—and not necessarily improved. It's a place where ecological changes have run rampant because ideas that seemed good at the time have proven to be bad, where an entire set of human values has changed, and where an honest ethic of pulling a hard living from the land has given way to a new economy that doesn't make sense to the working man, and perhaps not to the land itself.

It is through the practice of oral history that we have uncovered Reidhead's point of view. One of my students interviewed him in 2006 as part of an ongoing oral history project that I help coordinate at Northern Arizona University. My colleagues and I are interested in what primarily working-class people who have spent their lives living on the land have to say about environmental change. They're Native American farmers. They're the children of homesteaders. They're retired foresters. They have based an often hardscrabble living on learning the patterns of the place where they're rooted. Our project has added numerous recorded histories to our university library's archive, for use by future historians or environmental scientists. But it has also generated awareness among an increasingly urban public about how people who have worked the land see its changing patterns; we have used photos and excerpts from the interviews as the basis of several public exhibitions and events, as well as for a trade paperback book.[1]

Land of Federal Largesse

Only Native Americans have roots that go down farther into the rocky soil of the Little Colorado River Valley than Reidhead. His great-grandparents settled here in 1879, in the culmination of a great Mormon trek that helped stock the northern Arizona range with livestock they had driven from Utah. His great-grandfather was the first white child born in the area that would later become the town of Show Low—which received its name in honor of a card game that determined the owner of the area's first settlement.[2] Show Low stands at the edge of the ponderosa pine forests of the Mogollon Rim and the lower, open grasslands that slope down to the distant Little Colorado. By the time Reidhead was born here in 1933, the region had developed a modest but reliable economy based on lumbering and cattle. The town was tiny, the population entirely rural, the ethos strictly working class.

The archived video reveals Doy to be as plainspoken as his appearance is weather-beaten. "My dad was born in 1900, and he fell into the horses and cows," he told the interviewer, Norm Lowe. "In them days, that's all we knew. Horses was transportation, cows was livelihood. I remember Dad was a good cowboy. . . . When I come into the picture, I can remember horses and cows."[3]

It was a hard living, but at least it *was* a living. In the midst of the Great Depression, there was an advantage to a rural lifestyle: you could raise your own food. It was a lesson that imprinted on the young boy. And he really liked all those cattle and horses, always had it in the back of his mind that he wanted to work with them. It took him a while to find the opportunity. At age seventeen he married and had to find work. Before too long he was driving the winding roads down to the growing Sunbelt city of Phoenix, where a postwar building boom was creating an insatiable demand for lumber.

> My first job was a dollar-ten an hour, after I was married. That was 1951. We was married when we was seventeen, and you had to—there wasn't nothin' to make a livin' with except your two hands—work at the sawmill or work on the county roads. Jobs was scarce and hard to come by, and pay wasn't very big, but it didn't cost you much to live, either. And I fooled around and got in the truckin' business, buyin' and sellin' lumber, haulin' it to Phoenix. Then I went in the loggin' business. I worked for Southwest Forest Industries for twenty years, haulin' logs—loggin' contractor, do it all. But I always had this cow deal in the back of my head, and there it was, I wanted to go ranchin'.

After working part-time for other ranchers, in 1968 he finally had the opportunity to buy a small spread northeast of Show Low. A few years later he sold his trucking business so that he could devote himself to ranching full time. Almost a century after his forebears had arrived, he'd finally reached his goal of being a cowman.

But though he may have looked the part, Reidhead was scarcely akin to the independent cowboys of Hollywood's hazy cinematic sunsets. He was, rather, heir to a long tradition of dependence on the federal government. The pattern was set with the first Mormon settlers of the region, who despite their tradition of self-reliance in Utah were able to homestead the Mogollon Rim region only because federal troops were working to confine unruly members of the Apache tribe to designated reservations—which then became a good market for the dairy products Reidhead's grandfather raised.

The region's dependence on Washington only increased after that. It was the government that subsidized the development of the transcontinental railroads, including the Atlantic & Pacific line (later to become the Santa Fe, and still later the Burlington Northern Santa Fe) that paralleled the Little Colorado to the north of Show Low. It was this line that Reidhead's father used to ship loads of horses to Los Angeles during the Great Depression. The government provided railroad builders with incentives in the form of land grants comprising every other section along the rights of way, while retaining the other half of the sections under federal or state control. In the nineteenth and early twentieth centuries railroad companies received more than 130 million acres of federal land this way, or more than the total area of California.[4] The resulting checkerboard of public and private ownership continues to cause headaches for land managers, who have to deal with numerous artificial boundaries across wide-open landscapes that are, ecologically, all of a piece.

The two bulwarks of Doy Reidhead's personal economy—logging and cattle ranching—were also intimately tied to federal largesse. President Theodore Roosevelt created the modern US national forest system in 1905 to bring an end to what had been a free-for-all of clear-cutting and homesteading in the West's forested lands. That included the Sitgreaves National Forest in the region around Show Low.[5] When Reidhead trucked logs to Phoenix as a young man, they were coming primarily from either national forests or the two nearby Apache reservations, where the descendants of warriors who had held off American settlers for decades lived essentially as wards of the federal Bureau of Indian Affairs.

Finally, cattle grazing has long depended on the public lands held either by the federal government or the state of Arizona. On these arid plains and forests, livestock need a great deal of land to provide sufficient forage, and sites that could be productively and profitably homesteaded and ranched were few. As a result, ranchers typically claimed scattered sites around springs or along waterways, then grazed their herds on the common lands all around. This practice led to widespread overgrazing and, eventually, to the Taylor Grazing Act of 1934. Passed in response to the Dust Bowl, the act resulted in the fencing of much of the West's grasslands and ended, once and for all, the old cattleman's practice of allowing cattle to range freely across land of all ownerships before a roundup to separate the herds.[6] In its place came a permit system that allows a rancher to graze his cattle on designated federal or state lands, often at prices well below market rates.

The landscape that Doy Reidhead was born into, then, was not one in which rugged, working-class loners did what they thought was right, independent of central authority, but rather a place whose most important decisions were made by far-away federal bureaucrats. For a while those bureaucracies served as allies of the residents of Western rural areas; they got the railroads and highways built, developed the huge water projects that made possible cities like Phoenix, and kept low the fees for logging and grazing on federal lands. In exchange, Arizona's ranchers and loggers faced some restrictions—more or less onerous, depending on one's point of view—on how they could use the public domain. If there was a general sentiment to how Westerners saw the federal government in the mid-twentieth century, it was, as the historian and essayist Bernard DeVoto put it in a *Harper's* essay in 1947, "[G]et out and give us more money."[7] They wanted the federal dollars that subsidized their livelihoods and lifestyles, but they also wanted minimal interference in their day-to-day affairs.

That all changed—for Reidhead as for many others—with the flood of new federal land-management legislation that arrived in the 1960s and early 1970s. Roused by spreading evidence—such as that provided by Rachel Carson's *Silent Spring,* the burning of Ohio's Cuyahoga River, the building of Glen Canyon Dam in northern Arizona, and a notorious 1969 oil spill off the southern California coast—that their country's natural heritage was being unacceptably degraded by the pursuit of profit, Americans rallied to environmental causes as never before. In 1970 an estimated 20 million Americans took part in the first Earth Day. Legislators responded. In 1969 President Richard Nixon signed the watershed National Environmental Policy Act, which for the first time mandated a review of the environmental effects of management decisions on public lands. In the following year, he signed a bill authorizing the creation of the federal Environmental Protection Agency, as well as an important expansion in federal regulation of air pollution in the form of the Clean Air Act Extension. In 1972 Nixon signed the Clean Water Act, in 1973 the Endangered Species Act, in 1974 the Safe Drinking Water Act. He also presided over a suite of lesser decisions that affected federal land managers and rural residents, such as an executive order, in 1972, banning the use of poisons to control predators on federal lands. The tradition of environmental legislation continued through the Ford and Carter presidencies—especially, from the perspective of public-lands users in the West, in the 1976 passage of the

National Forest Management Act and the Federal Land Policy and Management Act. Together, these two pieces of legislation came to guide the management of the West's two biggest landholding agencies: the US Forest Service and the Bureau of Land Management.

The impact of all these new regulations was sweeping, but their overall import was clear: over the course of Reidhead's first decade as a full-time rancher, the set of residents and values over which the federal government had to exercise care suddenly expanded. It was no longer just ranchers, loggers, and livestock. Now the government's wards explicitly included endangered species as charismatic as bald eagles and as obscure as the Little Colorado spinedace, a small fish that inhabited the river's main stem and tributaries. The government also had to take into account any citizens, anywhere, who needed or wanted clean air, clean water, and unspoiled places. Suddenly local, working-class people were competing for resources and political attention with a more affluent, amenity-oriented group of Americans. If you had a ranch to sell, this change might bring you great profits. But if you wanted to keep working with your hands as you always had, producing food, lumber, or other primary resources, you were apt to find yourself hamstrung by new regulations and a changed set of priorities that viewed public lands as holding primarily recreational, even spiritual value.

Land of Unexpected Consequences

A century ago a young forest ranger named Aldo Leopold, newly posted to the sprawling Apache National Forest that runs east of Reidhead's ranch along the Arizona–New Mexico line, shot a wolf. That act was all in a day's work for a federal agent—or, indeed, for pretty much any white settler—at the time. But it had broad repercussions on Leopold's philosophy, which was to become an integral element of American thinking about wildlife and wildland management in the twentieth century. "I was young then, and full of trigger-itch," Leopold eventually wrote about the incident. "I thought that because fewer wolves meant more deer, that no wolves would mean hunters' paradise. But after seeing the green fire die, I sensed that neither the wolf nor the mountain agreed with such a view."[8] Leopold went on to become a high-ranking Forest Service official, then a pioneering professor of wildlife management at the University of Wisconsin, and finally a seminal environmental philosopher. His A Sand County Almanac espoused the idea that predators should be embraced, for both ecological and ethical reasons, as a critical part of ecosystems, and not eliminated as enemies.

Leopold is a classic example of an expert who had access to the historical record—he helped shape it through his policy decisions, teaching, and writings. But in Reidhead's oral history we can find valuable impressions of how evolving land-use policies shaped working-class lives throughout the twentieth century. In the early years of Reidhead's life, federal agencies strove to eliminate predators on the assumption, shared by the young Leopold, that doing so would improve conditions for livestock producers.[9] They failed even as they succeeded. Though they managed to extirpate wolves and grizzly bears from the Southwest, they weren't able to wipe out mountain lions or coyotes. Today, Reidhead said in his interview, packs of feral dogs constitute some of the principal predators on livestock in east-central Arizona. Meanwhile, conflicting desires about just what sort of animals ought to benefit from the land's forage worked against the interests of ranchers. For example, the state's native elk had been driven to extinction in the late nineteenth century by unregulated hunting for markets and personal subsistence. Beginning in 1913, state wildlife officials began relocating Rocky Mountain elk to northern Arizona to give state residents big game animals to hunt. They did well in a landscape scarce in predators—and newly rich in water sources thanks to the many stock tanks and check dams ranchers were placing on their spreads. Hunters were happy, but ranchers were not. They soon learned that there was no effective way to fence elk out. To this day ranchers and wildlife managers remain at loggerheads about how to deal with an elk population that has swelled to many tens of thousands.[10] As Reidhead said,

These elk go where the feed's at. . . . You don't rotate elk. . . . They go where they wanna go. . . . Everywhere you look. They'll take a browse country or a brush country that you use to winter on, and instead of just taking the leaves, they'll take the bark. Over there in that cliff rose country, and that mahogany— they just love to strip that mahogany to nothin'. It grows in these rock canyons, all these heavy sandstone rock canyons—beautiful place to winter cattle, you know. But the elk's pretty well ripped it.

For Reidhead, the burgeoning of the state's elk population represented a very literal government intrusion onto ranchland—one whose cost livestock producers were expected to shoulder without any compensation. It's a conflict that has, ironically, been made worse by the long campaign to rid the landscape of predators. Elk proliferated in large part because hunters and wildlife-control agents had wiped out their principal predators—wolves and grizzly bears. That did not make it any easier for most of the region's ranchers to support the current project to restore Mexican gray wolves to the Arizona–New Mexico border region, an effort that began with the release of captive-bred wolves in the area in 1996 and that continues today, dogged with much controversy.

For a diehard cattleman like Reidhead, allowing other animals to compete for forage has always been hard to stomach—even when the competitors are his otherwise beloved horses. One of the ranches he worked on and eventually managed was the Gibson Ranch, which bordered the Fort Apache Reservation, where wild horses roamed. When a snowstorm knocked the fences down, many of the horses turned up on the ranch, raising the prospect not only of competition for food, but also that these charismatic animals would, in the public's mind, warrant protection right where they were.

> We had lots of trees and canyons, and that Gibson Ranch was about twenty-five miles across the south boundary. And then you neighbored the Fort Apache Indian Reservation. Fences was always in bad shape, run more wild horses up there that come over the fence than you did cows. But that's some of the political politics we was into, see. . . .
>
> It had a big snowstorm just smashed the fences down, and them horses come up over there, got on the Forest Service, off the reservation. Nobody was cowboy enough to drive 'em back. They fixed the fence good, but left the horses on this side. So the old ranger that was up there, a great old guy, he just wanted the horses gone. And I'll tell you why he wanted 'em gone—he was afraid they'd make a wild horse refuge. Now here we're already gettin' into some stink. You see what I mean?
>
> He said, "If these horses don't get moved, we're gonna have trouble with this. They'll take this and make a wild horse refuge out of it."
>
> So he said, "I'll build the traps, and we'll salt and catch these horses."
>
> "All right, that's fine."
>
> "You take 'em to sale and sell 'em, and whatever you get is yours."
>
> They was unbranded, and on Forest Service land. So we built them traps

and salted. We caught 187 horses. I'd unload 'em out of the traps and load 'em in a trailer and haul 'em to sale. A hundred dollars was a big price on 'em. We had double the time we was gettin' paid for the horses, but it took a lot of time. . . . We pretty well cleaned it up. And then today—they had the big fire, three years ago, or four, the fire took out the fence, and now the horses, they got the same problem again.

For Reidhead, then, the values epitomizing the twentieth-century conservation movement countered how he wanted rangelands to operate. The federal Wild Horses and Burros Act (passed in 1971 as one of the Nixon-era environmental protection mandates) protected these iconic animals. Reidhead might be a horseman through and through, but in his pragmatic view these particular horses were pests rather than companions—competitors that would take forage away from valuable cattle.

But the conservation ideal that most affected how he was able to make a living was epitomized not by herds, but by a single animal: Smokey Bear. For most of the twentieth century, the Forest Service waged all-out war on fire. In the Southwest's arid forests, the agency firmly ignored a great deal of evidence that wildfire was a naturally occurring and ecologically important phenomenon that burned off dried grasses and fallen pine needles and thinned out young pine stands. Once firefighting began in earnest in Arizona, after World War II, those ecological services were lost. In response, the region's forests and woodlands grew much more dense, and as a result fires in recent decades have been far more damaging than those that came before.[11] The process culminated, at least in the Show Low region, in 2002 with the Rodeo-Chediski Fire, a monstrous conflagration of 468,000 acres that destroyed some 481 structures and forced the evacuation of Reidhead's old hometown.

But to ranchers the ecological changes forced by a new fire regime were worse than the threat to houses and neighborhoods. As trees proliferated, they both made it more difficult to conduct roundups and out-competed the grasses that cattle could eat. Reidhead tried to fight against this wave of ecological change by removing small piñon pines and juniper trees (known as cedars in local parlance). He burned them, pushed them over with a bulldozer, cleared swaths with a heavy cable stretched between two dozers. But, over many thousands of acres of ranchland, it was a losing battle.

I pushed thousands of acres of cedars. . . . It [the bulldozer] doubled your capacity. But, you know, one man can only do so much. I pushed thousands of acres of cedars on this ranch, on the Gibson Ranch—I kept a Cat workin' all the time. . . . Pushed and burned. Cables will just kill half of 'em and leave half of 'em roots in the ground. Tried that route. A lot of these trees are no higher than that chair, and you couldn't cable 'em. You could cable the mature trees, you couldn't cable the little saplings. In other words, all at once, in about a ten-year cycle, it just closed the country off with piñon and juniper. And this ain't changed a bit. I can take you up there and show you two-thirds of it; you can't even get through it a-horseback.

This, then, was the constellation of factors that Reidhead faced as he matured as a rancher. The federal government's long-running campaign to remove predators never quite succeeded; in the absence of wolves and grizzly bears, smaller predators continued to prey on livestock. Meanwhile, ever-growing herds of elk and some wild horses—that wolves or grizzly bears might have kept in check—continued to compete with his cattle for forage. Trees proliferated where grass had grown before, either because of fire-suppression policies or because of increasingly stringent logging regulations.

Perhaps most significant, the expectations that Americans had of their national forests—and of all public lands—were changing quickly. In Reidhead's youth, the Arizona forests and rangelands had functioned as storehouses of resources to be harvested by hardworking people. Now they were turning into scenic backdrops against which wealthy, white-collar urbanites could play at a Western idyll, while traditional livelihoods such as ranching were forced into the back seat.

If you look at the old pictures, you'll see big purdy pines and lots of open space. You see what I mean? That was the history, when the pioneers come to this forest, that's what it looked like. If you don't believe me, dig up some of the old pictures. . . . The Forest Service come in there and just took over this—put out all the fires, and did no thinning of any kind, just protect the trees. And they had the ways and means and could hire enough men to put the fires out, see. So it stopped the lightning fires. That's what happened then. Then we get into this period where we got all these people comin' to Arizona. All of 'em want to go to the pine trees and cool off. Ninety percent of the people live in the valley, the lowlands. And the big kick, everybody come to the mountains. Well, the Forest Service owned the whole danged thing. The Forest Service is tryin' to please the ranchers, and the Forest Service is tryin' to please the tourists.

Land of Scenery

Ranchers are tightly bound to the land, but Reidhead moved around as his career progressed. He bought his first ranch in 1968, then sold it in 1974 to buy a bigger spread made up of two other ranches that included a large percentage of state land. Working with his sons and with a few hired hands, he was able to run 2,300 head on it, and made a decent living for about a decade.

> It'd work good one year, and the next year it'd reverse itself, due to the market change. You know, you gotta live with the market. One year I could get sixty cents [a pound] for my calves, loaded on the truck, off the cows. And I'd take 'em to the feedlot and feed 'em, put corn and grain in 'em. The next spring when I had 'em weighin' seven hundred pounds, they was worth fifty cents. So I didn't make a dollar—I lost money. Feedin' cattle, when the market changes, calves can jump—in them days, ten cents was big. But it would usually drop ten cents one way or the other. Well, ten cents is the difference in success and failure. We operated this ranch that way for eleven years. It was doin' good, keepin' the bills paid, doin' great.

But it could not last. Once again decisions made in Washington cast a big shadow on the landscape. The federal government wanted to resolve a long-simmering land dispute between northern Arizona's Navajo and Hopi peoples—which was fueled largely by high-dollar politics involving the development of energy resources on those reservations—by engineering a land swap between the two tribes.[12] The complex deal involved purchasing some private ranch lands and transferring them to the tribes. Against his expectations, Reidhead became part of the deal when his land was purchased by another rancher whose own ranch was part of the land transferred to Navajo ownership. Because Reidhead ranched largely on public land, he had no choice in the matter.

But his life-long resilience allowed him to continue ranching. In the mid-1980s he bought the Gibson Ranch, which included a permit to graze livestock each summer on national forest land along the Mogollon Rim.

That worked for a few years, until the Forest Service cut the number of cattle that ranchers could run under the permit terms.

> Everybody was tryin' to run the Forest Service. Maybe you've been around enough to know what was goin' on. It was one guy bangin' here, and one guy bangin' there. Anyway, in three years, me runnin' the ranch to the best of my ability according to their speculations and expectations, keepin' my cattle clean, keepin' my fences up, keepin' the tanks clean, keepin' the work done, I thought I was doin' all I could do.
>
> Well, anyway, they decided the permit needed [to be] cut in half. So they cut it in half. Well, then my financiers that financed the whole thing, they got nervous. Here we buy a million-dollar forest permit, and now it's worth a half million dollars. So I had to compensate to that. And then, you know, just one thing led to another. After that, I decided to sell the damned place, try to pay the debts.

He did, and that unwanted opportunity suddenly forced Reidhead to settle down for good on some land he already owned along Silver Creek, near the town of Holbrook and the Little Colorado River. It's open grassland, far from the National Forest and its conflicts.

> I kept about 20,000 acres here, and I had a section of deeded land here, with this house on it. My brother built my fireplace, and I didn't want to leave my fireplace. We was too old to go anywhere else, so we decided to raise a few horses and a few cows and settle down so we could make a livin'. That's where we are today. . . . Yeah, and we've pretty well kept the debt paid on the whole place. . . . We've been big time, and now we're little time. But at my age, I'm about where I want to be.

Through much of his life Reidhead's story was hardly uncommon. Like much of the West, the Arizona hinterlands were full of men and women who worked with their hands, cut pines, wrangled livestock, drove trucks. But that has changed, too. As he looks back on more than seven decades on the land, what strikes Reidhead as the greatest transformation on the landscape is not visible, but rather hidden: namely, that his livelihood, and with it a long-worked set of skills and experiences, has become so rare. His story is one of loss. Working ranches have become scarce, and with them a way of life is vanishing. They dwindled in part because of the ecological, bureaucratic, and social changes with which Reidhead and other ranchers have had to contend, though the major factors were large-scale economic changes that made it far cheaper to raise cattle on massive feedlots in Colorado or Oklahoma—or to import beef from overseas. What ranches are left in the Show Low area tend to be hobby ranches, bought and managed as playgrounds or tax shelters for the wealthy.

> It don't hurt to be a millionaire to ranch, but it sure helps. I doubt seriously that—I think there might be only one ranch left in this country that was here when I come to this country. . . . I could show you probably 15,000 head of cattle runnin' here when I come here thirty-one years ago. There was probably 15,000, 20,000 head of cattle. And I don't believe you can go count 2,000 today. That's what a drastic change we've had. Can you believe that? . . . It just got too hard to survive on. . . . Most of the ol' boys who had ranches are dead, and their kids either didn't have it in their system—you gotta love it to do it—or else have some money siphoned in to you from somewhere. You know what I mean?

That's a profound change, as a landscape once given over almost entirely to resource extraction has turned into one that is valued primarily for recreation. "They found out that their scenery is worth more than their timber," Reidhead said of the neighboring Fort Apache Reservation, from which he hauled a lot of timber in the 1950s. The same is true of national forest land, and even the private lands embedded within the national forest landscape. What were hardscrabble, workaday surroundings have become a recreational playground for urban residents—especially from the Phoenix megalopolis—willing to spend big money for a weekend retreat among the Show Low area's tall pines.

> What the Apache–Sitgreaves produced—that's all they had to offer. That was the sole means of everybody's financial opportunities in this part of the state of Arizona, was the timber and the ranching. There wasn't no jobs, there wasn't no little-bitty towns. And then people would raise gardens and milk cows—you know, just existed. We're talkin' about the complete turnover. And what turned this over is all this population explosion, and then the money change[d the] picture. Anybody can finance a car, everybody can get a credit card. Well, you can't pay the damned credit cards off, you never get the car paid for, but you . . . pay it off on the credit card to get another-un. I don't know how it works, but it works.
>
> Let's take the town like Show Low—was the poorest town that I ever seen. And now it's the richest town you ever seen, property values 300 percent higher,

or 1,000 percent higher, and everybody can find a job. All kinda jobs. They got all these big schools to run. They got all the big-city jobs. . . . Anybody that had the property has more money than they can spend now. It's a different world. I don't think the Forest Service is interested in sellin' any grass, or sellin' any timber. I think them days has come and gone. They've pretty well proved it.

This, then, is Doy Reidhead's world as revealed to us through the window of oral history. From the vantage point of more than seven decades on the land, he looks back on an intimately experienced landscape that has, despite surface similarities, been transformed into something almost diametrically unlike what it was. Grasslands have grown into woodlands, livestock pastures have become homes for elk, ranches have become playgrounds for wealthy magnates from the construction or financial services industries. Expensive vacation homes dot the landscape. The towns are full of weekend visitors who bring their big-city values with them. And who produces the resources those people need? Not the residents of Show Low—rather, it is rural residents in British Columbia, Siberia, Brazil, and the other places that, in a globalized economy, have become vital nodes in the North American supply chain. It is, indeed, a different world. In this telling, Doy Reidhead is anything but the prototypical independent cowboy testing his will against nature's blank slate. He is, rather, a pawn—rich in land but still of the working class, and buffeted by large-scale ecological, economic, and social forces that have constantly tested his resilience. It is to his credit that he has, in their face, more or less stayed put (and, for that matter, stayed married to the same woman for six decades) while so many others have not.

Land of Common Ground

Oral history, the labor historian Alice Hoffman has written, "makes possible the preservation of the life experience of persons who do not have the literary talent or leisure to write their memoirs. In this way it facilitates a new kind of history—a history not of the captains, kings, and presidents but of farmers, workers, immigrants, and the like."[13] That close-to-the-ground experience is very much what we have wanted to capture through our oral history project. By recording and archiving stories of the land, we work toward an ideal of having the land speak for itself about how it functions and how it has changed over time. We fully recognize that this is an ideal we will never reach. But we are persuaded that the stories of those who have experienced and lived environmental change are an important way marker in pointing toward a more comprehensive understanding of that change than we might otherwise attain.

It is a particular virtue of oral history that the interviews we record are conducted without an agenda, except the very broad one of documenting stories of the land. As a journalist, I've conducted many interviews with rural residents like Doy Reidhead, but generally in pursuit of information or opinion about a particular theme or story. I might interview Reidhead about his thoughts on the reintroduction of Mexican wolves in eastern Arizona, or about changes in the management of state grazing lands, or about the prospect of the development of wind energy projects in his region. In all these cases I would probably at the outset of the interview have a preconceived notion about what to look for. I would remain highly conscious about how Reidhead's words and opinions fit into the larger societal context, and often controversy, that I am trying to report. I might well view Reidhead less as an individual than as an example: an example, say, of a working rancher opposed to the reintroduction of wolves, or in need of an economic boost from wind turbines. As a result, the conversation would likely be bounded, and perhaps guarded.

With oral history, our goal is different, because at least in the process of conducting the interview we ideally make no judgments about how what we are hearing fits into the larger context. We remain aware of the latter, of course, and may pose questions based on it, may prod memories or ask for more details or point out how one account agrees with or differs from others we have heard, but our goal is to the greatest extent possible to let narrators speak for themselves, to tell their own stories the way they remember and understand them.

There is a very fine line here: much of the best journalism is based on exactly the kind of open-ended interviewing I'm describing, and historians have pointed out that oral histories are shaped by who the interviewers and narrators are, what relationships and expectations exist between them, and what sort of questions the interviewer asks.[14] But in the continuum of ways in which a researcher of any stripe could go to rural, working-class residents in pursuit of information, an oral history interview can at least approach that ideal of letting those narrators speak for themselves, without ideological expectation.

One theme that we have found running through a number of the oral histories we've recorded is that ranchers (and other rural residents) and environmentalists share many areas of agreement. We journalists often focus on obvious points of controversy, such as opinions on the reintroduction of wolves, on the politics of climate change, or on stocking numbers for cattle on public rangelands. But we do so at the risk of ignoring the many points of agreement shared by environmentalists and members of the working class. Reidhead is no supporter of the Endangered Species Act, but he does decry the conversion of ranchland to vacation-home developments—which is a serious threat to the continued survival of some species—as thoroughly as any environmentalist might. Whether engaged in ecological restoration or in the redress of environmental injustices, activists might do well to take note of the unexpected alliances that may be the product of careful and unmediated listening. Even those perceived as opponents may have valuable stories and perspectives—and may in some cases prove to be allies. It's worth listening to learn where points of common ground may lie.

Our oral history project has certainly revealed many perspectives on the land, and different goals both for the land itself and for the people living on it. To be sure, controversies abound. But we've seen a couple of encouraging signs. First, a common theme that runs through the narratives is a profound love of place. Whether expressed, as Reidhead said, as a desire to remain by the fireplace his brother built, or as a respect for family tradition, or as a desire to see a creek or meadow or patch of forest revived to health, love of place appears to be more than circumstantially linked to long tenure. Second, a number of the narrators we have interviewed, such as ranchers and Native American farmers, are involved in projects aimed at restoring riparian areas, fish habitats, or healthy grasslands—and aimed, at the same time, at improving their bottom lines. To us, these are signs that point toward a connection between the ecological and the economic, and they hint that the many Doy Reidheads out there may, in the future, have a bit more to do with their own fate than was the case in the past.

Reidhead's story is a case study in how globalization has changed a rural landscape: the extraction of primary resources has been outsourced to other countries even as the local landscape has come to be valued primarily as a recreational amenity. But it may be that this trend does not point in only one direction. Connections between the ecological and economic health of agricultural areas are increasingly part of a public dialogue. Questions about oil prices, food security, and the safety of a heavily industrialized food supply are instilling an ever-greater interest in local production of food and other resources. Some of Reidhead's ranching neighbors have begun direct sales of grass-raised, local beef to locavore consumers—and a few have even begun raising organic vegetables for sale, too. Urban residents look to connect with the rural areas around them or to experience the open spaces and agricultural heritage that rangelands represent. In northern Arizona, some residents now volunteer their time on ranches so that they can monitor wildlife, control invasive plants, or remove old, poorly designed fences. Yes, stories from working-class, rural residents like Doy Reidhead may focus on large part on a perceived loss of local control to distant bureaucratic or economic forces, or outline how changes in values have exacerbated conflicts over western landscapes. Yet by casting light on some common values they might point the way to surprising new means of cooperation. Careful listening to such stories might yet inspire a broader spectrum of a region's people to decide, with their voices and with the work of their hands, what their place should look like.

NOTES

1. Transcripts and, in many cases, video versions of the interviews are available at http://archive.library.nau.edu/cdm/ (from there, search for "ecological oral histories"). Thirteen excerpted narratives from the project, including Doy Reidhead's, are collected in *What Has Passed and What Remains: Oral Histories of Northern Arizona's Changing Landscapes,* ed. Peter Friederici (Tucson: University of Arizona Press, 2010). More details about the project, including some video excerpts, are available at www.What HasPassed.net.

2. The Mormon settlement of the Little Colorado River Valley area, including the roles of some in the Reidhead family, is detailed in James H. McClintock, *Mormon Settlement in Arizona* (Tucson: University of Arizona Press, 1985); Will C. Barnes, *Arizona Place Names* (Tucson: University of Arizona Press, 1988; reissue of 1935 edition), 249.

3. All excerpts from Doy Reidhead are taken from his oral history interview with Norm Lowe, conducted April 3, 2006, at Reidhead's ranch near Holbrook, Arizona, and archived at the Northern Arizona University Cline Library Colorado Plateau Archives, http://archive.library.nau.edu/cdm/.

4. Lloyd J. Mercer, *Railroads and Land Grant Policy: A Study in Government Intervention* (New York: Academic Press, 1982), 6.

5. What later became the Sitgreaves was first set aside as the Black Mesa Forest Reserve in 1898, as described in Robert D. Baker et al., *Timeless Heritage: A History of the Forest Service in the Southwest,* USDA Forest Service publication FS-409 (College Station, TX: Intaglio, 1988), 25.

6. Some historians have argued that the Taylor Grazing Act essentially allowed private interests, especially ranchers, to capture Western public lands for their own purposes, as reviewed in Karen R. Merrill, *Public Lands and Political Meaning: Ranchers, the Government, and the Property Between Them* (Berkeley: University of California Press, 2002).

7. Bernard DeVoto, "The West against Itself," *Harper's,* January 1947, 1–13; "[G]et out," 8.

8. Aldo Leopold, *A Sand County Almanac, with Other Essays on Conservation from Round River* (New York: Oxford University Press, 1966), 130.

9. Michael J. Robinson provides the details about federal antipredator campaigns in *Predatory Bureaucracy: The Extermination of Wolves and the Transformation of the West* (Boulder: University Press of Colorado, 2005).

10. The controversy about managing elk in Arizona is well described by Lloyd Robert Breeding in "Livestock Grazing on Anderson Mesa and Its Impact on Wildlife in a Semi-Arid Grassland," MLS thesis, Northern Arizona University, 2005.

11. For Southwestern forests, twentieth-century ecological changes are described in Peter Friederici, ed., *Ecological Restoration of Southwestern Ponderosa Pine Forests* (Washington, DC: Island Press, 2003).

12. Created by Congress in 1974, the Navajo–Hopi relocation program authorized federal funding allowing the acquisition by the Navajo Nation of federal and private land as a partial means of resolving long-standing land disputes. Barry Goldwater helped pass the bill creating the program, which was and remains highly controversial, as Ward Churchill relates in *Struggle for the Land: Native American Resistance to Genocide, Ecocide, and Colonization* (San Francisco: City Lights Books, 2002).

13. Alice Hoffman, "Reliability and Validity in Oral History," in *Oral History: An Interdisciplinary Anthology,* ed. David K. Dunaway and Willa K. Baum (Nashville, TN: American Association for State and Local History in cooperation with the Oral History Association, 1984), 67–73; "makes possible the," 72.

14. For example, James West Davidson and Mark Hamilton Lytle describe the challenges in assessing the completeness of early oral histories of freed slaves: "The View from the Bottom Rail," in *After the Fact: The Art of Historical Detection* (New York: Knopf, 1985), 147–77.

10

Working Wilderness

Ranching, Proprietary Rights to Nature,
Environmental Justice, and Climate Change

JONI ADAMSON

R ising from the surrounding grasslands, the Peloncillo Mountains appear alternately blue or pink, depending on your angle of vision and the position of the sun. They are not steep and rough like the castellated Chiricahua Mountains to the west, but instead ramble for one hundred miles along the Arizona–New Mexico Border before they merge with the Sierra Madre in Mexico. Some refer to these mountains as "islands" because they seem to float in a golden sea of native grasses that cover the valley floors and line the creek beds and river banks. Native grasses, including Blue grama (*Bouteloua gracilis*), Black grama (*Bouteloua eriopoda*), Tabosa (*Hilaria mutica*), and Sacaton (*Sporobolus wrightii*), are not the only ones that can be found in the valleys. Lehmann lovegrass (*Eragrostis lehman-niana*), a perennial originally from southern Africa and often referred to as an "exotic," has spread rapidly since it was introduced in the 1930s as a remedy for erosion and overgrazing.

I learned more about these grassland seas, and how threats to their survival are linked to climate change, when I was working at the University of Arizona's Sierra Vista campus, which is five miles as the crow flies from the United States–Mexico border. While teaching a course on environmental issues in American nature writing, I invited an environmental activist to come and speak to my students; this activist advocated removing cattle from all public lands west of the Mississippi because of the damage grazing does to ecosystems. I also invited Bill Miller Jr., owner of the Post Office

Canyon Ranch, to speak to my students. I wanted students to hear both sides of debates over the effects of grazing. Miller is a past president of the Malpai Borderlands Group (MBG), an alliance of small-scale ranchers dedicated to protecting two things that are widely regarded as contradictory: arid grasslands ecosystems and the cattle-ranching way of life. Organized in 1993, the MBG immediately became controversial because the thirty-five ranchers who formed the alliance invited academic grasslands scientists, the Bureau of Land Management, the US Forest Service, and the Nature Conservancy, groups traditionally disdained by ranchers, to work with them as they sought to restore grasslands that had been seriously damaged by overgrazing and desertification.

In 1997 Miller invited me to come see for myself the results of the group's collaboration.[1] I had the pleasure of visiting his ranch and meeting his aunt and his ninety-year-old father, and listening to them talk about their experiences living in a "working wilderness." This term was coined by photographer and author Jay Dusard, who is also a member of the MBG. In the afterword to Dan Dagget's *Beyond the Rangeland Conflict,* Dusard observes that in arguing for a working wilderness, ranchers are not rearticulating the view that humans hold dominion over all nonhuman creatures. MBG ranchers do not claim that livestock grazing is innocent of blame for the damage that has occurred in western North American grasslands over the past century. In fact, they acknowledge the mistakes of their forebears. Today they are radically altering the ways in which they graze their cattle while continuing to claim the right to derive a living from the land. At the same time, they are working to sustain, in the words of Dusard, "wildlife and ecosystems, livestock and other productive uses."[2]

Over the course of the next five years, in interviews with Miller and other small-scale ranchers, I immersed myself in debates—pro and con—surrounding management of livestock and grasslands in the arid Southwest. In 1999, for example, I attended one of the workshops that the MBG held for the public. I do not claim to be an expert on land management. I defer to Dan Dagget and the work he is doing with ranchers all over America who are forming alliances to experiment with new methods of grazing and revegetation of arid grasslands. Dagget explains that the reason there is so much attention focused on the efforts of groups like the MBG—who are at the vanguard of a growing movement in the West—is that the Western range is "in worse shape than even some of the most alarming assessments would have us believe." The successes of these groups, which have been widely reported in news stories and peer-reviewed scientific journals, call attention to how much more work there is to do on the Western range.[3]

More recently, the grazing techniques being used by most of the ranching alliances in Dagget's book, first described in 1988 by Alan Savory in *Holistic Resource Management,* have returned dramatically to the public imagination because of a 2013 TED talk that Savory delivered, titled "How to Fight Desertification and Reverse Climate Change." In twenty-two minutes Savory argues that finding technological alternatives to fossil fuel will be only one part of the fight against climate change. This is because fossil fuels are not the only cause of climate change. One of the largest causes of climate change is desertification, which Savory defines as the process by which humans degrade arid grasslands so badly with their activities that it becomes bare ground. Savory goes on to advocate something that most environmentalists would consider unthinkable—using cattle, sheep, goats, and other vilified domesticated animals in desertified spaces to mimic the density of grazing herds of the wild animals that once populated most of the world's vast grasslands. These animals, he argues, if grazed properly, can be used to encourage revegetation. Savory specifies that he is referring to arid grassland ecosystems that have evolved in places that have months of humidity followed by months of dryness. These are the places where "modern range science," a term Savory uses ironically to refer to twentieth-century land management strategies, has been employed to bad results. Around the world, these strategies have been imposed on ranchers and traditional pastoralists, often by government scientists and managers. Over the past one hundred years, from the Navajo Nation in the American Southwest to the Horn of Africa, once-healthy pastoralist economies have been degraded to the point that war, homelessness, social breakdown, poverty, and hunger have resulted.[4]

Viewed from satellite images, Savory observes, it is easy to see that desertification is spreading so rapidly around the globe that it is now a problem on five continents. In some of these places, following Savory's methods, livestock managers are attempting to mimic the patterns of wild herds of animals, and in this way to effectively address desertification and encourage the regrowth of vegetation. Large wild herds, Savory argues, once traversed grasslands, never dwelling for too long in one place, as they sought to avoid predators through continuous movement and the safety of their own sheer density. Savory's theory is that by grazing their domesticated animals in similar patterns, humans might be able to reverse some of the worst effects of desertification.

Clearly, twenty-two-minute TED talks do not allow for in-depth exploration of any one topic. Environmental journalist Chris Clarke points to this problem as he rightly observes that Savory should have used the words "desert" and "desertification" more precisely.[5] Many deserts are not a phenomenon of anthropogenic activities. Some species of bunchgrasses, for example, can live for centuries if untrammeled, and did not evolve in relationship to grazing animals. The seemingly bare ground of many deserts is actually a result of cryptobiotic soil crusts: self-regulating systems that can often hold seed banks of diverse assemblages of annual plants. Clarke's point is that Savory should have emphasized that not all bare ground should be seen as an outcome of climate change. The Sonoran Desert of North America, for example, sits at a lower elevation than the high desert grasslands where the MBG graze their cattle, and did not evolve in relation to ungulates.

As Kimberly N. Ruffin and I argue in the introduction to *American Studies, Ecocriticism, and Citizenship: Thinking and Acting in the Local and Global Commons,* and as the case studies in that collection illustrate, discussion of climate change and resource depletion is becoming increasingly heated, and ecological politics are becoming more visible, even among the most recalcitrant national, cultural, corporate, and social groups, because of the monumental problems that have arisen from the catastrophic consequences of rapid environmental change. Glaciers are melting at alarming rates, and large swaths of the world's grazing lands are turning into dusty, unfertile ground that is not capable of holding greenhouse gases or moisture. In the face of these rapidly spreading environmental disasters, it is common to hear policy makers, corporate business leaders, scientists, and environmentalists referring to concepts such as "global ecological commons" or "the global citizen," and discussing who has the right to speak for nature. But those who talk about saving global ecological commons areas, including World Bank executives, corporate agribusiness executives, or mainstream environmental leaders, are not always local to a given commons area. Indeed, the knowledges of local peoples or workers-in-nature are often dismissed in favor of global financial imperatives.[6]

In this essay, then, I will illustrate how workers-in-nature who understand the principles of environmental justice are entering into the struggle over who has a right to own, manage, and speak for nature. I will focus on the ways that members of the MBG take their place as global citizens, and claim a right to be part of conversations dealing with the health of the world's commons—and more specifically, the world's arid grasslands. I will examine how members of this group are putting Alan Savory's controversial theories about holistic livestock management into practice as they seek to be part of the solution to some of the most complex causes of climate change. To set these theories, claims, and practices into a context where they can be better understood, I will place MBG activities into a longer history that accounts for the removal of the Chiricahua Apache from the United States–Mexico borderlands in the late nineteenth century and the subsequent colonization of the grasslands by MBG forebears from the southern American states, including Texas. I will then discuss how drought and human error led to the decline of "native" grasses and the spread of "exotic" grasses or trees, such as Lehmann lovegrass and the velvet mesquite tree (*Prosopis velutina*), and explain why the use of these two words to describe diverse species is becoming increasingly problematic. Finally, I offer an illustration of how "telling stories about our stories"—to paraphrase William Cronon's description of the analytical process—can lead to better environmental practices.[7] I demonstrate how MBG ranchers are entering into alliances with other groups of workers-in-nature. From Arizona to Kenya, these ranchers and pastoralists are confronting social justice problems as they attempt to be part of the solution to global climate change.

Small-Scale Ranching and Climate Change

Bill Miller Jr. talked to my students about the ranches located on both sides of the United States–Mexico border, in the Animas, San Bernardino, and San Pedro River Valleys, which all span the international boundary. Most of these ranches are family owned, and some families who live on them have been there for up to six generations. They are considered small-scale ranches because most run fewer than fifty head of cattle and require a second income to stay afloat. One member of the household might work for the Forest Service, at a public school, for the Cooperative Extension Service, at the local community college, or at a university. Unlike large corporate ranches that feed cattle corn to "finish" them at Concentrated Animal

Feeding Operations, or CAFOS, which are blamed for the increase of green-house gases (methane, in this case) caused by the collection of large amounts of animal waste in one place, most small-scale ranchers "grass feed" their cattle on the rangelands surrounding their homes, thus dispersing the animals' waste. As explained in his TED Talk, Savory argues that grass feeding cattle and keeping their waste out of concentrated feedlots contributes to revegetation of desertified land. The animals are herded in high densities and moved rapidly from one pasture to another so that they disperse the seeds of the grasses they eat in dung that they then trample into the soil, where it fertilizes the seeds. Cattle are also removing dead tissue from grass plants, and so exposing plants and soil to the warming rays of the sun. The pounding of hooves moving across the land also increases the soil's ability to absorb water and to support growing grasses that store carbon and methane. Some critics of Savory's methods rightly caution that field tests do not always verify his claims for water sequestration, nor will his methods work in every type of arid grassland; other commentators are cautiously optimistic about Savory's goals to reduce desertification, poverty, and hunger in regions where ranching and pastoralist populations make up the majority of people, such as in the Horn of Africa.[8]

Miller and some of his neighbors began experimenting with Savory's methods and formed the MBG during a decade when drought and passage of the North American Free Trade Agreement (NAFTA) combined to put a number of ranchers out of business. Conditions in the early 1990s had been generally dry but a strong La Niña intensified drought conditions in 1994, and the economic ripple effect was felt all across the border region and deep into Mexico. Politics also played a role in this crisis. The NAFTA went into effect in 1994 and reduced tariffs on trade in live cattle and beef products. Mexican livestock flooded US border state cattle auctions and prices plummeted.[9] This kept the profits ranchers could earn on each cow low, while at the same time the cost of their vehicles, equipment, feed, and fuel kept rising. This was an especially severe problem for Animas and San Bernardino ranchers, who had little financial margin in the face of environmental vagaries and competition from non-US ranchers.

Costs of ranching were also driven up by the unprecedented wave of migration spurred by the effects of NAFTA, militarization of the border, and the effects of climate change. This embroiled the region in heated debates over undocumented immigration and border management. Over the course of my fieldwork from 1997 to 2002, I interviewed ranchers who took positions on all sides of these issues and there is much disagreement from ranch to ranch. Approximately 20 percent of the immigrants who pass through the southern US border come through Cochise County, Arizona, where several of the MBG's ranchers live. In *Bird on Fire*, Andrew Ross notes that these immigrants might be more aptly referred to as "climate refugees" because the post-1994 wave of immigration was set in motion as much "by drought, desertification, and the proliferation of extreme weather events" such as La Niña in Mexico as it was by NAFTA. As I detail in "Seeking the Corn Mother," many of these refugees were corn farmers in Mexico, who, because of environmental forces, drought, and desertification in their own county, together with the political and economic effects of NAFTA, could not compete with large-scale agribusiness and federally subsidized corn production in the United States. Thus, climate refugees' lives are put at serious risk when they migrate, and many die on the US side of the international border. This illustrates that the same economic and environmental forces that drive immigration put stress on the livelihoods of small-scale US ranchers.[10]

To address the economic and environmental threat of drought and desertification, members of the MBG, in a joint legal agreement, turned their lands into a commons area by placing conservation easements on their lands that prevent each rancher who is part of the alliance from ever selling to developers. They have pledged to keep the land under their joint care—open, unfragmented, and undeveloped. In return for the conservation easements, members of the group gain the opportunity to share the resources of what they call a "grassbank" that can help them survive the ups and downs of the weather and the market.[11] If one rancher receives too little rain and is facing economic crisis because of lack of feed for his cattle, and another has been the recipient of the Southwest's often uneven rains and has grasses growing abundantly on his land, then the two ranchers share these grass resources and in this way protect each other from losing their land during bad years. Also, as Alan Savory discovered in Zimbabwe through decades of experimenting, resting the land or removing livestock from a piece of ground during drought, by itself, will not lead to the return or increase of the vegetation. As Dan Dagget explains, on land that has been severely degraded, in places where there is humidity for only part of the year, such as the Jornada Experimental Range north of Las Cruces, New

Mexico, cattle and sheep can be excluded for decades and the grasses will not come back. Where centuries of overgrazing and drought have caused grasses to disappear and allowed woody species such as creosote bush and mesquite to "invade," even massive interventions, in the form of bulldozing woody species and reseeding with native grasses, can fail. Field tests indicate, however, that the reintroduction of grazing patterns that mimic the movements of ancient herds can bring back or increase the growth of grasses, sometimes in as little as one year.

Proprietary Rights to Nature and Environmental Justice

In his study of the political resurgence of the notion of global commons areas, sociologist Michael Goldman points out that at the core of any ecological politics, be it radical or neoliberal, is the issue of proprietary rights to nature—who owns, manages, speaks for, and gets to make decisions about the future of "Nature" or "Wilderness." In this debate false dualisms are imagined that muddle environmental politics. "North is pitted against South, global versus local, economic growth versus subsistence, abundance versus scarcity and rational science versus irrational [local] beliefs [and practices]."[12] These dualisms then become the apparatus of institutions, such as the World Bank, World Trade Organization, or NAFTA, which often erase the significance of local knowledges, specific places, and particular groups of people in favor of global economic objectives.

Small-scale ranchers in the American Southwest enter the struggle over global economic objectives and ecological imperatives by redefining nature as what the MBG has called "working wilderness."[13] This is a controversial move because it weighs into ongoing debates about livestock grazing in national forests and public lands in the American West. Questions circle around the issue of whether livestock grazing is being conducted in ways that protect or damage global commons areas such as the world's carbon-sequestering grasslands. The MBG's redefinition of wilderness as a space in which a working-class community has a right to make a living confronts the notion that what others define as a global or national ecological treasure should be cordoned off and protected for the good of the planet as a whole. Since most ranchers in America are economically dependent on grazing their animals on public lands, the struggle over who gets to speak for common lands—ranchers or the public—can be quite fraught with controversy. The MBG argues that since private ranching lands and the health of public grasslands can only survive together, the fate of the nation's grasslands is bound up with the fate of the ranchers.

These ranchers understand that if they cannot show a profit they will lose their land. They fear that if they lose their land because of economics, the land will fall into the hands of developers. Sale and division of the land would result not only in a loss of cultural diversity when ranchers are forced to move to the cities and find other means of supporting themselves, but also in an accompanying loss of biodiversity. Fences, housing developments, or potentially dangerous paved roads prevent wildlife from roaming free through the open spaces between Mexico's Sierra Madre and the Peloncillo and Chiricahua Mountains, on which ranchers depend for their economic survival. Ecologically degraded grasslands can be restored, ranchers argue, but the land—and the nonhuman species that depend on this land for survival—can never recover once the land is subdivided and paved over.

The redefinition of desert grasslands as working wilderness has implications for both social and environmental justice. As I have written in *American Indian Literature, Environmental Justice and Ecocriticism,* oversimplified concepts of wilderness often excuse humans from accounting for how their own lives or work have impacts far outside the urban places where they live and lead to unjustified vilification of workers-in-nature such as ranchers, farmers, or loggers.[14] The environmental justice movement, since at least the early 1980s, has called attention to theories of distributive justice that problematize unequal allocation of environmental benefits and hazards in urban and rural places and illuminate discrimination based on the racial and economic characteristics of communities. However, as my coeditors and I emphasize in *The Environmental Justice Reader,* theories of distributive justice have not been the only foci of the movement. An equally and arguably stronger focus has been placed by both academics and activists on the revolutionary ways in which this movement has transformed the possibilities for fundamental change through emerging forms of political organization. Local communities and workers-in-nature are claiming their right to redefine limiting definitions of "environment" that deny them the ability to work for a responsible and sustainable livelihood. *The Environmental Justice Reader* includes a set of first-person "testimonies" by on-the-ground activists, hailing from Alaska to Arizona. The collection includes interviews with leading figures of the environmental justice movement and outlines the complexities of the issues they are addressing as it examines some of the reasons why alliances succeed or fail. These interviews and testimonies help to clarify why small-scale groups of ranchers, pastoralists, or farmers, who have been vilified in the past as "antienvironmentalist" might be seen today as ecopolitical allies working for social and environmental justice.[15]

As Alan Savory's TED talk emphasizes, groups of ranchers and pastoralists from around the world are working to address a complex mix of political, economic, and environmental issues that fall under the umbrella of climate change. While they must squarely contend with rhetoric common in environmental discourses that describes their activities as harmful or antienvironmentalist, Savory and other pastoralists and ranchers are transforming the most harmful practices of twentieth-century livestock management. They are grazing their animals in predator-friendly, high-density herds, in which the livestock move quickly through a range eating the seed heads of grasses and spreading seeds in their dung as they open the ground through trampling to hold more moisture which helps restore grasses by improving the conditions for seed growth. By "predator-friendly herds," Savory means large "herds that are dense enough that they offer protection to vulnerable animals" and "allow for occasional predation" which results in "overall healthier ecosystems." Larger herds, he argues, improve ecosystems by allowing for the possibility of reintroduction of predators such as wolves.[16]

These ideas counter the notion that too much disturbance of ecosystems by large numbers of animals—or by the reintroduction of predators—will necessarily have negative results. They challenge commonly accepted narratives once promoted by twentieth-century rangeland scientists about what contributes to grassland health or degradation. By employing media (TED talks, for example) and introducing new narratives, alliances such as the MBG see themselves working for better understanding of what contributes to rangeland health. The MBG ranchers understand that if the land they depend on is degraded, then the communities and cultures dependent on both domesticated and wild animals and plants they value could go extinct. They argue that ranching communities, like functioning ecosystems, must evolve and change if ranchers are to protect and even upgrade the public and private lands they deem to be their responsibility. As other pastoralists and ranchers in other places in the world take up the high-density, predator-friendly grazing strategies recommended by Savory, they are rejecting formerly accepted stories about "nature" and "balance" that have contributed to a century of decline, and telling new stories that are working to contribute to social and environmental resilience.

The Trouble with Stories About Nature and Balance

As environmental historian William Cronon observes, the trouble with most stories we tell about nature is that they are given a unity and order that neither "nature nor the past possesses so clearly."In most debates over nature, the causal relationships of an ecosystem are divided "with a rhetorical razor" that creates dichotomies between "included and excluded, relevant and irrelevant, empowered and disempowered." But the more we understand about nature and about history, the more we come to understand that the simple, heroic stories about a "balance" that we crave are constantly overwhelmed by long-dismissed or newly emerging details about "disturbance" that we cannot ignore. [17]

Stories about nature are often much too simplistic; an increasing number of scientists and researchers are telling us that in today's world we are going to have to deal not only with problems characterized by complexity, but also with problems characterized by uncertainty. In the Animas and San Bernardino Valleys, as early as the 1920s, overgrazing and rapid deterioration of the range led to a vociferous debate over causes and remedies that would rage for the next ninety years, with ranchers, foresters, and land managers telling competing stories—teeming with good guys and bad guys—about balance and disturbance. As Sally Fairfax and Lynn Huntsinger observe, early in the twentieth century the Forest Service and the Bureau of Land Management transformed the basic contours of Frederick Clement's theories of succession and progression toward a state of equilibrium or—in the management lexicon, "climax" or "balance"—into a simple story in which the good guys are the climax plants and the bad guys are the weedy upstarts at the beginning of the path of succession and disturbance.[18] In the Southwest, disturbance often takes the form of grazing, fire, and the incursion of exotic or alien species that are cast as scary villains that interrupt orderly progression toward climax or balance.

However, an increasing number of ranchers are practicing management-intensive grazing methods that challenge familiar stories about balance and disturbance. These ranchers are following models developed by

Savory. They have come to see that excluding all forms of disturbance (grazing, trampling, predators, fire) can "actually have a detrimental effect" on the land. Environmentalists often blame the deterioration of grasslands solely on cattle. Yet previously overgrazed pastures—even places lacking any vegetation—are again dense with native grasses. Ranchers, in consultation with grassland scientists and university resource managers, are experimenting with grazing cattle in high-density patterns that mimic now-extinct herds of megafauna ungulates with which the indigenous grasses evolved. According to noted grassland ecologist Tony Burgess, cattle, which are not native to North America, survive and proliferate because they are able to exploit niches that are vacant not only of bison, but also of other large, free-roaming grazers and browsers that lived during the Pleistocene Era. The time has been so short since those large grass eaters became extinct, he argues, that in terms of evolution, "The plants don't know they're gone." Claims that exotics, such as cattle, mimic the role of extinct megafauna ungulates are based on the 1970s discovery of in situ spear points in mammoth bones at a Paleo-Indian site in a borderland valley that date back 11,000 years. Bison bones have also been discovered that date from 1200 CE to 1450 CE. According to Conrad Bahre, this means not only that megafauna ungulates were a part of the desert grasslands ecosystems, but also were likely present until at least the seventeenth century.[19]

Savory's management-intensive grazing techniques require ranchers to learn about the numerous, complex, local variables involved with the grazing patterns and rotation of domesticated livestock that have neither the instincts of wild animals nor the ability to range freely as megafauna ungulates once did. Today, ranchers must acquire deep knowledge of each species of grass growing in a pasture—and there are usually many, whether native or exotic—and the amount of time it will take for that particular grass to regenerate after it has been grazed. All these variables depend on temperature, rainfall, exposure to sun, the time of the year, and the amount of forage a cow requires that, in turn, depends on the cow's size, age, and stage of life.

Understanding the complexity of rangeland management and the key role of grasses in arid ecosystems helped me better understand why my visits to nearly every ranch usually began with discussions of the critical importance of being able to distinguish between native and exotic grasses and to understand their relationship to grazers. These discussions occurred *before* I was offered any stories about folklore or wildlife. Often, while being shown pictures of long-dead relatives, such as grandmothers or uncles, the rancher I was interviewing would urge me to look behind the human subject and focus on the Sacaton grass ("That was the 'horse-high' grass my great, great grandpa used to tell me about"), or pictures of cowboys rounding up cattle ("Look at the density of that Blue grama! Cows love eating that"). What these storytellers wanted me to understand is that grasses are the key to the continued health of desert grasslands, and the economic future of ranching. They also wanted me to understand the connections between overgrazing and bare ground to climate change. These ranchers see grass as a keystone species that plays a critical role in maintaining the structure of the social and ecological community; they believe that if disturbance is managed through careful grazing patterns, grasslands will again play a major role in sequestering carbon.

Retelling Stories About Work-in-Nature

Other forms of disturbance, mainly in the form of fire and predators, were once an important part of arid grasslands ecosystems of the American Southwest; these disturbances continue to counter still-common "stories" about orderly progression or environmental stability and balance. When Bill Miller Jr. spoke to my students, he reminded them that when his fore-bears first came to the Animas and San Bernardino Valleys the land was blanketed with tall, dense native grasses as high as a horse's belly. But today ranchers are fighting the spread of woody species (mesquite trees, cholla cactus, and tall spiny ocotillo) and "exotic" grasses (such as Lehmann lovegrass) that suppress the growth of native grasses. After consulting with the scientists and environmentalists who are part of their alliance, MBG ranchers reintroduced fire to the ecology, a move that generated much controversy.[20]

To understand controversies over natives, exotics, and disturbance, Miller told us, one must look back in time to the ways in which indigenous peoples used fire to encourage the growth of new grasses and discourage the growth of woody species. In the Southwest, historical records and some fire scar data indicate that wildfires were once common. It is likely that, before Spanish migration to what is now the American Southwest, the dominant vegetation type may well have been grassland or open forest savannah, the result of the deliberate use of fire to create and expand familiar and useful environments and to attract wildlife to freshly burnt pastures where new shoots of grass were growing, a practice referred to as fire hunting. By the seventeenth century people from two different cultures, traveling along the north-south migration routes of the Americas, arrived in the Animas and San Bernardino Valleys and, over time, displaced the indigenous Opata and O'odham (also known as Sobaipuri) cultures that had long inhabited the region. From the east came the Athabascan-speaking Apache, with a culture based on raiding, and from the south came the Spanish, with a culture based on colonization and domesticated livestock. The Apache were probably first attracted to the area by the abundant grassland fauna they encountered and then by the rich cattle and sheep herds introduced by the Spanish. They began an intense predation on Spanish livestock that was so widespread that they effectively kept cattle numbers in check.[21]

In 1886 the US Cavalry forcibly (and many would argue unjustly) removed the Apache to reservations in Florida and Central Arizona. This left the Texan and Kansan forebears of the MBG ranchers without any check on their cattle-grazing activities; these early ranchers had been dislocated by the Civil War and drought in the southern American plains, and lured to the Animas and San Bernardino Valleys by an offer of free land from the Southern Pacific Railroad. Faced with a burgeoning market for livestock created by the growing number of Indian reservations, military bases, and mining camps of the West, these ranchers dramatically increased the numbers of their herds but did not understand that cattle could not be left to graze continuously in the same pastures because doing so would kill the grasses. With the Apache no longer one of the variables in the fire regime of the Southwest, individual families took up ownership of delineated parcels of land; in pursuit of profit, they failed to understand the ancient processes through which the grasses had evolved in relationship with occasional fires and quickly moving, high-density grazers.[22] They also did not understand the role of predators such as wolves and mountain lions in ecosystem health and began systematically removing predators considered a threat to cattle from the entire region. The result was overgrazing on a colossal scale, lands denuded of vegetation, and deeply eroded riparian zones.

Before 1900 both Mexican and American stockmen were still familiar with the tradition they called the "the Indian way" or "Paiute burning"; they practiced light burning to encourage the growth of new grasses. When a fire broke out in the back country, they let it burn. After 1900 the US

Forest Service began arguing that light burning would leave the torch in the hands of so-called uneducated ranchers. Trained to emulate European foresters, American forest rangers argued that fire was wasteful, destructive, irrational, and politically subversive because it destroyed valuable trees. Ironically, the story guiding European and American foresters—that the tree is a talisman of land health—became a subplot in a narrative that historian Richard White has called the myth of the "first white men" about the bringing of supposedly superior knowledge to Western lands.[23] The notion of superior knowledge—that the more cattle and fewer predators on a piece of land the better—ironically drove the environmental degradation of the Southwest's once-dense, relatively treeless grasslands. By suppressing these older fire regimes and overgrazing, ranchers unwittingly encouraged the spread of woody species, like the mesquite tree. Cattle then helped disseminate these trees throughout the arid grasslands by eating their seed pods and spreading them in their dung.

As White explains, from the nineteenth century forward, when Americans wanted to think about their relation to nature, they relied on conceptions of "first white men," entering newly "discovered" lands for the first time, and surveying a world with no previous marks of human culture on the landscape. The most popular "first white men" were Meriwether Lewis, William Clark, and Daniel Boone. In the Southwest, Alvar Núñez Cabeza de Vaca, a Spanish conquistador who wandered lost in what is now Texas, New Mexico, and northern Mexico for nine years in the late fifteenth century, became one of these fascinatingly sympathetic mythical viewers of the natural world who exist somewhere outside human history. The problem is that closer readings of the journals of men such as Lewis and Clark and Cabeza de Vaca do not bear out the myth that native people did not make changes to the land or that only white men had the knowledge to intelligently alter nature. In their journals, Lewis and Clark were quite aware of and note that they were moving through landscapes where native peoples were "farming, hunting, fishing, and grazing their animals." Similarly, Cabeza de Vaca reported in his travel narrative, "Natives run with firebrands in their hands, burning the woods and fields . . . both to drive away the mosquitoes and force lizards . . . out of the ground, to eat them" and to encourage the growth of new grasses.[24]

Since the mid-nineteenth century, other narratives have also been called upon to romanticize notions of "natural balance." Henry David Thoreau's so-called higher laws, for example, have been used by some readers and environmentalists to ascribe to wilderness an immutable order to which the human world can only aspire. Later, in the 1960s, citing some of these romanticized narratives, many environmentalists came to reverence wilderness and vilify workers-in-nature, losing sight of the fact that all the materials needed for an urban existence are dependent on the farmers, ranchers, loggers, or miners who provide them. This is not to say that workers-in-nature or indigenous peoples always work in ways that are uniformly beneficial to vital ecosystems. The MBG acknowledge, for example, that systematic removal of predators has ultimately been devastating to ecosystems. To address human error in previous generations and proceed more wisely, they are bringing together diverse groups of people who recognize the value and necessity of land management practices that benefit people and the multiple species that depend on healthy, functioning ecosystems.

Telling Stories About Stories

The trouble with competing stories about natives and exotics is that the more we come to understand about nature, the more we see how simplistic stories about ecological balance play almost no role in shaping the characteristics of an arid environment. This is why William Cronon advises us to tell stories about our stories. In a region where the Chiricahua Apache were forcibly removed by the US military and by ranchers who desired ownership of the rich grasslands for the benefit of their "exotic" cattle, we must ask, "Why do recent environmentalist stories about the removal of exotic species and the protection and enhancement of native ones seem so satisfying? Does storytelling about natives and exotics cause us to ignore elements of the environment that need additional or more complex responses?" As John Rodman reminds us in a study of the complexities surrounding restoration of lands that have been ravaged by exotics, the ultimate issue is "not whether or when a species is (labeled) native or exotic" but "to what extent [do] species behave as members of communities?" In some cases, Rodman writes, restoring ecosystems to previous states may be impossible because a species may have gone extinct. In that case, another species (perhaps an exotic) might need to be introduced by conservationists to preserve the long-term systemic health of the ecological community.[25]

On long drives through basin and range country with the ranchers I interviewed, I was introduced to the complexity that my untrained urban eyes constantly missed. Ranchers directed my attention not only to native grasses, such as Blue and Black grama, but also to exotics, including Lehmann lovegrass, and to woody species, such as the velvet mesquite tree. I came to see how the landscape was a diverse mosaic of colors that indicated different species of indigenous grasses, such as Sacaton and Tabosa, and exotic grasses. They showed me places where native Black grama grasses were growing up through the fast-growing Lehmann lovegrass, which was providing the right conditions for the native grasses to return. However, they also told me that the aggressive, adventive Lehmann lovegrass tends to burn with a high intensity when a fire breaks out, so in some cases it is blamed for complicating the success of prescribed burns and hindering the success of reintroduction of native grasses.[26] This is just one example of the reasons why fire, used to control the spread of mesquite, cannot be considered a panacea in range restoration. A complex array of elements in the natural world, such as wind, humidity, type of grasses being burned, and the time that has elapsed since the last fire, must all be taken into account. To plan for all these complexities, MBG ranchers have forged alliances with the Nature Conservancy, university scientists, grassland ecologists, and Forest Service and Bureau of Land Management professionals, with whom they consult on all prescribed burns. Like other ecopolitical groups around the world, MBG ranchers insist that in all debates about proprietary rights to nature and proper management of the land, expert opinion must be carefully weighed against generations of accumulated local knowledges for best results.

As John Rodman suggests, it is here, in the midst of such complexities, that we recognize that we are living in a time when thousands of organisms are intermingling and there is a terrific dislocation in nature and many uncertainties about restoration and conservation.[27] Perhaps there is no better illustration of Rodman's point than competing stories told about the place of mesquite in desert grasslands. The spread of mesquite is often associated with desertification and the decline of native grasses. Blame for the spread of mesquite is often laid on cattle that ingest the pod and seeds of the trees and spread them through the grasslands. In the twentieth century, stories about the mesquite—which has always been present along river bottoms and arroyos in the American Southwest—changed from narratives about its status as a "native" into narratives about its transformation into an "exotic invader." Mesquite spread from the waterways throughout the grasslands where it began competing successfully for nutrients with native grasses. Because the germination rate of the beans increases dramatically after passing through the digestive track of cattle and horses, mesquite populations began spreading more rapidly when the introduction of cattle increased the means of dissemination. While this benefitted the birds of the region that were sheltered by the expanding *bosques*, the trees began to be blamed for depriving the grasses of sunlight and the livestock of forage. Ranchers began to engage in massive restoration efforts by bulldozing mesquite and intensively reseeding native grasses. These efforts, for the most part, have failed.

Competing stories about grasses and mesquite, then, illustrate why ecological restoration requires us to retell stories and ask better questions, including, How will we "help reconstruct communities using new parts," and what will "membership in a multispecies community involve"? These questions shy away from oversimplified dualistic stories about native and exotic species. We begin to see that ecological restoration must be more about deepening our awareness of what it would take to build self-regulating communities "in a disturbed world" than it is about heroes winning out over villains.[28] This has implications not only for the grasses and the mesquite, but also for the rancher and the cow, which have both been described as either natives or exotics, depending on who is telling the story.

The Role of Human Values in Social and Environmental Justice

By listening to stories told by local people, I came to a better understanding of how community members interpret working wilderness as a set of cultural and environmental values. Environmental historian Donald Worster reminds us that we should never forget the role that humans and their values play in shaping environments. Humans have "a right to derive a living from the earth and to participate in the processes of natural creativity"; however, Worster adds, "no one, no matter how desperate his condition of elevated ambition, has any right to diminish the complexity, diversity, stability, fruitfulness, wholeness, and beauty" of the natural world.[29]

I would argue that the MBG's sense of obligation to conserve and protect the grasslands grows, in part, out of the kind of worldview that Worster describes. When I have asked these hardworking men and women why they continue working the land and their livestock, despite the daily backbreaking labor, the climatological unpredictability, the economic uncertainty, the legal wrangling, and the media pummeling, they sweep an arm across the valley between the Peloncillos and the Chiricahuas and say, "Look at this. The mountains look different in every light." They want to protect their lands because they want to continue to see that beauty and continue to see themselves as participants in the ceaseless processes of natural creativity that surrounds them. They understand that grazing animals are an important part of keeping arid grasslands healthy and that healthy grasses are a key component in the fight against rising levels of greenhouse gases.

Since the early 1990s, MBG ranchers have been working to deal with problems characterized by complexity and uncertainty. By redefining the land where they live as a working wilderness, they are calling attention to the ways in which disputes arise among diverse groups about what nature is and should be, and about what the human role in nature is and should be. They have become what Ruffin and I call "global ecological citizens" by forming alliances that reach out not only to US ranching groups, but also to other pastoralists in other parts of the world. In April of 2004 six Maasai herders from Kenya, from one of the hardest-hit, desertified regions in the Horn of Africa, came to the United States–Mexico borderlands to visit local MBG ranchers.[30] These six have seen firsthand the war, poverty, displacement, and hunger that can result from desertification. On their seven-day trip, they visited several ranches, observed cattle and wildlife, and discussed predators. They rode mules for the first time, learned how to rope a calf, joined in the life of the community, and exchanged dances, songs, and stories. Many hours of discussions concerning problems common to both the Maasai and the MBG ranchers took place. This is exactly what people who are working for environmental justice do: they identify linked social and environmental problems, form loose alliances, and come together to discuss "differently situated human practices and perspectives on nature," as they work toward consensus in order to create a more livable and just world.[31] Then they share what they have learned with others.

NOTES

1. My visit to the Post Office Ranch was the beginning of a project to collect ranching folklore about snakes, mountain lions, and other wildlife. However, interviews with families, and my time spent living in the Animas, San Bernardino, and San Pedro Valleys, would lead me away from the subject of folklore and toward the complex subject of grasses and land management. There remains much rancor against those who choose to write about and/or support ranching or ranching conservation alliances like the MBG from some academics, environmental groups, and property rights activists who oppose government regulation of public lands. For this reason, I will name and quote only those ranchers—both pro and con—who have chosen to have their words published in the books and articles that I cite in this essay. For a definitive history of MBG, see Nathan Sayer's *Working Wilderness: The Malpai Borderlands Group and the Future of the Western Range* (Tucson, AZ: Rio Nuevo Publishers, 2005). See also *Conservation Action*, MBG, http://www.malpaiborderlandsgroup.org/?section=conservation-action. For more discussion of Bill Miller Jr. and the Post Office Ranch, see Jonathan Adams, *The Future of the Wild: Radical Conservation for a Crowded World* (Boston: Beacon Press, 2006), 119–20.

2 Jay Dusard, afterword to *Beyond the Rangeland Conflict: Toward a West that Works*, by Dan Dagget (Layton, UT: Gibbs Smith, The Grand Canyon Trust, 1995),"wildlife and ecosystems," 103.

3. Dagget, *Beyond the Rangeland Conflict*, "in worse shape," 1. The MBG is not without its detractors. For criticisms, see Terry Greene Sterling, "'Radical Center' Tries to Shield Ranch Land: Diverse Interests Unite behind Common Goals," *Washington Post*, November 13, 2004, A03. For an example of a recent peer-reviewed article in a scientific journal supporting MBG claims, see Gerald J. Gottfried, Larry S. Allen, Peter L. Warren, Bill McDonald, Ronald J. Bemis, and Carleton B. Edminster, "Private-Public Collaboration to Reintroduce Fire into the Changing Ecosystems of the Southwestern Borderlands Region," *Fire Ecology: Special Issue* 5, no. 1 (2009): 85–99.

4. See Allan Savory, *Holistic Resource Management* (Washington, DC: Island Press, 1988); Allan Savory, "How to Fight Desertification and Reverse Climate Change," http://www.ted.com/talks/allan_savory_how_to_green_the_world_s_deserts_and_reverse_climate_change; Traci Brynn Voyles, "Intimate Cartographies: Navajo Ecological Citizenship, Soil Conservation, and Livestock Reduction," in *American Studies, Ecocriticism, and Citizenship: Thinking and Acting in the Local and Global Commons*, ed. Joni Adamson and Kimberly N. Ruffin (New York: Routledge, 2012), 50–63.

5. Chris Clarke, "TED Talk Teaches us to Disparage the Desert," http://www.kcet.org/updaily/socal_focus/commentary/east-ca/learn-how-to-hate-the-desert-with-ted.html.

6. Adamson and Ruffin, introduction to *American Studies, Ecocriticism, and Citizenship*, 1–17.

7. William Cronon, "A Place for Stories: Nature, History, and Narrative," *Journal of American History* (March 1992): 1347.

8. James McWilliams in "All Sizzle and No Steak: Why Allan Savory's TED Talk about How Cattle Can Reverse Global Warming Is Dead Wrong," http://www.slate.com /articles/life/food/2013/04/allan_savory_s_ted_talk_is_wrong_and_the_benefits_of _holistic_grazing_have.2.html, is openly skeptical; while Michael Tobias, in "Alan Savory, Freeman Dyson and Soil Sequestration," http://planet3.org/2013/03/17/alan-savory-freeman-dyson-and-soil-sequestration/, is cautiously open to some of Savory's claims while noting that his methods are not scalable.

9. Hallie Eakin and Diana Liverman, "Drought and Ranching in Arizona: A Case of Vulnerability," *Impact of Climate Change on Society*, USGS http://geochange.er.usgs.gov /sw/impacts/society/ranching/, July 10, 1997, 3.

10. For a more in-depth look at these debates, see Sterling, " 'Radical Center' Tries to Shield Ranch Land"; Andrew Ross, *Bird on Fire: Lessons from the World's Least Sustainable City* (New York: Oxford University Press, 2011), "by drought, desertification," 187; Joni Adamson, "Seeking the Corn Mother: Transnational Indigenous Community Building and Organizing, Food Sovereignty and Native Literary Studies," in *We the Peoples: Indigenous Rights in the Age of the Declaration*, ed. Elvira Pulitano (New York: Cambridge University Press, 2012): 228–49.

11. For more on grassbanking and other initiatives of the MBG, see Jake Page, "Finding Common Ground in the Range War," *Smithsonian* 28, no. 3 (July 1997): 50–61; also see Dagget, *Beyond the Rangeland Conflict*, 13–23.

12. Michael Goldman, introduction to *Privatizing Nature: Political Struggles for the Global Commons*, ed. Michael Goldman (London: Pluto Press, 1998), "North is pitted against South," 13.

13. Dagget, *Beyond the Rangeland Conflict*, "working wilderness," 103.

14. Joni Adamson, *American Indian Literature, Environmental Justice, and Ecocriticism: The Middle Place* (Tucson: University of Arizona Press, 2001), 53–58.

15. For more on oversimplified concepts of "wilderness," see Adamson, *American Indian Literature*, 66. For more on the relationship between work-in-nature and workers-in-nature and environmental justice, see ibid., 51–88. For the interviews discussed in this paragraph, see Joni Adamson, Mei Mei Evans, and Rachel Stein, eds., *The Environmental Justice Reader: Poetics, Politics, and Pedagogy* (Tucson: University of Arizona Press, 2002), 7, 15–57, 163–80, 194–212.

16. Allan Savory, "How to Fight Desertification and Reverse Climate Change," TED Talk, February 2013, http://www.ted.com/talks/allan_savory_how_to_green_the_world _s_deserts_and_reverse_climate_change, "predator-friendly herds," "herds that are dense," "allow for occasional predation," "overall healthier ecosystems."

17. Cronon, "A Place for Stories," 1349.

18. Sally Fairfax and Lynn Huntsinger, "An Essay from the Woods (and Rangelands)," *Arizona Quarterly* 53, no. 2 (Summer 1997): 202–3.

19. Dagget, *Beyond the Rangeland Conflict,* "actually have a detrimental," 10; Tony Burgess quoted in ibid., "The plants don't know," 9–10; Conrad Bahre, "Human Impacts on the Grasslands of Southeastern Arizona," in *The Desert Grassland,* ed. Mitchel P. McClaran and Thomas R. Van Devender (Tucson: University of Arizona Press, 1995), 215.

20. See "History of Fire in the Malpai Region" http://www.malpaiborderlandsgroup .org/?section=conservation-action.

21. Stephen J. Pyne, *Fire in America: A Cultural History of Wildland and Rural Fire* (1982) (Seattle: University of Washington Press, 1997), "likely that before Spanish migration," 74; Bahre, "Human Impacts on the Grasslands of Southeastern Arizona," "From the east came the Athabascan-speaking," 240; Pyne, *Fire in America,* "cattle numbers in check," 518–19.

22. Bahre, "Human Impacts on the Grasslands of Southeastern Arizona," "increased the numbers," 245; Pyne, *Fire in America,* 518–19.

23. Richard White, "'Are You an Environmentalist?,' or Do You Work for a Living?" in *Uncommon Ground: Rethinking the Human Place in Nature,* ed. William Cronon (New York: W. W. Norton, 1996), 171–85; "first white men," 175.

24. Ibid., "first white men," "most popular first white men's," 175; "journals, Lewis and Clark" and "farming, hunting, fishing," 176; Alvar Núñez Cabeza de Vaca, *Castaways,* ed. Enrique Pupo-Walker, trans. Frances M. López-Morillas (Berkeley: University of California Press, 1993), "Natives run with firebrands," 62.

25. John Rodman, "Restoring Nature: Natives and Exotics," in *The Nature of Things: Language, Politics and the Environment,* ed. Jane Bennett and William Chaloupka (Minneapolis: University of Minnesota Press, 1993), "not whether or when" and "to what extent," 51.

26. Bahre, "Human Impacts on the Grasslands of Southeastern Arizona," 216.

27. Rodman, "Restoring Nature," 151.

28. Ibid., "help reconstruct communities" and "membership in a multispecies," 151; "in a disturbed world," 153.

29. Donald Worster, *The Wealth of Nature: Environmental History and the Ecological Imagination* (New York: Oxford University Press, 1993), "a right to derive" and "no one, no matter," 183.

30. See Tom Maliti, "Arizona Cowboys, Masai Warriors Are Equally at Home on the Range," *LA Times,* May 2, 2004. http://articles.latimes.com/2004/may/02/news /adfg-cowboys2.

31. Adamson, *American Indian Literature,* "differently situated human," 184.

11

"Survival Is Triumph Enough"

Class, Environmental Consciousness,
and the Southern Memoir

SCOTT HICKS

"**W**e're land poor," my mother has always told my father, especially during times of financial decision making: taxes, a new car, college tuition, retirement. "We've got land, but we don't have money." The land, however, inscribes family history: sixty-eight acres in northern Orange County, North Carolina, the site of my grandfather's home place and deeded jointly to my mother and her two sisters, and seven acres on the eastern side of the county, my father's inheritance from his father, where my parents moved after their wedding and where they raised my brother and me. I realize now how burdensome the land is: the unceasing work to keep at bay the honeysuckle, brush, and woods that my late grandfather, working alongside his son-in-law, cleared at the old home place; the taxes my parents pay in a well-heeled county; and a home, thanks to its location near Durham and Chapel Hill, worth more in its sale than in its occupation, a truism that compels my family's do-it-yourself work ethic. At the same time, I've always wondered why my family has treated its land as it did: spreading oil on our driveway to keep down the dust, burning trash we could recycle curbside, logging the postage stamp of woods on our property. Part of my discomfort, I'm convinced, grew out of my unease with the socioeconomic status of my family. We were, to quote Jeff Foxworthy, redneck: a car or two on blocks surrounded by stacks of pipes, girders, wood pallets, coils of wire, buckets and drums, and parts of engines and machines cast off by Duke University Hospital, where my father worked as an electrician from 1976 to 2009. The promise of our land—rolling hills in the central North Carolina piedmont, an area metastatically suburbanizing —seemed disrespected by my mother's complaint, the oil we spread and smoke we spewed, the clutter we disgorged.

But as I look back now, from my own home in Laurinburg, in the North Carolina sandhills, with a spouse and two children, I see a complexity to the landscape not only of my raising, but also of my class status. My father can grow a cornucopia of vegetables (under black plastic, a method he heard about somewhere and has perfected) and my mother can freeze and can the fruits of this labor more deliciously than anyone else I know. What I once saw as embarrassing junk has become a testament of my father's resourcefulness to transform detritus into usefulness, to divert garbage from the landfill—evidenced, for instance, in the charcoal grills he has welded for us out of fifty-five gallon oil drums Duke discarded. The landscape my parents have inhabited and, piece by piece, created since 1974 is a place that—seen through compassionate, empathetic, open-minded eyes— symbolizes a disappearing grace in a changing world.

Though this essay could draw on any number of texts to explore environmental consciousness and working-class experience, I am drawn to the twentieth-century memoirs of white US southerners Harry Crews, Tim McLaurin, and Bobbie Ann Mason.[1] For one reason, their narratives explicitly mirror the stories my grandparents have told me of their childhoods, of making ends meet, staying close to home, and seeing to a better life for their children and grandchildren. For another reason, I write as a scholar of African American and environmental literatures, and these memoirs reveal the role that racism plays in socioeconomic inequality and environmental injustice. That is, racism sanctions the relegation of people of color to the least workable lands and the importation of pollution, hazard, and toxicity into their communities. For those who have the privilege of whiteness without the privilege of wealth, it stimulates the infliction of violence, born of fear and anger, against life (human and otherwise) and place. In *A Childhood: The Biography of a Place* (1978), Crews describes his Depression-era youth in Bacon County, Georgia, coming of age in a hard landscape of poverty, racism, and disease. In *Keeper of the Moon: A Southern Boyhood* (1991), McLaurin tells of his childhood in mid-century Fayetteville, North Carolina, punctuated by the classed realities of tough manual labor in tobacco fields and factories; the release provided by drugs, sex, and dogfighting; and an uneasy truce among the area's whites, blacks, and American Indians. Mason's *Clear Springs: A Memoir* (1999) chronicles the Pulitzer-nominated author's childhood on her family's farm near Mayfield, Kentucky, in the 1940s and 1950s, her escape to New York City, and her eventual return. Though my experiences growing up during the 1980s and 1990s cannot compare to what it was like to survive the Great Depression in the rural South, my history, framed through my elders' lives, is a history shaped by Southern working-class white experience—just as it also is a history of my own making, anchored in my scholarship and pedagogy.

Despite their commonalities of working-class white experience, these texts cover a wide swath of geography and history, from Crews' birth in south Georgia in 1935 to Mason's Kentucky homecoming in the mid-1990s. Nonetheless, the stories my own parents and grandparents have passed down help me see the interconnectivity of Crews's, Mason's, and McLaurin's work. My own history, like the histories these texts foreground, begins in the Depression-era rural South, in an era before wide-scale agricultural mechanization, electrification, and modernization. The realities of life for these writers and my own family spurred migration from the country to the city, from sharecropping to so-called public work in cigarette or textile factories. The choices available to these writers, as well as to my grandparents and parents, and the decisions they made result directly from their adaptation to new landscapes, new economies, and new communities. For Crews and McLaurin, the military provided a path. For Mason, college and cosmopolitan countercultures provided an exit. For my parents, my grandparents' long careers in Cone Mills and Liggett & Myers Tobacco provided a future for their children that included homeownership and technical school. Most important, however, these narratives cohere because they explore the difficulties of simultaneously narrating socioeconomic poverty and environmental antagonism. These personal histories challenge what it means to be of the rough South and what it means to write what we call grit lit—not only for the working class, but for the ecologies they inhabit as well.[2]

In these memoirs, land and class intersect in ways both insidious and benevolent. For Crews and McLaurin, antagonisms of land and class give them bona fide credentials as inhabitants of the rough South—their survival depends on winning the war of man versus nature, be it soil infertility, boll weevils or tobacco borers, pyorrhea, pit bulls, or snakes. They assert the South as a landscape of ecological violence and poverty, and thus they and their families assail the land with increasing violence as they struggle to wrest a living from the degraded soils. Their success (they live to tell the story, if this truth be proof of victory) consists in their grit, and the stories they write define grit lit as vanquishing the environment that would otherwise crush them, their communities, and their cultures. Yet in the crevices of Crews's and McLaurin's rough South, in the niches of their grit lit, lies an abiding love of homeland, of place, so ingrained that they cannot exist outside of the environment that eviscerates them. As Crews puts it, "All I had going for me in the world or would ever have was that swamp, all those goddamn mules, all those screwworms that I'd dug out of pigs and all the other beautiful and dreadful and sorry circumstances that had made me the Grit I am and will always be. Once I realized that the way I saw the world and man's condition in it would always be exactly and inevitably shaped by everything which up to that moment had only shamed me, once I realized that, I was home free."[3] Although Mason's gender ostensibly would exclude her from the battle of man versus nature, she inhabits the rough South and calls out its misogynist and ecocidal tendencies, just as she presents an alternative grit response. In *Clear Springs*, the fertility of northern Kentucky soils sustains the family, and although Mason's working-class and feminist identity compel her to leave the land, she returns on terms that revise the intersection of land, class, gender, and labor.

Indeed, as these memoirs and my own self-understanding suggest, to tell a story of environmental inequity and working-class experience is to tell a story of personal shame and guilt. Perhaps this hypothesis explains why outsiders are prone to declare that the poor are not environmentalists, or maybe it explains the pervasive conflation of the South with environmental devastation. But telling a story of environment and class records a way of life and work in place. This synthesis is indispensable, for cleaving understandings of class from understandings of environmentalism perpetuates violence against poor people and the landscapes they inhabit—and worse, as John Foster Bellamy writes, "reinforc[es] the dominant relations of power in global capitalism, with their bias toward the unlimited commodification of human productive energy, land, and . . . the ecology of the planet itself."[4] The planet needs working-class people to tell the stories of their environmental consciousness and practice, and scholars and citizens need to listen to those stories and work together in pursuit of economic and environmental justice. The narratives of Crews, Mason, and McLaurin underscore this point, and I hope we scholars and critics can unite our diverse disciplinary perspectives, join our voices with the working class and the planet, and sustain ourselves and the places we inhabit for the long-term fight against socioeconomic inequality and environmental devastation.

"A Theater of Environmental Disasters"—and Unable to Turn Away

Since the early twentieth century, when the events of these narratives begin and when my own grandparents were born on small farms in rural Orange County, the South has witnessed major economic and environmental transformation. In *This Land, This South: An Environmental History* (1996), Albert E. Cowdrey catalogues "a theater of environmental disasters" in the South in the early twentieth century: the boll weevil, logging and deforestation, and malaria. Similarly, Pete Daniel's *Toxic Drift: Pesticides and Health in the Post–World War II South* (2005) zeroes in on "the pesticide wreckage" of the second half of the twentieth century, when Southern farmers sought to leverage new chemicals for greater yields of intensive crops such as cotton. Jack Temple Kirby elasticizes environmental and Southern history through his rich interplay of places and personalities, artifacts and theories, in *Mockingbird Song: Ecological Landscapes of the South* (2006). The South's environmental history, recounted by these historians and others, reflects the upheaval of the region's economic order—in particular, its metamorphosis into a region of factory workers, because of contractions in agricultural work thanks to mechanization and modernization.[5] Such migrations characterize my own family's history: my maternal grandparents moved from sharecropping near outlying crossroads to Hillsborough and its Eno Mills; my paternal grandfather moved only a few steps from my grandmother's birthplace and took a job in a tobacco factory in Durham. The industries they joined—tobacco and textiles—have since departed, the result of globalization, leaving places like the county where I live now with North Carolina's highest unemployment numbers—a fact I can't help but see in the many acres of clear-cut alongside Scotland County's roads. From environmental (un)consciousness to economic (non)opportunity, the stories that Crews, McLaurin, and Mason narrate record and interrogate profound transformations of the manywheres of their various Souths.

To start at the beginning, as it were, Crews's *Childhood* narrates the

infertility of Bacon County's land and the poverty of its human inhabitants. "The timber in the county was of no consequence, and there was very
little rich bottomland," he writes. "Most of the soil was poor and leached
out, and commercial fertilizer was dear as blood." Because of the land's
infertility, eking a living from farming is near impossible for many. Crews
recounts his family's farm tenancy, "from one patch of farmed-out land
to another, from one failed crop to a place where they thought there was
hope of making a good one" as they try to wrest a living from the land.
The Crewses' sharecrop thirty acres of Luther Carter's farm, "as much as
one man and one mule could tend, and even then they had to step smart
from first sun to last to do it." The sharecropping system keeps tenants and
their families impoverished and imprisoned in a corrupt cycle: "Whether
on shares or on standing rent, they were still tenant farmers and survival
was a day-to-day crisis as real as rickets in the bones of their children or
the worms that would sometimes rise out of their children's stomachs and
nest in their throats so that they had to be pulled out by hand to keep the
children from choking." Though "[h]e worked harder than the mule he
plowed" and "did everything a man could to bring something out of the
sorry soil he worked," Ray Crews can escape neither poverty nor death, cut
down after a hard day's work in 1937 by a heart attack.[6] Life is not much
easier for Harry after his mother remarries, though the family is able to
remain on the same land for several years.

The poverty of the land and its people compels a hard antagonism in the
men and women of *Childhood*. Reduced into a primarily economic asset,
forced on them by the transition from subsistence farming to cash crops,
the land becomes eminently exchangeable. The Crewses thus cannot root
themselves in the land, and it sustains neither crops nor humans. When
Ray Crews finally owns land, it is "nothing but pine trees and palmetto
thickets and stands of gallberry bushes and dog fennel." Like the rest of the
county, known for its infertile swampiness, the plot manifests the untamed
wildness of the area. Taming it takes more work, it seems, than actual
cultivation—and any taming they accomplish serves only to expose the soil
to erosion, infertility, and desertification. What's more, devoting time to
making the land suitable for agriculture diverts time away from farming—
labor that can actually put food on the table and clothing on the children.
To make the land cultivable, Ray and Myrtice must clear it "with an ax and
a saw and a grubbing hoe and [family mare] Daisy. Daisy pulled what she

could from the ground. What she couldn't pull out, mama and daddy dug out. What they couldn't dig out, they burned out. There were a few people, very few, who could afford dynamite to blow stumps out."[7] Crews' destructive, obliterating verbs—pulling out, digging out, burning out, dynamiting out—reinforce the profound enmity and hostility between humankind and earth. Thanks to their poverty, the people's violence against the wilderness is immediate and bodily. Thanks also to their poverty, their violence is marginally tempered, unable as they are to afford dynamite and unleash all-out shock and awe war. Their occupation of the land continues with conventionalized violence: a transition from biodiverse, polycultural farming to the no-holds-barred imposition of tobacco, a cash crop grown in monocultures with increasingly intense inputs of toxic chemicals (including lead poison, which, in Crews' memoir, claims the lives of two yearling cattle) and leads to greater soil erosion and compaction.[8] Rather than nurture and sustain his place on earth, rather than build soil—a way of life and labor celebrated by Wendell Berry, Gene Logsdon, Wes Jackson, Joel Salatin, and a host of other agrarian contrarians—Ray and thousands like him extract what they can and move on when they cannot. Put simply, the Crewses confront a dual injustice: their poverty and social marginalization drive their necessity to degrade landscapes already marginal to begin with, a necessity that further destabilizes their place on the land.

Yet the alienability of the land paradoxically embeds it more deeply in the psyche of the maturing Crews. Just as he candidly tells of his family's offenses against the soil, so too does he tell of his culture's love and defense of the soil. Despite the land's worthlessness, private property "was inviolate, and you were always very careful about what you said to another man if you were on his land. A man could shoot you with impunity if you were on his property and he managed to get you dead enough so you couldn't tell what actually happened." Similarly, the primacy of private property mirrors a more emotional sense of home. For the poor whites of Bacon County, the land serves as a way of identifying themselves, of giving themselves some sense of meaning and place in the world. "I come from people who believe the *home place* [emphasis in original] is as vital and necessary as the beating of your own heart. It is that single house where you were born, where you lived out your childhood, where you grew into young manhood. It is your anchor in the world, that place, along with the memory of your kinsmen at the long supper table every night and the knowledge that it would always exist, if nowhere but in memory." As he concludes his memoir, recounting his return home after three years in the Marine Corps, Crews pays homage to the primacy of home place even as he, subconsciously, cannot express it otherwise than "Goddamn sun," "what, in Bacon County, was unthinkable." "I had cursed the sun. And in Bacon County you don't curse the sun or the rain or the land or God. They are all the same thing. To curse any of them is an ultimate blasphemy."[9] In much the same way, my own family sometimes has cursed its inheritance, angry that while we see ourselves as blessed to own my grandfather's home place, such capital does not translate into a life that transcends a mean attention to making do with dollars and cents.

It is thus on a contradictory note that the memoir ends. Crews—after 181 pages of recounting the hostility of the south Georgia ecology, the backbreaking labor of his parents to provide a place for him and his brother, and his near-fatal bouts with injury and disease—cannot remain in Bacon County, just as he cannot leave. He cannot cleave his familial and cultural history from the landscape that, in spite of itself, somehow has seen him to adulthood. Taken together, these traumas and sins are markers of a landscape that neither welcomes nor rejects him—and they are traumas that, in ways small and large, are reinscribed on the landscape for generations to come in a labor structure that bears the violence of socioeconomic inequality. From my perspective, Crews' paradoxical inability to stay or leave mirrors my own conundrum: just as I cannot remain within the landscape of my birth—my job keeps me two hours away, and I lack my father's know-how, strength, and ease around machines—neither can I forsake it, for I am responsible both for what my family has done to the land in my name as well as for what will become of it, when my father no longer can take care of things.

Out of Reach, yet in Sight

Unlike *Childhood* though inspired by it, Tim McLaurin's *Keeper of the Moon* negotiates rural and urban places, working-class and middle-class spaces, and agricultural and industrial labor. Set in Fayetteville, in southeastern North Carolina, this narrative of Wild Man Mac (the name McLaurin used while handling and demonstrating snakes to fearful audiences) complicates and rewilds the hard relationships between human and environment that Crews imagines and narrates in his autobiography.[10] A sustainable and just life, however, remains out of reach.

In *Childhood*'s Bacon County, no family seems any better off than another; every family's land is equally hard. In McLaurin's Fayetteville and surrounding Cumberland County, there exist spaces of natural fecundity as well as spaces of natural infertility. In *Keeper of the Moon,* those spaces demarcate and are demarcated by socioeconomic status, as the lay of the land and quality of soil telegraph privilege and the lack thereof. In the migration to urban centers and suburban blurs, rural people leave behind family home places and resettle in the marginal spaces of the expanding industrial geographies. Where the landscape is higher and more temperate, the people are tonier. McLaurin writes, "The fall line of the Piedmont stops on the west side of the Cape Fear River on the fancy side of Fayetteville, the high land where dogwoods and azaleas bloom." Yet "[o]ne has only to cross the old span bridge on Person Street to enter the working world. The land is damp there, holds the heat, and runs flat and wet toward the coast. East Fayetteville is a community of squat frame houses, pool halls, fish markets, auto parts stores and 7-Elevens, men who work with their hands, women who fret over their children and the bills. Laws are generally observed, but interpreted according to one's situation and opportunity." Just as the high ground of Fayetteville excludes the working classes, so too does East Fayetteville create a social, economic, and juridical world of its own. Yet its world, juxtaposed against upper-class neighborhoods such as Haymount, also functions as a sort of colony of wealthy Fayetteville where less desirable land uses can be outsourced—smelly fish markets, auto parts stores—and where less-desirable people (because they are less desirable to the upper class) can be paid less, worked harder, and otherwise oppressed. The depth of McLaurin's narrative of class and geography affirm Don Mitchell's assertion that "class . . . is necessarily marked by geographically complex patterns, textures, and strategies."[11] Indeed, the bewildering, paradoxical complexity that pervades his narrative underscores the academic and psychosocial impossibility of anchoring any subject's identity, class, and place. As *Keeper of the Moon* suggests, one cannot rightly appraise one's own place, for its appraisal cannot help but rise or fall in its comparison to other places, its history irrelevant in the here and now. In a way, what McLaurin and his fellow working-class whites do to and with the land—again, the

dual injustice of poverty and necessity—cannot be severed from the specter of those ever-blooming dogwoods and azaleas in Haymount, no matter
how great or small the literal and figurative mileage between them.

McLaurin's memoir and other fiction—such as *The Acorn Plan* (1988),
a novel that likewise faces the violence and traumas of working-class life
in a world where the poor are consigned to the bottoms—illustrate the
profound ways that the roots and symptoms of human oppression express
themselves in the construction and deconstruction of unequal spaces.
Thus *Keeper of the Moon* celebrates sites of working-class liberation and
freedom, where McLaurin and his kinfolk escape, gather, and connect. For
example, he describes Yellow Island, a "bramble of trees and vines . . . in
the delta of Cape Fear [River], approximately twelve square miles of some
of the most junglelike terrain north of the equator," as untamed, exotic,
and escapist, a wild retreat where rural men prove their masculinity and
throw off the chains of industrial drudgery: "Yellow Island was a haven for
raccoons and deer, fox and possums, the thick tangles of reed and brier
topped by hardwoods, a fortress against man and his hunting tools. For
every coon shot from a treetop, probably a dozen slipped the dogs. A savvy
buck could shed many racks and live until his muzzle was gray as long
as he stayed in the deep woods." What's more, working-class whites construct spaces in the wildness of rural Cumberland and surrounding counties that, outside the surveillance of the job or the law, express their values
and customs. In *The Keeper of the Moon,* "a quarter-acre clearing that had
been cut of undergrowth with a bush-hog mower and raked clean," down
a "small dirt lane . . . cutting between two tobacco barns and leading into
the woods," becomes a refuge for cockfights, dogfights, dope smoking, and
moonshine, outside the reach of the law.[12] For McLaurin's working-class
whites, such clearings—fallow fields, perhaps abandoned when farming no
longer can provide for a family—become sites of collective memory and
community. Their gathering in these out-of-the-way places re-members
them as a people united by work and sustains them as they weather a new
economy defined by downsizing, outsourcing, union busting, and chronic
joblessness. These out-of-the-way spaces, however, are threatened with
extinction. The suburbanization of Cumberland County (thanks to the
rapid expansion of Fort Bragg) and regions across the Sunbelt is transforming fields and woods into orderly subdivisions whose names recall only the
natures they replaced, not the families removed from the landscape.

To be sure, McLaurin cannot retreat to nostalgia, nor can he make himself comfortable in the new industrial landscape, a terrain defined by factory work, the chasm between rich and poor, the depopulation and divestment of the countryside, and the inscription of unjust economies on the land. He is both proud to be working class and critical of its conscriptions: "I might look the part of a laborer in my pinstriped uniform, but I was a man who milked rattlesnakes and rode monkeys on his shoulder," he writes. "Such a man I imagined could never become permanently mired." Like Crews, he holds deep esteem for old ways of life, yet unlike his predecessor, he confronts the reality that he cannot and will not replant himself in this place: "It is far easier to chase the stars than to hunker down on a piece of solid land and love it and hate it. With acreage comes commitment—sticking to one woman, your children, working a job that pays the bills and keeps you fed and clothed. I fear I am not the same man as my brothers or father, could not continue to punch that clock every day."[13] In this lamentation, the memoir communicates a searing honesty that encompasses both the desire for belonging and the hard realities of geographic, bodily, and cultural exile.

Considered alongside *Childhood* and *Keeper of the Moon,* Mason's *Clear Springs* reflects an alternative consciousness that shifts the terms of the debate and gestures toward recuperative understandings of place. Similar to the way that Crews reconstructs his late father's life, Mason reconstructs her mother's life as a means of understanding her own migration from and return to her family farmstead. Her eventual homecoming takes place only on her terms, terms that aren't easy, as my own confrontation with my family's history makes clear. On the one hand, I know that I am a channel for the lives who have created and shaped me. Yet I cannot repeat the ecological mistakes they have made, just as I cannot embalm my home place as it exists in my memory and the memories of my forebears—even though to fail to do so feels like turning my back on my upbringing. My reading, thinking, and writing give me a sense of the value of wildness; I cannot tame, clear cut, litter, or stockpile the landscapes I inhabit as if they are some sort of bulwark against hard times. Rather, I have come to believe that I must make reparations, even as those amends seem, on the surface, contradictory to the culture I have inherited.

Published at the close of the twentieth century, Mason's memoir depicts the postmodern complexity of place, even a place as ostensibly simple as an old farmstead: "A lane cuts through the middle, from front to back, and two creeks divide it crosswise. The ground is rich, but it washes down the creeks." Black walnut trees and blackberry bushes have been planted as windbreakers and bulwarks against soil erosion, and generations have dumped trash in the creeks "to prevent hard rains—gully-washers—from carrying the place away." As an author working after the publication of Rachel Carson's *Silent Spring* (1962), Mason acknowledges the complexity of the place as an ecosystem and the way it has been affected by pollution, paying close attention to a quarter-acre pond her father built for her mother's fishing enjoyment. The pond, she describes, hides a lively ecosystem of pondweed, snails, spiders, water striders, crawfish, worms, and larvae. Yet it also registers environmental disasters, the result of encroaching industrial and commercial development, in the fish kills that have occurred there: "a fuel spill from the highway, warmwater runoff from a tobacco-warehouse fire, and a flood that washed the fish out into the creek." Bordered by railroads and highways that connect New Orleans, Chicago, Mobile, and Tupelo, "[t]he landscape is still changing, [and] [m]y birthplace is now at the hub of industrial growth in the county," along with subdivisions, a Soviet-like set of feed mills, an air-compressor factory, and an influx of new Latino workers.[14]

Just as she underlines the complexity of the place, so too does she expose the farm as a site of masculine privilege. Throughout, *Clear Springs* responds to and repudiates this misogyny, an injustice that for Mason constructs a rough South that causes an impassable chasm between human beings and the environment. In a signal passage, Mason describes, through the point of view of her mother, Christy, the family's decision not to buy a neighboring piece of land in the 1940s. It is a prime parcel, "a fine piece of land. It had an easy roll to it, no troublesome creeks, easy access to the highway. It wouldn't even need a barn or a house, since it was adjacent to the present farm."[15] But traditional notions of agrarianism, women's roles, and family duties, at their heart male-normative, derail the purchase, even though the family can afford it—with Christy Mason's savings. Wilburn Mason's decision against the purchase means defeat for Christy, who then resigns herself to trying to improve the family's lot through a more or less traditional role as a farmer's wife. Each time she moves outside those boundaries to provide a better life for her family, she fails, though her off-farm work brings in much-needed money.

The ramifications of Wilburn's decision become clear, as Mason realizes that buying the neighboring property might have kept the family on the farm, rather than sending children to work off the farm. Moreover, it might have preserved the landscape's agricultural character: "In the 1940s, . . . my family could have bought that land for what would now seem mere chicken feed. And where would the chicken tower be now? What if? It is frustrating, even now, to think of my father's unwillingness to take the smallest risk. . . . [M]aybe we would not have ultimately dispersed. Maybe the larger farm would have been enough to hold us there." The suppression and dismissal of women's voices and experiences on the farm ripple into sublimations and repudiations in other realms. For one, Mason builds walls against poverty or classing herself with working-class people. "Of course we weren't poor at all," she declares. "Poor people had too many kids, and they weren't landowners; they rented decrepit little houses with plank floors and trash in the yard. 'Poor people are wormy and eat wild onions,' Mama said. We weren't poor, but we were country." In Mason's narrative, the possession and assiduous upkeep of land function to safeguard her family's place in society. For another, Mason can root herself neither in the land of her family history nor in the urban landscape of town. She writes,

> [I] want[ed] desperately to live near the stores and library, yet I was so unsure of myself when I went to town that I didn't know how to act. I wouldn't talk to anyone or look anyone in the eye. One version of me was a little queen on a throne. But another was a clodhopper. At heart was the inferiority country people felt because they worked the soil. . . .
>
> . . . As I picked blackberries or hoed vegetables in the scorching morning sun, Hilltopper music playing in my head made me feel there was a way out— some release from the cycle of the seasons.[16]

Refusing to imagine a shared bond with her working-class peers, yearning to escape the psychological poverty she felt, and listening to popular bands allow her to escape not only the misogyny of her home in particular, but also country people, country places, and country time in general. As I read Mason's memoir, I cannot help but think of the quick smile that comes to my mother's face when she speaks of her first car, a red Volkswagen Beetle; it is an image that, as I think about it in the terms of *Clear Springs,* becomes an escape from the place she knew, a sort of exotic difference that set her apart from her sisters, her mother, and the home place she has never left. Now that my father has retired, my parents have talked of moving into a new house, for neither has lived in their own house. A new house, a red Beetle: these symbolize flight, escape, and transcendence, even as they symbolize ordinariness, compromise, and staying close to home.

At the reflective and circumspective close of the narrative, Mason offers a socially and environmentally just solution: organic agriculture. Her vision symbolizes her reconceptualization of the land, at the same time that it offers reclamation and redemption of the old ways of farming. Through their decision to farm organically, she and her husband Roger couple their respect for her Kentucky forebears with a modern sensitivity for steward-ship. Inspired by Thoreau's *Walden* (1854) and *The Whole Earth Catalog*, they begin their rebirth in Connecticut, shortly after their wedding. They

> were on the cusp of the back-to-nature-movement, the natural look, the real thing. I was ready to hoe. Roger didn't know a shelly bean from a marigold, but ambitiously we launched into growing a garden. . . . By hand, we broke sod for our garden. When I plunged my hands into the black New England soil, I felt I was touching a rich nourishment that I hadn't had since I was a small child. It had been years since I helped Mama in the garden. Yet the feel of dirt seemed so familiar. This was real. It was true. I wheeled around and faced home.

Her return home and to farming happens on her terms alone:

> I had mercifully escaped the hardship of the old ways—no lye soap or wash-boards, no hog-killing. I wouldn't have to carry water. I wanted blackberries, but not the cruel, thorny ones; botanists had discovered better ones now. I had grandiose visions of an asparagus bed. I was optimistic, just as I had been when I moved to New York years before. Now I could rediscover and celebrate the Kentucky springtime. . . . I wanted to return, but not relapse. . . . Finally, I thought, I could live there now on my own terms.[17]

Mason's new vision lays to rest a lost way of life—hog killing, domes-tic drudgery—and replaces it with a hopeful future—user-friendly black-berries, asparagus instead of callous cash crops. In this way, *Clear Springs* seeks to move forward in a way that will heal the landscape that now sur-rounds her ancestral home—a landscape scarred by corporate agribusiness, a fossil fuel–addicted transportation system, and low-wage grunt work. In this way, too, *Clear Springs* moves us beyond the paralyses that end *Child-hood* and *Keeper of the Moon* and suggests alternatives that build both soil and wealth—alternatives that might, Mason implies, rectify the growing chasm between rich and poor and the alienation between humankind and terra firma. To be sure, the reality might be less rosy than the dream—as I can attest, having joined and dropped out of a community garden near my house—but without the dream, even a minor transformation becomes impossible. Thanks to that community garden, I have met people I would never have met before, resurrected what I learned of gardening from my father, put in a small vegetable patch in my backyard, and joined a group of people trying to create a more locavorous community.

Red Sky at Morning: Challenges, Inheritances, and Opportunities

Like Crews and McLaurin before her, Mason thematizes socioeconomic and cultural relationships to the environment and the problems that stem from those interactions. In earlier interpretive frameworks, their memoirs might have been easily comprehended through theorizations of pastoralism and antipastoralism, southern compulsions to tell about race and place, and defenses of southern exceptionalism. Today's crisis of climate change and concomitant ecological insecurity, compounded by increasing chasms between rich and poor, compel a new, more critical, more pressing interpretation. In *Red Sky at Morning: America and the Crisis of the Global Environment* (2004), James G. Speth provides a framework with which we might couple ecocritical and new critical realist sensibilities in our readings of these US Southern memoirists. In his wide-ranging book, Speth outlines nine "threats to biodiversity and to healthy ecosystems": land use conversion, land degradation, freshwater shortages, watercourse modifications, invasive species, overharvesting, climate change, ozone depletion, and pollution. These devastations appear in each memoir: the transformation of wilderness to cultivated farmland, the overapplication of toxic chemicals to cash crops, the exhaustion of the soil through overcultivation, and the hints of climate change. Exacerbating these destructive changes, in these memoirs and the world over, are "the pressures generated by large populations of the poor. . . . They should be thought of as victims of economic systems that have not provided alternatives" to deforestation and agricultural conversion—and whether they seek subsistent survival or keeping up with the overdeveloped world's Joneses, capitalism compels an exploitative relationship to the land, as Crews, McLaurin, and Mason make clear.[18]

Worse, power inequities between the Global North and the Global

South—mirrored in the subordination of the US South to the US North—make environmental reparations doubly difficult: "Important asymmetries exist between the countries of the well-to-do North and those of the poorer South," Speth writes, "easily contribut[ing] to social tensions, violent conflicts, humanitarian emergencies, and the creation of ecological refugees" —conflicts that pervade, in one form or another, the three narratives explored here. He continues, "To generalize, the poorer countries of the global South have perceived the global environmental agenda as an agenda of the wealthy North and, indeed, international environmental regimes have typically been pushed by the richer countries. The poorer countries have not only given these concerns a lower priority, they have feared that agreement would undermine their growth potential or impose high costs of compliance."[19] Beset by perceptions of worthlessness and powerlessness, these voices of the US South strain to be heard and appreciated. To be sure, US southerners enjoy greater geopolitical and socioeconomic privilege than the denizens of the Global South worldwide, and white US southerners enjoy greater privilege than nonwhite US southerners. Yet the solution, both political and environmental, consists in empowering US southerners in the same way and measure as all people of the Global South, Speth and others argue.

Indeed, as Mason's example in turning to local, sustainable, organic farming suggests, the solution lies with those who have taken the blame, rightly and wrongly, for environmental devastation. Speth quotes Roger Stone and Claudia D'Andrea of the Sustainable Development Institute who "conclude that the only solution, imperfect though it may be, is 'the relatively simple act of allocating responsibility for managing and protecting forests to the local groups and communities that depend upon their healthy survival rather than on their destruction.'"[20] In a world facing unknown climatic alteration, the specter of intensive, biodiverse, small-scale farms (like those that predated the Crewses' fated-to-fail, get-big-or-get-out, cash-crop monocultures), of full-time stewardship of the land by those most connected to it (not half-time factory work and half-time farming, as was the case for McLaurin's father), and of organic agriculture (as Mason comes to appreciate) offers optimism and hope.

As Crews, McLaurin, and Mason reveal, to be working class and Southern is to bear a heavy environmental burden. It is to be mired in toxicity, both of one's own making and not, to be relegated to the most difficult of landscapes, and to be imprisoned in struggle to wrest something from that landscape—a specter of labor that functions to reinscribe one as poor, dirty, worthless, and expendable. Reading their provocative memoirs makes clear that the Earth needs an invigorated, and invigorating, environmental justice activism, a movement Southern born and raised. It must reject the dichotomy of "jobs *or* the planet," and it needs to be able to channel the clannish tendencies of working-class whites to retreat to hidden spaces of the countryside (either as rednecks or as crunchy granola types) into equitable partnerships with people of color in a shared public commons. What's more, it must dream into being a systemic vision of agriculture that builds soil rather than destroying human lives and local communities, uplifting and coalescing the many groups that work toward labor rights for farmworkers, sustainable agriculture, and progressive environmental law. Only when we work across the issues can we appreciate the diversities and complexities of working-class relationships to labor and land and reimagine those relationships in ecologically, culturally, and economically sustainable ways—and to tell our life stories without shame or guilt, creating a world that nurtures and enriches.

In the end, we need each other most because we can't do it alone—and, equally important, we need memoirs like Crews's, Mason's, and McLaurin's, because they compel us to understand our place (environmental and socioeconomical place) for the infinite complexity it entails. We need these stories and these groups so that we can acknowledge the environmental abuse done in our names and act to make lasting reparations. For these stories are by people like us, and as such, they open our eyes to the possibilities that exist.

Before the spring 2010 semester ended, my parents visited. As we ate lunch, we talked about when Mom and Dad would have to mow Grandpa's old home place and whether our cousins, who dairy farmed and lived nearer the property than my parents, planned to plant any field cover there this year. Mom and Dad got around to telling me that they had been working with a state forestry service agent to come up with a timber plan for the property, a requirement for keeping the land in a tax bracket my mother and her sisters could afford. The forestry service agent, they explained, would survey the property and estimate the value of timber it contained, using the information as the basis of a plan for managing its resources. As they talked, I thought of the many fall and spring days my dad and I spent at the farm cutting firewood, splitting it, and hauling it home—usually going into the woods and removing a fallen tree, rarely having to cut one down. I felt sad, then, to imagine the place, full of mature oak, sycamore, poplar, hickory, walnut, and pine, could be clear cut; only now had the scars of an earlier round of logging—thanks to an infestation of pine beetles—begun to fade.

"Well, do you want to inherit it?" she asked, abruptly.

"Do I want to inherit it?" I repeated her question to myself. Of course I wanted to inherit it, I thought; as Janisse Ray says in *Ecology of a Cracker Childhood* of the woods of her own youth: "The memory . . . is scrawled on my bones, so that I carry the landscape inside." But then I imagined what that inheritance could be: a ravaged landscape, a mockery of my memories, a curse. As Ray laments the lost pinewoods, she acknowledges that "[o]ne day that timberland may be mine. It will be truly and unforgivably mine."[21] Whether my inheritance would be intact or clear-cut, I realized, depended on my taking responsibility for this land, now, even a hundred miles from home.

"Yes, I want to inherit it," I said. "I'll take care of it."

How I'll take care of it, if it is handed down to me, I haven't decided, and thankfully it's not a conversation that my parents, wife, and I had that day. Will I hire someone to mow once a month, when my parents are no longer able to do the work themselves, thus preserving the fields my forebears wrought from the woods? Or will I let those fields return gently to woodland, and provide a home for the blacksnakes, turkey, and deer I've had the good fortune of seeing there? Will I connect with groups like the Triangle Land Conservancy, or work with county officials on securing a conservation easement to preserve the property in perpetuity? Will I come to the point, as my mother sometimes does, that I curse it, as a weight that keeps me from providing for my family? Whatever happens, I hope I can begin, like Crews, McLaurin, and Mason, to rewrite the story that I inherited, to tell it without personal shame or guilt, and to leave for the generations that follow a record of work, life, and memory, inscribed and sustained on the land—in sum, a heritage worth preserving for the future.

NOTES

For their careful readings and incisive suggestions in the long journey of this essay, I wish to thank the editors of this volume, Jennifer Westerman and Christina Robertson; my colleagues, Teagan Decker, Jane Haladay, and Mary Ann Jacobs of the University of North Carolina, Pembroke; and my undergraduate honors thesis adviser, Joséph Flora, emeritus, of the University of North Carolina, Chapel Hill.

1. Whereas I, as someone of working-class white experience, can historicize my forebears' existence in a racialized, and racializing, culture, I cannot countenance sentiments of prejudice, just as I cannot pardon expressions (even if unwitting) of racism in *Childhood* (in which Crews describes his father's sexual conquest of a Seminole Indian woman and his own tormenting of his African American friend) and *Keeper of the Moon,* in which a young Tim McLaurin mocks Dr. Martin Luther King Jr. in front of an African American friend and, later, urinates on two Lumbee Indian boys. Harry Crews, *A Childhood: The Biography of a Place* (Athens: University of Georgia Press, 1978); Tim McLaurin, *Keeper of the Moon: A Southern Boyhood* (Asheboro, N.C.: Down Home Press, 1991); Bobbie Ann Mason, *Clear Springs: A Memoir* (New York: Random House, 1999). Although I do not foreground the complications of race and racism in this essay, and while I approach these three texts ethnographically, I ground this analysis in theories of environmental justice and thus do not contend that race and racial oppression should be excluded from analysis of working-class whiteness and environmental consciousness. I am profoundly grateful to the members of my family and to my teachers who have opened my eyes to horizons far beyond my seven acres in eastern Orange County and who have supported the kind of work I do.

2. I see these narratives as exceptionally rich texts for ecocritical analysis, and I hope future ecocritics will continue to explore the territory of the rough South and the grit lit it spawns for deeper insights into the interpenetrations of socioeconomic class, environmentalism, and a South whose environmental practices transcend political, cultural, and historical boundaries. Such future work will carry on the work begun by J. Bill Berry and Fred Hobson in their analyses of Southern autobiographical impulses; Jay Watson in ecocriticism of class and landscape; and Eric Gary Anderson, Martyn Bone, Deborah Cohn, Leigh Ann Duck, George Handley, Riche Richardson, and Jon Smith in new Southern studies. Like Watson, I too "want . . . to lobby . . . for the value of incorporating Southern texts, landscapes, and perspectives more fully and actively in the ongoing project of American environmental studies," interrogating how "the region's long, highly visible history of poverty and its rich and troubled history of land use intertwine to foreground poverty itself as an environmental issue." As Watson argues, "the social lives and identities of Southerners must be understood in an environmental context," just as "the converse is also true, that the Southern environment demands a thoroughgoing socioeconomic analysis: because natural history in the South so pointedly *is* social history and vice versa [emphasis in original], an ecology of a cracker childhood

must be accompanied by an economics of the cracker landscape" (Jay Watson, "Economics of a Cracker Landscape: Poverty as an Issue in Two Southern Writers," *Mississippi Quarterly: The Journal of Southern Cultures* 55, no. 4, 497).

3. Robert Gingher offers a helpful definition of grit lit, despite his limitation of it to fiction: " 'Grit lit' is a facetious shorthand for fiction devoted to the rough edges ('grit') of life, . . . homespun stories grounded in the grime or 'grit' of reality [that] typically deploy stark, sometimes violent narratives of poor white southerners." Naming Dorothy Allison, Doris Betts, Larry Brown, Crews, Mason, Cormac McCarthy, McLaurin, and Lee Smith, Gingher writes that "[t]hese writers exploit the full power of the gritty mundane particular, their voices and visions finely attuned to the extent that their humankind resists or re-invents what-is in order to survive. . . . Grit lit writers find such stark, often violent conditions as necessary for reaching an essentially hostile audience as for startling constitutionally hard-headed characters (and, by extension, readers) into some shocking new valuation of their true position on earth" (Robert Gingher, "Grit Lit," in Joséph M. Flora and Lucinda H. McKethan, eds., *The Companion to Southern Literature: Themes, Genres, Places, People, Movements, and Motifs* (Baton Rouge: Louisiana State University Press, 2002), 319–20; Crews, *Blood and Grits,* New York: Harper & Row, 1979, "All I had," 145.

4. John Foster Bellamy, "The Limits of Environmentalism without Class: Lessons from the Ancient Forest Struggle in the Pacific Northwest," in Daniel Faber, ed., *The Struggle for Ecological Democracy: Environmental Justice Movements in the United States* (New York: The Guilford Press, 1998), 188.

5. Cowdrey, *This Land, This South: An Environmental History* (Lexington: University Press of Kentucky, 1996), "a theater of," 127; Daniel, *Toxic Drift: Pesticides and Health in the Post-World War II South* (Baton Rouge: Louisiana State University Press, 2005), "the pesticide wreckage," 170; Kirby, *Mockingbird Song: Ecological Landscapes of the South* (Chapel Hill: University of North Carolina Press, 2006).

6. Crews, *Childhood,* "The timber in," 16, "from one patch," 40, "as much as," 30, "Whether on shares," 11, "[h]e worked harder," 31.

7. Ibid., "nothing but pine," 37; "with an ax," 38.

8. Andrew Kimbrell et al. in *The Fatal Harvest Reader: The Tragedy of Industrial Agriculture* (Washington, DC: Island Press, 2002) examine these interpenetrating impacts.

9. As Amy E. Weldon writes, "[F]or Crews, then, words can define not only the physical place inhabited by poor white Southerners but also the imaginative and spiritual spaces, including the interconnected web of music, religion, manners and customs, and ways of storytelling—so that, as the title of *A Childhood: The Biography of a Place* indicates, telling the story of a place and telling the story of its people are nearly the same thing." " 'When Fantasy Meant Survival,' " *Mississippi Quarterly* 53, no. 1 (Winter 1999), 95; Crews, *Childhood,* "was inviolate," 28, "I come from people," 16, "Goddamn sun," 182.

10. McLaurin calls Crews his "favorite writer," whose "raw honesty" in *Childhood* inspired the North Carolinian to write *The Keeper of the Moon*. McLaurin continues, "Harry Crews taught me that I should write what I know about, and that the characters and their words should be true to the reality of their lives. . . . He also taught me that if a man writes of the affected, of those who live hard and hope mightily, he is usually himself of that caste and should not live too insulated from his past." " 'Is Your Novel Worth a Damn?'": Meeting Harry Crews," in Erick Bledsoe, ed., *Perspectives on Harry Crews* (Jackson, MS: University Press of Mississippi, 2001), 12–13. For a full discussion of rewilding, see Dave Foreman, *Rewilding North America: A Vision for Conservation in the 21st Century* (Washington, DC: Island Press, 2004).

11. McLaurin, *Keeper of the Moon,* "The fall line," 130; Mitchell, "Working-Class Geographies: Capital, Space, and Place," in John Russo and Sherry Lee Linkon, eds., *New Working-Class Studies* (Ithaca, NY: ILR Press, 2005), "class is necessarily," 95. He continues, "Working-class histories and geographies—the geographies of capitalism— are complex, contradictory, and confusing. There is still much to be learned about them" (95).

12. McLaurin, *Keeper of the Moon,* "bramble of trees," 246, "Yellow Island," 248–49. To my mind, passages such as these confirm Larry Brown's appreciation that McLaurin's "love of the natural world resonated through everything he wrote, the seasons, storms, clouds and sunshine, sky and rain, the bright stars in their constellations. The smallest of God's creatures had their place in Tim's work" ("Tim," *Pembroke Magazine* 36 (2004), 67; McLaurin, *Keeper of the Moon,* "a quarter-acre," 90.

13. Ibid., "I might look," 217, "It is far," 227.

14. Mason, *Clear Springs,* "A lane cuts," 5, "a fuel spill," 3, "[t]he landscape is," 7. In " 'I Keep Looking Back to See Where I've Been': Bobbie Ann Mason's *Clear Springs* and Henry David Thoreau's *Walden*," (*Southern Literary Journal* 36, no. 2 (March 2004), Laurie Champion locates the complexity of Mason's memoir in its deep structural, ideological, and aesthetic relationship to the transcendentalist's masterwork.

15. Mason, *Clear Springs,* 45–46.

16. Ibid., "In the 1940s," 46, "Of course we," 83, "[I] wanted desperately," 97, "As I picked," 102.

17. Mason, *Clear Springs,* "were on the," 157, "I had mercifully," 182.

18. Speth, *Red Sky at Morning: America and the Crisis of the Global Environment* (New Haven, CT: Yale University Press, 2004), 30–34; "the pressures generated," 38.

19. Ibid., "Important asymmetries exist," 61, "To generalize," 107–8.

20. Ibid., "conclude that the," 40.

21. Ray, *Ecology of a Cracker Childhood* (Minneapolis: Milkweed Press, 1999), "The memory," 4, "[o]ne day that," 103.

12

Reinhabiting the Poor Farm in
Memory and Landscape

JENNIFER WESTERMAN

⏤⏤⏤⏤⏤⏤⏤⏤⏤⏤⏤⏤⏤⏤⏤⏤⏤⏤⏤⏤⏤⏤⏤⏤⏤⏤⏤⏤⏤⏤⏤

Perhaps you have seen the rambling outline of a dilapidated clapboard house against a rural sky and a nearby sign: Poor Farm Road. Or a grainy black-and-white photo of a brick manor house, its upright shoulders the hallmark of a long-forgotten institution. There were the Vanderburgh County Poor Farm in Illinois, the Frederick County Poor Farm in Virginia, the City Poor Farm in New Hampshire, the Lee County Poor Farm in Iowa, the Jackson County Poor Farm in Michigan, and throughout the nation, poorhouses in almost every county. Less familiar are the faces and voices of the people who once lived in these places, including poor workers who had fallen on hard times, single mothers paid insufficient wages, skilled laborers who had become disabled, orphaned children, farmers whose crops had failed, the insane for want of treatment facilities, the unwell, the elderly—too old to work and displaced by the speed of factory systems—and widows left alone. I have often wondered what the West Virginia poor farm where my great-great grandmother grew up looked like and how it was that she and her mother came to live there.

I am drawn to the history of the poor farm because I see in its past the story of working-class people marginalized from society in rural landscapes sidelined by urban industrialization. I am interested in how working-class identities have shaped and been shaped by the dual forces of social welfare institutions and environment, particularly in southern Appalachia. The care-taking social programs that emerged in the United States in the early to mid-nineteenth century—and that endured into the early twentieth century—responded first to prevailing economic conditions, and later to the unintended consequences of the programs' designs. Inherent in these systems has been the view that the environment is separate from humans and thus exploitable, and that working-class people exist on the outskirts of landscapes of power and are thus expendable.

The social history of the poor farm in the United States illustrates how conditions of poverty helped to create a particular view of working-class people and poor workers. This perception, one that in many ways persists in our modern times, absolves dominant economic and social agents from accountability and places culpability for poverty in the character failings of individuals. While reasons for poverty varied during the poorhouse era, historian and author of *In the Shadow of the Poorhouse: A Social History of Welfare in America* Michael B. Katz contends that the majority of explanations "may be traced in one way or another to the organization of work."[1] Environmental historians Richard White, Chad Montrie, and others have shown that this work is performed within an ecological context. As poorhouses became the dominant institution for social welfare, working-class people and poor workers were regarded as part of the machinery of industry, whether in extractive labor in nature or in factory environments, or as social deviants when unemployed. These perceptions aided in their economic and physical marginalization—even as in some cases their bodily labor connected them to landscape—or wrote them out of the narratives that have dominated our environmental thinking.

Revisiting the poor farm can illuminate connections between the ways we have valued the land and working people and the social and environmental policies that have influenced these cultural beliefs. Environmental historian Stephen Mosley noted in 2006 that "working-class voices have been too rarely heard in environmental history," and that "very few social historians have made the effort [to recognize] the environment as 'a critical factor affecting human agency.'" Linking working-class experiences of poverty with environmental conditions suggests one method for attending to this gap. One purpose for recovering working-class stories, suggests American studies scholar Janet Zandy, is "to recall the fragile filaments and necessary bonds of human relationships, as well as to critique those economic and societal forces that blunt or block human development."[2] This recovery work begins when the stories of working-class people are reinscribed into the narrative of human development. It is a narrative that comprises not only economic and social structures, but also the natural environment on which we depend.

A more thorough integration of social justice concerns into the idea and practice of bioregionalism offers one such possibility for telling new stories about workers and the land. A bioregion is a physical and cultural territory defined "by natural (rather than political) boundaries with a geographic, climatic, hydrological, and ecological character capable of supporting unique human and nonhuman living communities." "By foregrounding natural factors as a way to envision place," suggest the editors of *The Bioregional Imagination: Literature, Ecology, Place,* "bioregionalism proposes that human identity may be constituted by our residence in a larger community of natural beings—our local bioregion—rather than, or at least supplementary to, national, state, ethnic, or other more common bases of identity."[3] In other words, for bioregionalists human identity is situated in relation to the geographical parameters and cultural contexts of a particular place. One possible limitation of bioregionalism is that in positing the primacy of a natural community rather than a social one, it risks separating nature and identity from the larger, class-based economic system and marginalizing working-class experiences of place. A social justice–oriented bioregionalism would account for ways that identity formations are politicized in a particular region, especially in terms of social class and how that status, in turn, impacts our experiences of place, our levels of exposure to environmental hazards, and our economic well-being.

Another significant tenet of bioregionalism addresses links between environmental degradation and human separation, both physical and emotional, from nature. The solution proposed by bioregional thinkers is to develop a bioregional identity through the process of reinhabitation: "learning to live-in-place in an area that has been disrupted and injured through past exploitation [and] becoming native to a place through becoming aware of the particular ecological relationships that operate within and around it." The emphasis has historically been placed on restoring environmental damages via living-in-place in order to facilitate an ecological way of seeing. "But while bioregionalism has so far attempted to bridge the divide between humans and non-human nature," researchers studying the Oak Ridges Moraine bioregion assert, "it has yet to confront the more profound challenges posed by the continuing perception of a nature-culture divide and the social and environmental inequities between and within human communities themselves." I see an opportunity to deepen reinhabitory thinking by considering how reinhabitation engages with structures of power that have institutionalized forms of class-based discrimination in social welfare policies, economic systems, and the public imagination.[4]

The idea and practice of a social justice–oriented bioregionalism, and of a corresponding reinhabitory model, might serve to elevate the concerns of working-class people and poor workers and their experiences of place. This approach recognizes that landscapes also hold violence done to people in addition to that done to natural systems, such as mountains, streams, plains, and deserts. The bioregional project has the potential to do restorative work in the service of bridging the nature–labor divide, but it must confront class categories as they relate to environmental histories, place-based knowledge, and environmental and social problems. As environmental writer Joshua Dolezal reasons, "Social disenfranchisement, a familiar theme to the working poor, contributes to both environmental degradation and societal collapse." Working class is a category defined by occupation and in relation to income, race, gender, ethnicity, place, power, access, and exposures to risk, and it is also an identity mutually defined by relationships to the land. The bioregional frame could call attention to the ways that class is not simply an economic or social classification, but also an environmental category. If "the concept of reinhabitation is a response to the conditions of detachment," the necessary healing work cannot begin until working-class people are visible on the landscape. By the act of bearing witness, as Bernie Glassman calls us to practice, the memories and lived experiences of working-class people and the landscapes of their labor come into view.[5]

Memory and Landscape in Southern Appalachia

When my sister and I met Jim Helmick at his home in Brandywine, West Virginia, he was eighty-seven years old. Complications from eye surgery had left him legally blind in one eye, and he said in a matter-of-fact way that his hips bothered him, and that walking was painful at times. He sat in a worn blue recliner amidst a modest scattering of accumulated possessions, nearly all of them covered in a thick layer of brown dust. Cobwebs that hung in long swooping chains from the mustard-colored fireplace mantle to window, then window to aqua-blue wall, were also covered in dust. Although the afternoon was bright outside, a single overhead light cast a hazy glow throughout the front room of the weathered farmhouse where he had lived since age fourteen.[6]

Before then, Helmick had spent his childhood about twenty miles north at the Pendleton County poor farm in Upper Tract, West Virginia. "Well, I was, I think I went there when I was two but I never did know what time of year we went to the county farm," he recalled. "I was born in '26 and we went down to the county farm in '28, and we was there until November of '36. That's when we went to Elkins. . . . I come here in 1947, [so I've been here] seventy-three years," he said. The Pendleton County poor farm was built in 1900. In the decades that followed, it served as one of several social welfare institutions in the state, known first as poorhouses, and later, as poor farms.

The poorhouse was the dominant institution of public welfare in the United States throughout the century before the New Deal. The structure and management of poorhouses were originally based on English Common Law and the 1601 Elizabethan Poor Law that mandated government responsibility for the poor. The system of state-run homes for the poor was designed to replace outdoor relief, a type of aid for paupers that depended on their placement in local homes. Despite these intentions, the two systems of relief continued together for many years. Auctioning of the poor to farmers was also a common form of social welfare. Poorhouses were managed by boards of state charities, county commissioners, local county officials (who were usually referred to as Overseers of the Poor), and county welfare boards. The goals of poorhouses, explains Katz, were to provide a more economical method for dealing with poor people, to discourage the working class from seeking relief programs, and to "transform the behavior and character of their inmates."[7] Essential to the poorhouse system were the rehabilitative vision of character reform and the desire to reduce demand for relief.

Poorhouses were established to provide basic needs and to reform through work what society perceived as a lack of morality that led to poverty. One result of this system was that the poor were categorized according to external social constructions of deviance. Poverty was itself considered to be a deviant condition. In the existing poor farm records found in county archives or in genealogies, the cause of admittance to the poorhouse was often plainly listed as poverty. Elizabeth Gaspar Brown, who examined county records of a poor farm in Wisconsin, noted that there was considerable discussion in the documents about the distinction between town poor and county poor. As county officials deliberated whether to purchase a rural farm for use as a poorhouse—and much of their deliberations had to do with cost—they also reinforced prevailing divisions between the worthy poor and the unworthy poor, further ostracizing some members of an already stigmatized population. These distinctions were rooted in a mid-nineteenth century report whose author made distinctions between poverty and pauperism. Katz writes, "Poverty resulted not from 'our faults' but from our 'misfortunes,' [but pauperism was] 'the consequence of willful error, of shameful indolence, of vicious habits.'" For many counties, care of the poor was primarily an economic issue and categorizing the poor in this way served to marginalize many working-class people and poor workers who experienced periods of unemployment. "In essence," writes Katz, "social policy advocated shutting up the old and sick away from their friends and relatives to deter the working class from seeking poor-relief. In this way, fear of the poorhouse became the key to sustaining the work ethic in nineteenth-century America."[8]

When we asked Jim Helmick about his childhood memories of life at the Pendleton County poor farm, he offered this recollection:

> You don't know better because that's the way you live. That's the way it was. When you don't have nothing different, you don't know whether it's good or bad. You don't have nothing, you never miss it. That's the way it was. You never got to go nowhere. You stayed on the farm all the time and you never got no Christmas. Christmas is something I just heard other people talk about. You hardly knew that that ever happened. I never knew what Christmas was. I never got nothing. The county was the one who had to buy the presents, and I guess they felt like they didn't have the money. When you don't have it, you never miss anything. You're just as happy as anywhere else, that's the way it was. You don't have the same lifestyle at a place like that as you do in a home where you go where you want to go and do what you want to do. . . . [T]here they tell you what to do. . . . [W]e didn't have any money to buy anything with so we couldn't even walk to the store.

I interviewed Jim Helmick as part of my research on the farm colony model, a practice that integrated agricultural labor into the structure of poor farms in the late-nineteenth and early-twentieth centuries. I had read several harrowing accounts of poorhouse conditions, such as this one from an 1870 report by Dr. G. W. Blacknall: "Thousands have been, many are even now, cast into that common receptacle, the County Poor House, where amid filth and neglect they do not live but only languish out the burden of an existence that is scarcely more than physical." And I had also encountered some research, personal stories, and the memoir of an overseer's child, *How I Grew Up Rich on the Poor Farm,* suggesting that poor farms may have had a divergent history from poorhouses, perhaps one that was not as dehumanizing as the institutions Blacknall witnessed.[9] Reading these histories through an environmental and social justice lens, I wondered if the self-sufficient communities described in some of this literature accurately reflected life for county farm residents who had little choice in their residency.

In his contemporary study of six New England poorhouses and poor farms, sociologist David Wagner suggests that the history of poorhouses in America diverged in the mid-nineteenth century when poor farms were created and that "historians and social scientists have failed to follow the name change from 'poorhouse' or 'poor farm' to explore exactly what this change actually entailed." Poor farms were rural poorhouses that adopted the farm colony model. Wagner contends that the story of the poorhouse "is not a depressing sob story, though it contains many things we regret; it is just as profoundly, and perhaps more importantly, a story of how poor people and others came to change the nature of an institution." The poor farm model, Wagner argues, had a separate history of aligning work in nature with improved mental and physical health: "The loss of this history suggests, too, a whole other side of the history of the poorhouse or poor farm. . . . [T]he poorhouse was a community for many people. Not only was its role important to those who stayed there but in some counties and towns, the poor farm also grew to play a major role as an agricultural center, a producer of revenue for government and of food products for the poor and others."[10] The poor farm, or farm colony, gave able-bodied poor and mentally ill patients an opportunity to work the land and to create self-sustaining food systems for poor farm residents. In addition, Wagner asserts, poor farms created a sense of community among the residents and helped to reform social and cultural misperceptions about the poor and mentally ill. However, county records examined by Katz and others indicate that the success of these programs varied widely. Occupancy at poor farms tended to increase in winter when unskilled laborers whose work was primarily performed outdoors in warmer months became unemployed and when the growing season had ended.

When we asked Jim Helmick how his family came to live at the Pendleton County poor farm, he said, "Well, they didn't have no home anywhere else. I don't know why they brought us there but that's where we wound up. They didn't have no place else to go. . . . [T]hat was a home for people who didn't have a home. . . . It wasn't the best place in the world, but it was a place that you got a roof over your head and a place to eat and a place to sleep even though the food wasn't that great."

Helmick remembered that there were "quite a few people there," at the Pendleton County poor farm. "[M]ost of them were mentally incompetent. They were not really able to do a lot of work." His father, a skilled farmer and manual laborer who had lost his job, "did virtually all the work with the horses and there was no one else much capable of doing it," Helmick said. I was curious if he also worked on the farm. The children, he said, "just had to wait 'til you got big enough to work 'fore you could do anything. When we got big enough, old enough, we had to take the cows to pasture of a morning and go get them of the evening; we had to carry water out to the hens, pull weeds out of the garden." Helmick also recalled that the products of his father's farm labor were rarely eaten by the residents. Blue john milk and ribble soup stood out in his memory of the poor farm kitchen, and he laughed warmly at the thought that my sister and I were not familiar with these names for skim milk and a thin flour dumpling soup.

Like Helmick's father, working-class people and poor workers of all ages lacked long-term job opportunities and federally guaranteed social and occupational safety nets, such as unemployment insurance and compensation for workplace injuries, in the late-nineteenth and early-twentieth centuries. The seasonality of labor demand and influxes of immigrant laborers meant that workers were also highly mobile, and this transiency fueled irregular patterns of economic development. Contrary to the belief that poor farm residents were derelict in their work ethic, many working-class people and poor workers faced economic hardship after a lifetime of work in a particular occupation, and the poor farm offered a shelter against homelessness and hunger. According to a 1937 comparative study of poor farm residents (called inmates) and poor workers in San José, California, researchers H. Dewey Anderson and Percy E. Davidson found, "Almost a

fourth of these poor-farm people had followed a single occupation during their working lifetime, yet such unusual steadiness had not prevented
them from ending their days in the poorhouse." These were men who had
"worked largely in the lowest levels of unskilled or semi-skilled labor where
pay is relatively small and possibilities of providing for a 'rainy day' few." As
modes of industrial production were adopted, economic development was
inconsistent across the nation's rural areas, towns, and cities. Throughout
the poor farm era, suggests Katz, "no clear line separated ordinary working people from those in need of help, because periodic destitution was
one structural result of the great social and economic transformations in
American life."[11]

For many poor workers, the factory system changed both the idea and
practice of work. Individual skills were devalued and high rates of production were prized. Mechanization, such as the development and use of steel
plows and mechanical reapers in agriculture, led to the dehumanization of
work, including lack of autonomy and ownership, and for many, entry into
the world of wage work. Inconsistent demand for industrial workers led to
transiency and lack of family stability. These factors were especially problematic for the working poor, women, those facing racial injustice, and the
elderly. According to one historical study of elderly working-class laborers in the South, "[B]lack, white, and Hispanic tenant farmers labored well
into old age. However, the advent of the mechanical cotton picker eventually pushed sharecroppers off the land. As a result, older blacks migrated
to cities for employment. For those who remained, there were few government services and persistent poverty." Wages for working women were disproportionately low, and many were dependent on the wages of men. In his
study of the Jefferson County Poor Farm in Alabama, James Tuten identifies a dual injustice experienced by poor, working-class African Americans:
"Not only did blacks suffer a higher rate of poverty, but they also endured
further stigma through the segregation system within the poor farm itself."
As workers aged and participation in the factory system became less likely
for them, the elderly were excluded from the prevailing economic model.
By 1930 "fully 30% of the elderly population was in poverty. This number
rose to 50% in 1935 and to two thirds by 1940."[12] Despite their level of skill
or their work histories, many elderly Americans found themselves displaced by industrial modernization.

These social and economic shifts were connected to the environmental changes that developed concomitantly. At the same time that economic insecurity often resulted in their participation in extractive industries, working-class people and poor workers came to be viewed as separate from or disinterested in an environment that was either depeopled or commoditized. The poor farm experience was chronologically framed by frontier narratives of unlimited American expansionism and the economic and environmental realities of the Great Depression and the Dust Bowl. The poor farm period paralleled the rise in industrialization, tremendous natural resources exploitation, rising population, and increasing migration to urban areas. Each of these environmental and social conditions changed the way we used and valued nature and more firmly entrenched a mechanistic worldview that depended on and perpetuated the separation of nature and culture.

During the late-nineteenth and early-twentieth centuries, exploitation of the natural world intensified across the nation. As rail lines opened interior spaces to development and lands were degraded, nature's labor and human labor were shaping American culture in significant ways. Deforestation caused rural communities to splinter, and resulting floods fragmented them even further. Extractive human labor in nature, such as iron manufacturing and coal mining, threatened the health of both the land and the people. Nature's labor in one of its most powerful forms—water—was bridled for human use. In the southern Appalachian bioregion, environmental historian Donald Edward Davis identifies logging as "the single greatest human activity to affect environmental and cultural change in the southern Appalachians." He adds, "While corporate logging operations did much to alter the mountain landscape, reducing forest cover and contributing to flooding and soil erosion, industrial logging had an important impact on the subsistence economy of the region, removing much needed farmland from the community land base as well as eliminating from the forest the native plants and animals that mountain families had long depended upon for survival" (including ginseng, goldenseal, mayapple, and galax).[13] When unemployed industrial workers attempted to return to their farmland, they often found that the soils were no longer viable, and even a return to traditional agriculture did not guarantee that Appalachian families would escape the conditions of poverty that led many to the poor farm.

While some urban poor farms did exist, the majority of these institutions were located in rural areas on the margins of economic development.

Working-class people and the working poor were removed, literally and figuratively, from the emerging industrial landscape. The poor farm thus serves as a cultural representation of both the commodification of labor and nature and the alienation of labor in nature. The isolation of the poor in the rural, agricultural spaces of poor farms contributed to their invisibility. In turn, forms of violence against people and the land were consequences of the ideological and actual separation of social and environmental problems.

The US Department of Labor commissioned a nationwide study of poor farm conditions in 1925. *The American Poor Farm and Its Inmates,* written by Harry C. Evans, was a scathing indictment of the poor farm system. "We have reported the worst," Evans wrote, "but by no means all the worst. There are many farms that are maintained and conducted in as decent a manner as possible, but decency is rarely possible under the system."[14] Evans described his grim observations: poor farms were unclean, unsanitary, filthy, rat infested, a cesspool. He was particularly appalled by the housing of physically sick and mentally ill inmates alongside women and children. Some records reveal that forced sterilization occurred. Poorhouses, Katz asserts, were ostensibly the "backwaters of social policy, stagnant and festering exceptions to the progressive spirit in American life." Although Michael Harrington's *The Other America* (1962) illuminated conditions of poverty in the United States and influenced President Lyndon B. Johnson's "War on Poverty," Frances Fox Piven and Richard Cloward's 1971 volume, *Regulating the Poor: The Functions of Public Welfare,* further advanced the idea that poorhouses were abhorrent and degrading modes of social control by political elites.[15]

As Jim Helmick recollected conditions on the poor farm where he grew up, he held an old pink rag in his hands. I noticed that he kneaded it between his hands as he spoke, and I felt we were pursuing questions whose answers, after seventy-three years, might still be raw. "I've been separated from my parents most of my life," Helmick recalled. He continued to recount his childhood at the poor farm: "I didn't stay in the same house as they did. I stayed with the older people. I never stayed with them. You never stayed with your parents. It wouldn't natural be that way but that's the way it was. It wasn't an ideal place, but it was a place they had for people who didn't have no place to stay. I don't think I'd want to go back and do it again, but it's unfortunate you have to go, but that's the way it was." I was reminded of something I had read in Katz's history: children in poorhouses often lived among adults who were strangers and with the mentally incompetent in ways that denied their humanity. After the *Charleston Gazette* published an article on the deplorable conditions of the Kanawha County poor farm, the director of Public Welfare in West Virginia, Major Francis Turner, decided to "remove children from all the poor farms in the state."[16] Helmick was relocated to a children's camp, and later was placed by the state at the farm where he worked the land for the rest of his life: "They brought me from the children's camp out at Elkins," he remembered. "I didn't have any say to my coming here, but the county put me here."

The demise of poor farms began with workers' compensation programs in the early twentieth century, followed by retirement programs for teachers, police officers, and fire fighters. On August 14, 1935, the Social Security Act granted benefits for elderly retired workers who had been employed in industry and commerce, and the act established a federal and state partnership system of unemployment insurance. The rise of labor unions supported some workers. Yet the Social Security Act left out large numbers of working-class people, including agricultural workers and poor farm residents, and opposition to organized labor grew. And some reformers questioned whether financial support alone, outside of poor farm communities or other means of holistic care, would truly provide for the well-being of the nation's poor.

Before our interview concluded, my sister asked Jim Helmick how he thought growing up on a poor farm had influenced the person he became as an adult. "Well, I never had much the rest of my life," he began in the same earnest and humble way that was the hallmark of our interview.

> I never missed anything because I never had nothing. I never really wished I had this or wished I had that. . . . Well, I can't speak for other people, but I guess other people would be angry because of the way—the life they had to live—or blame people who put 'em there or have some regret about being there, which I never did because I never got used to anything any better there than I did after I got away . . . and I didn't set the world on fire after I got away from there. . . . [T]hat's the way it was, that's the way it was. . . . [J]ust unlucky I was born to parents that didn't have anything to begin with.

As we talked, I became aware that the voices of former poor farm residents like Helmick's are being silenced by old age and time. During our interview, he was remarkably sharp and incredibly kind and an excellent storyteller. His recollections represent only one voice out of many, and I realize that these are the time-worn memories of a child. But when my sister thanked him for helping us to understand what life may have been like for our great-great grandmother, for children raised on a poor farm, Helmick drew the rag to his eyes and wiped away his tears. His is a landscape story shaped by poverty and class identity that is worth remembering.

Reinhabiting the Poor Farm in Appalachia and Beyond

The expansion of state-run institutions for the mentally ill was "another legacy of the campaign to transform poorhouses," according to Katz.[17] The State Hospital at Morgantown opened in 1883 to provide psychiatric services—serving as an asylum for the insane—for thirty-seven western North Carolina counties. In 1893 the campus comprised more than three hundred acres of rolling Appalachian foothills. Building on the poor farm structure, the hospital property included a bake house, dairy, greenhouse, and stables. Small residences, constructed in the style of traditional Appalachian farmhouses, were surrounded by vegetable gardens, vineyards, and orchards. The author of a 1906 *Charlotte Observer* article praised superintendent Dr. Patrick Livingston Murphy for adopting the farm colony model, declaring, "The colony system, after two years trial [*sic*] has proved a success beyond all hope." According to historian Lynne Getz, Murphy felt "most proud of the colony system that he implemented at Morganton. In his view, the colony system represented a natural extension of moral treatment that was better suited to the changing circumstances of growing hospitals." Interestingly, "Murphy decried the social and economic changes he thought contributed to greater rates of insanity in the population, particularly the rise of factories." While Murphy never made broad therapeutic claims for the colony system, writes Getz, he recognized its pragmatic functions, such as assisting with overcrowding and the therapeutic value of work in nature.[18]

According to Getz, Murphy relied on traditional patriarchal ideas, including beliefs in segregation and that education for women led to their insanity. Despite the fact that the Board of Public Charities of North Carolina proclaimed that "Employment is the best remedy for insanity, and farming is the best and most remunerative form of labor. . . . [I]t is not only a curative measure, but an economical one," Murphy did not allow women to participate in outdoor labor; in fact, he did not allow them out-side. Getz notes that Murphy succeeded in the state because "many North Carolinians remained comfortable with a hierarchical social structure in which the well born and well educated exercised a paternalistic authority over the members of the lower class." While many documents describe that conditions were like a family, Getz questions how family was defined and understood.[19]

In the early twenty-first century, Morganton's Western Piedmont Community College (wpcc) entered into an agreement with the former State Hospital at Morganton (now called Broughton Hospital) to lease its historic farm colony land. The Richardson Campus is the living laboratory for the College's new associate's degree program in sustainable agriculture. Eager students, many of whom are from working-class backgrounds, have built a new barn and passive solar greenhouse, cultivated heirloom vegetables, and planted an apple orchard on a portion of the land they now call The Farmstead.

I traveled to wpcc to meet with the faculty who are shaping this new project. We sat beneath a massive oak tree on a knoll overlooking a vast expanse of agricultural land, eating ripe tomatoes, plump figs from old trees near the horticultural building, slices of thick local cheese, and homemade bread. As we talked about the college's plans for the teaching and research farm and an allied crafts enrichment program, I began to consider what reinhabitation of this landscape might mean. The program's director is a dynamic and joyful man named Chip Hope. His passion for sustainable agriculture grew out of gardening with his mom, a degree in horticulture, research on heirloom tomatoes, and, eventually, his own heirloom seed business, Appalachian Seeds Farm & Nursery. He joined the faculty at wpcc with a vision for helping people learn to grow more of their own food and medicines and to promote sustainable agriculture in the region. When I asked him about the history of the Richardson campus land and his current work, he replied that reinhabitation

is an integral part of what we are doing in our program, sometimes consciously, sometimes not. The very first time I saw the farm I knew that we could/should bring it back to life . . . to fruition, and I knew that it was a part of my job to do that. We are reinhabiting a once viable farm and giving it life and purpose again. I talk about the history. I think about it all the time. I can't be on this property hardly without thinking about it. . . . [There is] an incredible presence, very strong, powerful. Who were the people and what did they do? I try to imagine. Occasionally, we dig up pieces of old dinnerware and iron bed frames.[20]

Farming, says Hope, "is one of the greatest ways to connect with life, nature, spirit, health."[21] As we walked around the campus, we saw reminders of the institutional past: chicken house, caretaker's residence, brick dormitory, barn. This is a storied landscape that contains more than an agricultural past. It holds as well the history of social welfare and land use.

Similar to the academic program Hope stewards, efforts to reinhabit both rural and urban spaces via sustainable agriculture projects that link social justice with restorative work in nature are being developed across the United States. The Serving Ourselves Farm at Boston's Long Island Shelter is a homeless shelter and organic vegetable and herb farm with fruit trees, laying hens, and an apiary. The Homeless Garden Project in Santa Cruz, California, is an urban organic garden to "provide job-training and meaningful work in a therapeutic environment." The North End Opportunity Farm in Charlotte, North Carolina, plans to hire homeless people to plant, tend, and harvest fruits and vegetables and to produce farm-raised tilapia to sell locally. The Urban Farm at HELP USA serves residents as a vocational training tool for the on-site Culinary Arts Job Training and Placement Program at the two hundred–bed transitional shelter.[22]

A 1999 case study of the Farm Project, a voluntary program for empowering the homeless and working poor run by a New England social services agency, illustrates the promise of reinhabitation. Participants raised vegetables, donated food to local food pantry programs, tended their own gardens, and sold produce at a weekly farmers market. According to the researchers, some participants felt these activities "added to their sense of personal pride, hope, a sense of ownership, and responsibility." Some participants also reported a sense of nostalgia for their own childhood farms, and many expressed joy in helping others. Many recent studies have reached similar conclusions: interactions with nature promote human health and well-being and engender an ecological way of seeing, perhaps even a bioregional identity. In *Earth in Mind: On Education, Environment, and the Human Prospect*, David Orr asks what might happen if we see "farming not as a production problem to be fixed, but as a more complex activity, at once cultural, ethical, ecological, and political."[23] A social justice–oriented bioregionalism seems poised to enable this work.

■ Was the poor farm an abject failure, as Katz defines the poorhouse model of social welfare? Or did the poor farm have a separate history as a place of refuge where residents farmed the land, cultivating self-sufficiency and community? American poor farms have been mostly paved over, though some have been preserved, marked by road signs on rural byways or in the genealogy notebooks of intrepid family historians. Still, the legacy of poverty endures. Historic poor farms and contemporary farm and shelter programs treat the symptoms of a larger disease.

The most recent US Census Bureau finds that 46.2 million Americans live in poverty and that children under the age of eighteen experience poverty rates greater than those for all adults eighteen to sixty-four years old, and nearly three times as high as those sixty-five and older. Today, "the majority of the working poor (54 percent) do not escape poverty despite working full-time, year-round." As political economist Jeanette Wicks-Lim asserts, "Without aggressively addressing the issue of low-wage work, a large share of workers and their households will continue to live in poverty." Michael Zweig, director of the Center for Study of Working Class Life at Stony Brook University, argues that the term *the poor* is not a class identity, but rather that poverty is a condition, one that working-class people experience more often than the capitalist or middle classes. "[M]ost of the poor don't stay poor for long periods," Zweig writes. "They cycle in and out of poverty, depending on employment, family situation, changes in earnings on the job. . . . [M]ore than half the working class experiences poverty in a ten-year period. The poor are not some persistent lump at the bottom of society; they are working people who have hit hard times."[24] As the gap widens between those who live lives of abundance and those who struggle every day simply to live at all, we must examine why our society continues to permit such imbalances.

And as these disparities increase, environmental crises continue to disproportionately impact working-class people and poor communities. The conditions of poverty and the social, economic, and political institutions created to address them must be understood within their broader ecological context. How will we define fair labor standards, regulate occupational and environmental hazards, and calculate the minimum wage in the United States in the coming years? What social safety nets will we choose, and will they make us more resilient or less sustainable? The world of work is highly mutable, and it will be made even more so by the ways a warming planet will shape the lives of workers and the land, of present and future generations.

The "culture of reinhabitation is a life-place culture: the rediscovery of a way to live well, with grace and permanence, in place."[25] To live rightly in any place, this vision must include the stories of working-class people and the land, link environmental and social history, and question how class and power define opportunities and assign risk in social and environmental contexts. The ways that people live and labor in nature and the ways we value people and the land have the capacity to create suffering or inspire wellness. It's simply not enough to ask, "What are the standards by which we as a society will choose to take care of poor workers and the working poor?" We must ask, instead, why poverty exists, and then work to end it.

NOTES

1. Michael B. Katz, *In the Shadow of the Poorhouse: A Social History of Welfare in America,* 10th ed. (New York: Basic Books, 1996), "may be traced," 4.

2. Stephen Mosley, "Common Ground: Integrating Social and Environmental History," *Journal of Social History* 39, no. 3 (2006), "working-class voices," 922, "very few social," 924; Janet Zandy, ed., "Introduction," in Zandy, *What We Hold In Common: An Introduction to Working-Class Studies* (New York: Feminist Press at CUNY, 2001), "to recall the," xiv.

3. Robert L. Thayer, *LifePlace: Bioregional Thought and Practice* (Berkeley: University of California Press, 2003), "by natural," 3; Tom Lynch, Cheryll Glotfelty, and Karla Armbruster, eds., *The Bioregional Imagination: Literature, Ecology, Place* (Athens: University of Georgia Press, 2012), "By foregrounding natural," 4.

4. Peter Berg and Raymond Dasmann, "Reinhabiting California," *Ecologist* 7, no. 10 (1977), "learning to live," 399; Liette L. Gilbert, Anders Sandberg, and Gerda R. Wekerle, "Building Bioregional Citizenship: The Case of the Oak Ridges Moraine, Ontario, Canada," *Local Environment* 14, no. 5 (2009), "But while bioregionalism," 399.

5. Joshua A. Dolezal, "Literary Activism, Social Justice, and the Future of Bioregionalism," *Ethics & The Environment* 13, no. 1 (2008): "Social disenfranchisement," 9; Perlita R. Dicochea, "Between Borderlands and Bioregionalism: Life-Place Lessons along a

Polluted River," *Journal of Borderland Studies* 25, no. 1 (2010), "the concept of reinhabitation," 22; Bernie Glassman, *Bearing Witness: A Zen Master's Lessons in Making Peace* (New York: Bell Tower, 1998).

6. I am indebted to my sister, Emily Corio, freelance journalist and teaching assistant professor of journalism at West Virginia University, for her gracious help in arranging and conducting this interview. James Helmick, interview with Emily Corio and Jennifer Westerman, August 4, 2013; quotes from the transcript.

7. Katz, *In the Shadow of the Poorhouse*, "transform the behavior," 23.

8. Elizabeth Gaspar-Brown, "Poor Relief in a Wisconsin County, 1846–1866: Administration and Recipients," *American Journal of Legal History* 20, no. 2 (1976), 82; Katz, *In the Shadow of the Poorhouse*, "Poverty resulted not," 19, "In essence," 25.

9. G. W. Blacknall, "Report of North Carolina State Board of Public Charities" (Raleigh: State Board of Public Charities, 1870): 7, quoted in Roy M. Brown, *Public Poor Relief in North Carolina* (Chapel Hill: University of North Carolina Press, 1928), "Thousands have been," 73; Betty Groth Syverson, *How I Grew Up Rich on the Poor Farm* (Minneapolis, MN: Betty Groth Syverson Publishing, 1997).

10. David Wagner, *The Poorhouse: America's Forgotten Institution* (New York: Rowman & Littlefield, 2005), "historians and social," 10; "is not a depressing," 3; TThe loss of," 2.

11. H. Dewey Anderson and Percy E. Davidson, "County Poor Farm Inmates Compared with Their Brothers and the Working Population of the Same Community," *Social Forces* 16, no. 2 (1937), "Almost a fourth," 234, "have worked largely," 236; Katz, *In the Shadow of the Poorhouse*, "no clear line," 4.

12. Kevin C. Fleming, Johnathan M. Evans, and Darryl S. Chutka, "A Cultural and Economic History of Old Age in America," *Mayo Clinic Symposium on Geriatrics Proceedings* 78, no. 7 (2003), "Black, white, and Hispanic," 916; James Tuten, "Regulating the Poor in Alabama: The Jefferson County Poor Farm, 1885–1945," in *Before the New Deal: Social Welfare in the South, 1830–1930*, ed. Elna C. Green (Athens: University of Georgia Press, 1999), "Not only did," 56; Fleming et al., "A Cultural and Economic History," "fully 30%," 917.

13. Donald Edward Davis, *Where There Are Mountains: An Environmental History of the Southern Appalachians* (Athens: University of Georgia Press, 2003), "the single greatest," 166, "While corporate logging," 175.

14. Harry C. Evans, *The American Poor Farm and Its Inmates* (Des Moines, IA: Loyal Order of the Moose, 1926); quoted in Dan Gunderson and Chris Julin, "Over the Hill to the Poorhouse," Minnesota Public Radio, July 29, 2002, "We have reported," http://news.minnesota.publicradio.org/features/200207/29_gundersond_poorfarm-m/index.shtml.

15. Katz, *In the Shadow of the Poorhouse*, "backwaters of social," 88. Michael Harrington, *The Other America* (New York: MacMillan, 1962); Frances Fox Piven and

Richard Cloward, *Regulating the Poor: The Functions of Public Welfare* (New York: Pantheon, 1971).

16. Jerry Bruce Thomas, *An Appalachian New Deal: West Virginia in the Great Depression* (Lexington: University Press of Kentucky, 1998), "remove children from," 197.

17. Katz, *In the Shadow of the Poorhouse,* "another legacy of," 102.

18. "Farm Work for the Insane: The Colony System Conducted by Dr. P. L. Murphy at Morganton in Line With the Most Advanced Methods," *Charlotte Observer* (January 5, 1906), "The colony system"; Lynne M. Getz, "'A Strong Man of Large Human Sympathy': Dr. Patrick L. Murphy and the Challenges of Nineteenth-Century Asylum Psychiatry in North Carolina," *North Carolina Historical Review* 86, no. 1 (2009), "most proud of," 55; "Murphy decried the," 40.

19. Ibid., "Employment is the best," 47; "many North Carolinians," 38.

20. Chip Hope, interview with Jennifer Westerman, September 4, 2013, quote from the transcript; Chip Hope, interview with Jennifer Westerman, May 20, 2011.

21. Chip Hope, interview, September 4, 2013.

22. Friends of Boston's Homeless, "The Serving Ourselves Farm at Boston's Long Island Shelter," 2013, http://www.fobh.org/the-farm—long-island; Homeless Garden Project, 2013, http://www.homelessgardenproject.org/; Tenikka Smith, "Farm Near Uptown Will Employ People from Homeless Shelter," WSOC-TV, January 30, 2013, http://www.wsoctv.com/news/news/local/farm-near-uptown-will-employee-staff-homeless -shel/nWBJk/; Kate McDonald, "HELP USA Unveils Innovative Urban Farm at Local New York Homeless Shelter," June 29, 2012, press release, http://www.helpusa.org/help-usa-unveils-innovative-urban-farm-at-local-new-york-homeless-shelter/.

23. Eric Brandt-Meyer and Sandra S. Butler, "Food for People, Not for Profit," *Journal of Progressive Human Services* 10, no. 1 (2008), "added to their sense," 58; "nostalgia," 63; David W. Orr, *Earth in Mind: On Education, Environment, and the Human Prospect* (Washington, DC: Island Press, 2004), "farming not as," 119–20.

24. Carmen DeNavas-Walt, Bernadette D. Proctor, and Jessica C. Smith, "Income, Poverty, and Health Insurance Coverage in the United States: 2011," Current Population Reports of the US Census, September 2012, http://www.census.gov/prod/2012pubs /p60-243.pdf; Jeannette Wicks-Lim, "The Working Poor," *New Labor Forum* 21, no. 3 (2012), "the majority of the," 19; "Without aggressively," 18; Michael Zweig, *The Working Class Majority: America's Best Kept Secret* (Ithaca, NY: Cornell University Press, 2000), "Most of the poor," 90.

25. Thayer, *LifePlace,* "culture of reinhabitation," 68.

CONTRIBUTORS

JONI ADAMSON is associate professor of English and environmental humanities at Arizona State University. She is the author of *American Indian Literature, Environmental Justice, and Ecocriticism: The Middle Place* (University of Arizona Press, 2001) and coeditor of *American Studies, Ecocriticism, and Citizenship: Thinking and Acting in the Local and Global Commons* (Routledge, 2012) and *The Environmental Justice Reader: Politics, Poetics, and Pedagogy* (University of Arizona Press, 2002).

PAUL BOGARD is assistant professor of creative nonfiction at James Madison University in Harrisonburg, Virginia. He is the author of *The End of Night: Searching for Natural Darkness in an Age of Artificial Light* (Little, Brown, 2013) and editor of *Let There Be Night: Testimony on Behalf of the Dark* (University of Nevada Press, 2008).

JAMES W. FELDMAN is associate professor of history and environmental studies at the University of Wisconsin, Oshkosh. He is the author of *A Storied Wilderness: Rewilding the Apostle Islands* (University of Washington Press, 2011).

PETER FRIEDERICI is associate professor of journalism at Northern Arizona University. His books include *Nature's Restoration* (Island Press, 2006) and the edited collection *What Has Passed and What Remains: Oral*

Histories of Northern Arizona's Changing Landscapes (University of Arizona Press, 2010).

SCOTT HICKS is associate professor of English at the University of North Carolina, Pembroke, where he teaches classes in first-year composition, literature, and the humanities. His articles on African American and environmental literatures and ecocritical theory and pedagogy have appeared in *Arizona Quarterly, Callaloo, Environmental Humanities, ISLE: Interdisciplinary Studies in Literature & Environment,* and *North Carolina Literary Review.*

JASON ROBERTS is a doctoral candidate in environmental anthropology at the University of Texas at San Antonio. His dissertation research examines the social and environmental effects of industrial logging in New Ireland province, Papua New Guinea.

CHRISTINA ROBERTSON teaches first-year composition, environmental humanities, and literature at the University of Nevada, Reno. Her non-fiction appears in *Trash Animals: How We Live with Nature's Filthy, Feral, Invasive, and Unwanted Species* (University of Minnesota Press, 2013), *Lake: A Journal of Art and Environment, The Pacific Crest Trailside Reader* (Mountaineers Books, 2011), and *Let There Be Night: Testimony on Behalf of the Dark* (University of Nevada Press, 2008).

TERRE RYAN is assistant professor of writing at Loyola University Maryland, in Baltimore. She is the author of *This Ecstatic Nation: The American Landscape and the Aesthetics of Patriotism* (University of Massachusetts Press, 2011).

DEBRA J. SALAZAR is professor of political science and affiliate professor of environmental studies at Western Washington University, Bellingham. She is coeditor of *Sustaining the Forests of the Pacific Coast* with Donald Alper (University of British Columbia Press, 2000). Her articles have appeared in *Organization & Environment, B.C. Studies,* the *Canadian Journal of Political Science, Society and Natural Resources,* the *Journal of*

Borderland Studies, and *Social Science Quarterly.* She has published creative nonfiction in *Witness* and the *Other Journal.*

EDIE STEINER is a doctoral candidate in environmental cultural studies at York University, Toronto. She teaches arts-based and media practices in Canadian college and university programs. Her photographs are in the permanent collection of the National Gallery of Canada, and her films have won international film festival awards.

CHARLES WAUGH is associate professor of English at Utah State University, where he teaches courses in fiction writing and American studies. He is the author of "Refuge to Refuse: Seeking Balance in the Vietnamese Environmental Imagination," in *Four Decades On* (Duke University Press, 2013), and along with Nguyen Lien is the coeditor and cotranslator of *Family of Fallen Leaves: Stories of Agent Orange by Vietnamese Writers* (University of Georgia Press, 2010).

JENNIFER WESTERMAN is assistant professor of sustainable development at Appalachian State University, where she teaches courses in environmental justice, environmental humanities, and sustainability studies. Her creative nonfiction appears in *Let There Be Night: Testimony on Behalf of the Dark* (University of Nevada Press, 2008), and her articles have appeared in the *Journal of Management Education* and the *International Journal of Innovation and Sustainable Development.*

INDEX